Arthur E. Dell Orto, Ph.D.
Chairman, Department of
Rehabilitation Counseling
Sargent College
University Rd.
Boston, Ma. 02215

# Substance Abuse Counseling
# An Individualized Approach

# Substance Abuse Counseling
# An Individualized Approach

**Judith A. Lewis**
*Governors State University*

**Robert Q. Dana**
*University of Maine at Orono*

**Gregory A. Blevins**
*Governors State University*

Brooks/Cole Publishing Company
Pacific Grove, California

**Brooks/Cole Publishing Company**
A Division of Wadsworth, Inc.

© 1988 by Wadsworth, Inc., Belmont, California 94002.
All rights reserved. No part of this book may be reproduced,
stored in a retrieval system, or transcribed, in any form
or by any means — electronic, mechanical, photocopying, recording,
or otherwise — without the prior written permission of the
publisher, Brooks/Cole Publishing Company, Pacific Grove,
California 93950, a division of Wadsworth, Inc.

Printed in the United States of America
10 9 8 7 6 5 4 3 2 1

**Library of Congress Cataloging in Publication Data**

Lewis, Judith A. [date]
  Substance abuse counseling: an individualized approach/Judith A. Lewis, Robert Q. Dana,
Gregory A. Blevins.
      p.    cm.
  Includes index.
  ISBN 0-534-08448-6
  1. Substance abuse — Treatment.    2. Substance abuse — Patients — Counseling of.
I. Dana, Robert Q. [date]    II. Blevins, Gregory A.    III. Title.
RC564.L49 1987
616.86 — dc19                                                                    87-24618
                                                                                    CIP


Sponsoring Editor: *Claire Verduin*
Marketing Representative: *Dr. T. L. Feelgood*
Editorial Associate: *Linda Ruth Wright*
Production Editor: *Penelope Sky*
Manuscript Editor: *William Waller*
Permissions Editor: *Carline Haga*
Interior Design: *Katherine Minerva*
Cover Design: *Stephanie Workman*
Art Coordinator: *Sue C. Howard*
Interior Illustration: *Maggie Stevens*
Typesetting: *Beacon Graphics, Ashland, Ohio*
Printing and Binding: *The Maple–Vail Book Manufacturing Group,
        Manchester, Pennsylvania*

**FOR**

Michael and Keith Lewis
Cookie, Jennifer, Jacob, and Lenora Dana
Vicki and Stacy Blevins

# PREFACE

In the 1980s we have seen the substance abuse field become a "growth industry," characterized by an increase in both the number and the diversity of clients, programs, and service providers. With this expansion has come a degree of controversy about the appropriate goals of treatment, the best methodologies, and the kinds of knowledge and skills that are necessary for effective practice. Professionals who might once have felt comfortable with a single treatment model have had to face the demand for change.

In the future the substance abuse field will undoubtedly include services offered in a variety of inpatient and outpatient settings to clients with highly diverse interests and needs. In this context, substance abuse counselors will need to be as skilled in assessing individual and community needs as they are in providing direct services. The purpose of this book is to help counselors develop these skills, whether they plan to work as substance abuse specialists or as generalists who deal with heterogeneous populations and address substance abuse problems as they arise.

*Substance Abuse Counseling: An Individualized Approach* is based on the fundamental assumption that substance abusers and their families are members of a heterogeneous population and must be treated from an individualized perspective. The heterogeneity among substance abusers is not surprising given the diversity of antecedents, correlates, and consequences of substance abuse; the differences among the drugs of choice; the variations in the patterns of use; and the variety of sociocultural environments within which substance use and abuse occur. Accordingly, we focus on empirically validated approaches for treating substance abusers. Our aim is not to endorse any one model but rather to describe the methods that are best supported by current research and to identify those issues that remain unresolved.

In Chapter 1, "An Introduction to Substance Abuse Counseling," we establish the basic framework for counseling substance-abusing clients, providing guidelines for professional practice and describing the settings in which treatment might occur. In Chapter 2, "Drugs and Their Effects," we offer an overview of the psychopharmacological principles that are essential to understanding the variability and commonalities of drug effects. In Chapter 3, "Assessment and Diagnosis of Substance Use Disorders," and Chapter 4, "Counseling Individual Substance Abusers," we focus on the importance of the assessment process in developing individualized treatment plans and on the diversity of techniques that enable counselors to provide the services indicated by the treatment planning process. In Chapter 5, "Family and Group Counseling," we address important treatment issues that transcend the individual client. In Chapter 6, "Relapse and Relapse Prevention," we discuss a way of breaking the "revolving door" cycle that is so often encountered in working with substance abusers. In Chapter 7, "Prevention," we suggest that substance abuse prevention activities and programs be established as essential components of the service delivery system. Finally, in Chapter 8, "Program Planning and Evaluation," we shift our analysis from a focus on the counselor–client relationship to a broader examination of programmatic issues.

All counselors find themselves facing problems related to substance abuse on a regular basis. We hope that they will feel more competent to confront this pressing concern after reading this book.

## Acknowledgments

This book could not have been completed without the support and help of a number of people. Our students and colleagues at Governors State University and the University of Maine helped by providing fresh perspectives and by allowing us to share our earliest conceptualizations. Our families, Michael and Keith Lewis, Cookie Dana, and Vicki and Stacy Blevins, provided support and encouragement throughout the project. The reviewers of an earlier draft of the manuscript gave us valuable insights that led to significant improvements; they include John E. Harrigan, Portland, Maine; Neal Pinckney, California State University, Sacramento; Howard J. Shaffer, Harvard Medical School; William A. Troth, East Texas State University; and Thomas D. Watts, University of Texas at Arlington. Michael Lewis lent enthusiastic support to this project from the beginning, providing much of the initial impetus and then critiquing the manuscript at each stage in its development. Finally, the talented staff at Brooks/Cole has been, as always, highly professional, efficient, and enthusiastic.

*Judith A. Lewis*
*Robert Q. Dana*
*Gregory A. Blevins*

# CONTENTS

# Substance Abuse Counseling
# An Individualized Approach

# An Introduction to Substance Abuse Counseling

All counselors, whether or not they consider themselves "addiction specialists," are forced to deal with the problems caused by substance abuse. The elementary school counselor who sees the devastating effects of parental alcoholism on young children, the high school counselor who hopes to prevent the negative consequences of adolescent drug use, the family therapist who wonders why a particular family system seems unusually rigid and secretive, and the mental health counselor facing a client's steady deterioration—all these people confront substance abuse issues every day. Dealing appropriately with these issues depends on the ability to recognize the abuse of alcohol and other drugs and to use counseling or referral skills in helping clients.

The primary purpose of this book is to help counselors develop the basic knowledge and skills they will need to deal with their clients' substance abuse problems. Some counselors will choose to specialize, devoting a major portion of their professional careers to substance abuse issues. For them this text will provide an introductory framework on which to base further study. Other practitioners will see themselves as generalists, working with heterogeneous

1

client populations and addressing substance abuse problems as they arise. These counselors will find here guidelines for adapting their current skills and techniques to the special needs of substance-dependent clients. Our intention is not to promote any one theory at the expense of others but, rather, to describe the methods that are best supported by current research and, above all, to encourage an individualized approach based on the unique needs of each client.

## ▌ Substance Abuse: A Working Definition

A counselor who wants to make appropriate assessments and action plans for clients needs to begin with at least a working definition of the term *substance abuse*. One of the most widely accepted conceptualizations is provided by the American Psychiatric Association's *Diagnostic and Statistical Manual of Mental Disorders* (1980). In approaching the question of substance use disorders, the manual explains:

> This diagnostic class deals with behavioral changes associated with more or less regular use of substances that affect the central nervous system. These behavioral changes in almost all subcultures would be viewed as extremely undesirable. Examples of such behavioral changes include impairment in social or occupational functioning as a consequence of substance use, inability to control use of or to stop taking the substance, and the development of serious withdrawal symptoms after cessation of or reduction in substance use [p. 163].

The *Diagnostic and Statistical Manual,* the third edition of which is commonly called the "DSM III" by clinicians, distinguishes between nonpathological substance use and substance *abuse* through three criteria: the pattern of pathological use, impairment in social or occupational functioning caused by the pattern of pathological use, and duration of abuse (at least one month). Pathological use is termed *dependence* in the presence of one additional criterion—physiological dependence, as evidenced by either tolerance to the substance or withdrawal symptoms.

Thus, use of a substance that modifies mood or behavior is *not* considered a substance abuse problem unless the user's functioning is negatively affected.

> Social relations can be disturbed by the individual's failure to meet important obligations to friends and family, by display of erratic and impulsive behavior, and by inappropriate expression of aggressive feelings. The individual may have legal difficulties because of complications of the intoxicated state (e.g., car accidents) or because of criminal behavior to obtain money to purchase the substance. . . . Occupational functioning can deteriorate if the indi-

vidual misses work or school, or is unable to function effectively because of being intoxicated. When impairment is severe, the individual's life can become totally dominated by use of the substance, with marked deterioration in physical and psychological functioning [American Psychiatric Association, 1980, p. 164].

For general counseling purposes, then, we can think of a client's problem as related to *substance abuse* if continuous use of alcohol or another mood- or behavior-altering drug is affecting his or her social or occupational functioning. We can assess a client as being *dependent* on the substance if signs of physiological withdrawal or tolerance are also present. Among the psychoactive substances associated with abuse or dependence are alcohol, sedative hypnotics, opioids, amphetamines, cannabis, cocaine, and tobacco.

Of the substances likely to cause problems among clients, alcohol is the most common.

> The use, misuse, and abuse of alcohol is one of the major health problems in the United States. Alcoholism ranks as the third most prevalent public health problem in this society. But the problems associated with alcohol are not limited to the health problems of alcoholic persons, because their alcoholismic behavior leads to familial, social, vocational, and legal problems. . . . People use, misuse, and abuse alcohol, yet may never become alcohol dependent nor defined as alcoholic. Yet these patterns of alcohol utilization contribute to health impairment, vehicular and pedestrian accidents, criminal behavior, destructive social behavior, and other adverse community consequences. Alcohol problems are therefore not limited to just alcoholics. . . . Everyone encounters the use, misuse, and abuse of alcohol in daily life [Pattison & Kaufman, 1982, pp. 3–4].

Clearly, a problem of this magnitude affects so many clients in so many ways that it cannot be overlooked by a competent counselor.

Counselors in virtually any setting can also expect to see a large number of clients affected by other drugs.

> Drug use is a mass phenomenon in the United States. Projections from a 1982 national household survey indicate that 32 million Americans smoke marijuana at least once a year; 20 million smoke it at least once a month. Annual cocaine users number over 12 million. Several million others take hallucinogens, stimulants, sedatives, and tranquilizers without medical supervision. And of course, these figures are dwarfed by the number of people who use legal drugs, including alcoholic beverages (125 million) and tobacco cigarettes (70 million) [Polich, Ellickson, Reuter, & Kahan, 1984, p. v].

Obviously, the mere use of a drug is not, in itself, problematic from a psychological perspective. The substance users who need the assistance of counselors are those who have developed life problems or health risks from using drugs. Thus, the counselor must recognize individual differences among substance-abusing clients and must try to address drug use in the context of the client's total life functioning.

# ▌ Guidelines for Substance Abuse Counseling

Counselors are using a wide variety of approaches to substance abuse problems, and controversy in the field will probably always exist. Even in the absence of absolutes, however, some generalizations about the most promising practices can be made. Counselors would do well to consider the following general guidelines as likely to stand the test of time. Counselors should:

1. View substance abuse problems on a continuum from nonproblematic to problematic use, rather than as an either/or situation.
2. Provide treatment that is individualized, both in goals and in methods.
3. Use methods and approaches that enhance each client's sense of "self-efficacy."
4. Provide multidimensional treatment that focuses on the social and environmental aspects of long-term recovery.
5. Support selection of the least intrusive treatment possible for each client.
6. Remain open to new methods and goals as research findings become available.
7. Be sensitive to the varying needs of diverse client populations.

## Substance Abuse Diagnosis: Continuum, Not Dichotomy

Treatment professionals sometimes oversimplify the assessment of substance abuse problems, creating a dichotomy that fails to confront the complexity of the diagnostic process. Such oversimplification is especially inadequate in dealing with alcoholism. Diagnosticians tend to assume that they can identify alcoholism as a unitary disease and that, once this identification has been made, a particular course of treatment can be prescribed. In fact, however,

> This theoretical assumption has little utility, and the search for an unequivocal method of accurate binary diagnosis has failed because the term "alcoholism" does not refer to a concrete entity, but rather to a diverse set of behaviors and problems. . . . The unitary concept assumes that there is a distinct class of persons who have the specific disease of alcoholism, who are substantively different from problem drinkers, heavy drinkers, prodromal alco-

holics, and prealcoholics. . . . Most scientific authorities in the field
of alcoholism now concur that the construct of alcoholism is most
accurately construed as a multivariate syndrome. That is, there are
multiple patterns of dysfunctional alcohol use that occur in multiple types of personalities, with multiple combinations of adverse
consequences, with multiple prognoses, that may require different
types of treatment interventions [Pattison & Kaufman, 1982, p. 13].

The counselor who turns away from the either/or diagnosis of alcoholism is not necessarily denying the definition of alcoholism as
a disease.

The question of whether alcoholism is to be considered a disease is
*not at debate*. Rather, the issue is whether alcoholism is a unitary
phenomenon or a multivariant syndrome. . . . To consider alcoholism a disease does not necessarily require a unitary set of
symptoms, nor does it require a uniform clinical course [Pattison,
1985, p. 197].

The difficulty with the dichotomous classification of yes or no for
alcoholism lies less in its classification of the dysfunction than in its
assumption that, because we know that a client is "alcoholic," we
know everything we need to know in order to treat him or her. If we
are to make appropriate treatment decisions, we need to do a great
deal more than label the client's dysfunction, and this is equally important whether the substance abused is alcohol or another drug.

It is now generally accepted that nonmedical drug users comprise a
great diversity of individuals who are drug dependent in different
ways and degrees, use drugs to meet different needs, have different
socio-economic backgrounds, are of both sexes, and represent a
wide range of ages, races, and ethnic groups. No single treatment
response will work for all: we need to match a particular approach
to each individual [Brill, 1981, pp. 5–6].

Use of a simple diagnosis of alcoholism or drug addiction actually
*interferes with* treatment planning by masking individual differences. This simplistic approach to assessment also lessens the
potential effectiveness of treatment by discouraging early intervention in cases of problem drinking or drug use. An either/or diagnosis leads inexorably to a generalized, diffuse treatment package
that, at worst, brings results "no better than the natural history of
the disorder" (Vaillant, 1983, p. 285) and, at best, meets the needs
only of individuals with serious, chronic, long-standing substance
abuse disorders. Insistence on a clear diagnosis of "alcoholism," for
instance, drives away from treatment many people who are not necessarily alcohol-dependent but who could benefit from assistance in
dealing with life problems associated with incipient alcohol abuse.

> Hundreds of thousands of families live with family members whose alcohol escapades affect them negatively, in greater or lesser degree, without the drinker ever becoming a heavier, or more badly affected, individual — or even coming close to the 2–5% who are in severe and chronic trouble. . . . If we wait for a progression to occur, we will unfortunately never notice that these people need and are entitled to receive help, and so do their families [Willoughby, 1979, pp. 133–134].

Suppose that, instead of conceptualizing substance abuse disorders merely as present or absent, we view drug or alcohol use along a continuum from nonproblematic to highly problematic, as shown in Figure 1.1. Figure 1.1 shows, in continuum from left to right, six categories of substance use:

1. nonuse
2. moderate, nonproblematic use
3. heavy, nonproblematic use
4. heavy use associated with moderate life problems
5. heavy use associated with serious life problems
6. substance dependence associated with life and health problems

Such a continuum does not imply progression in the sense that an individual who begins to develop problems automatically moves along the continuum from left to right. On the contrary, the various points on the continuum may represent different individuals, some of whom move from less serious to more serious involvement, some of whom stay at one point indefinitely, and some of whom move back and forth. In a discussion of alcoholism as a chronic disorder, for instance, Vaillant (1983) points out:

> The first stage is heavy "social" drinking — frequent ingestion of 2 to 3 ounces of ethanol (3 to 5 drinks) a day for several years. This stage can continue asymptomatically for a lifetime; or because of a change of circumstances or peer group it can reverse to a more moderate pattern of drinking; or it can "progress" into a pattern of alcohol abuse (multiple medical, legal, social, and occupational complications), usually associated with frequent ingestion of more than 4 ounces of ethanol (8 or more drinks) a day. At some point in their lives, perhaps 10–15 percent of American men reach this second stage. Perhaps half of such alcohol abusers either return to

| Nonuse | Moderate, nonproblematic use | Heavy, nonproblematic use | Heavy use; moderate problems | Heavy use; serious problems | Dependence; life and health problems |
|--------|------------------------------|---------------------------|------------------------------|-----------------------------|--------------------------------------|

**Figure 1.1**   Continuum of substance use

asymptomatic (controlled) drinking or achieve stable abstinence. In a small number of such cases . . . such alcohol abuse can persist intermittently for decades with minor morbidity and even become milder with time [p. 309].

Because of the impossibility of predicting the course of substance use for any one individual, counselors need to be as helpful as possible in responding to the client's needs at the time of first contact. The notion that substance abuse problems *will* worsen over time is, understandably, difficult for clients with minor difficulties to accept. Many treatment providers label such clients' hesitance "denial" and wait for them to develop a sufficient number of problems to warrant acceptance of the "alcoholic" or "addict" label. More appropriately, counselors should attempt to devise treatment plans that fit the nature and seriousness of clients' current difficulties.

It is possible to estimate where to place an individual client on the continuum without making the error of assuming that he or she will necessarily "progress" into more serious problems. One way of identifying the seriousness of a client's substance abuse is through examining the number of life problems associated with the individual's drinking or drug use. For example, Vaillant (1983) developed a Problem Drinking Scale (PDS) to identify the number of alcohol-related problems exhibited by the individuals interviewed in a longitudinal study. The problems, all of which are weighted equally by Vaillant, are listed (p. 25) as:

- complaints by employer
- multiple job losses
- complaints by family or friends
- marital problems
- a medical problem
- multiple medical problems
- diagnosis by clinician
- alcohol-related arrest
- three or more alcohol-related arrests
- two or more blackouts
- going on the wagon
- morning tremulousness or drinking
- tardiness or sick leave
- admission of a problem with control

Vaillant's perception that "it is the number and frequency of alcohol-related problems, not just their specificity, that define the clinical phenomenon known as alcoholism" (pp. 34–35) has led him to define alcohol abuse in terms of the number of problems exhibited. Individual drinkers can be placed on a continuum, depending on the number of alcohol-related problems they show. However, a drinker with a score of 4 or more on the PDS (that is, one who has at least four of the problems listed above) is considered a substance abuser and remains in that category until spending a full year free of problems.

In a classic national survey Cahalan (1970) also defined problem drinkers in terms of the number and severity of alcohol-related problems they exhibited. His purpose was epidemiological rather than clinical, but his list of problems can shed light on a client's life situation for counselors. His problem list (p. 37) includes the following:

- index of frequent intoxication
- binge drinking
- symptomatic drinking (difficulty stopping drinking, blackouts, sneaking drinks)
- psychological dependence
- problems with spouse or relatives
- problems with friends or neighbors
- job problems
- problems with police or accidents
- health
- financial problems
- belligerence associated with drinking

Cahalan's overall current problems score is derived by scoring each problem as to its severity on the basis of the number of question-naire items answered affirmatively. For purposes of studying the prevalence of drinking problems, Cahalan recommends "the combined current problems score of seven or higher as denoting a fair likelihood that this level of overall score isolates most of those with a recognizable problem (or set of problems) related to drinking" (1970, p. 38). Normally, an individual could score 7 or higher on this scale only by exhibiting "problems in two or more areas, with at least one being rated as being in severe form; or problems in three or more areas, with at least two being at least moderate in severity; or problems in five or more areas, with at least one being moderate or severe; or slight problems in seven or more areas" (p. 36).

A counselor can, by using Vaillant's PDS score, Cahalan's current problems score, or any one of a number of other methods and cutoff points, determine approximately where a client stands on the continuum from nonproblematic to severely problematic alcohol or drug use. It is *not* possible, however, to determine through the use of any objective measure whether an individual should be helped. The fact that traditional treatment approaches tend to be appropriate only for those clients clustered at the far right of the continuum has meant, in effect, the withholding of services from people with minor or moderate problems. An individual scoring 7 or higher on the Cahalan scale may clearly need assistance. But where is the cutoff point, below which a client should be rejected? Someone with a score of 4 or above on Vaillant's PDS has a definite problem, but an individual who scores 2 or 3 on the same scale may also benefit from assistance, albeit of a less intensive nature than a seriously troubled, substance-dependent client would need. Thus, an individual who has been arrested for driving under the influence of alcohol deserves a chance to learn how to discriminate his or her blood alcohol level. A young person developing problems associated with careless use of substances deserves an opportunity to learn responsible decision making. A person who has learned to abuse drugs as a way of dealing with grief or stress deserves the services of a counselor who can help him or her develop more appropriate coping methods. These clients need help that is not sullied by the process of labeling or by the assumption that their problems will necessarily get worse. They need to be seen as individuals who can be assisted without being forced to accept diagnoses that may be inappropriate.

## Individualized Goals and Methods

Counselors who move away from dichotomous diagnoses find themselves increasingly able to provide help tailored to the individual needs of their clients. When we begin to think of the people we serve as complex, multifaceted human beings, we can develop treatment plans that are as unique as the clients themselves. This process begins with the counselor's recognition that no one goal or treatment outcome is likely to be appropriate for every client.

One of the goals of substance abuse counseling, by its very definition, is a change from a problematic level of substance use (abuse or dependence) to a nonproblematic level (abstinence or responsible use). Yet even this one generalization is subject to adaptation from client to client. In each case the client and counselor must work together to decide on the most desirable outcome in terms of substance use. This decision is especially complex when the drug of choice is alcohol. A debate is raging in the alcoholism literature over the efficacy of controlled drinking as opposed to abstinence (Fisher, 1982; Heather & Robertson, 1981; Marlatt, 1983; Pendery, Maltzman, & West, 1982; Sobell & Sobell, 1984). Yet much of the controversy surrounding "controlled drinking" arises from a misunderstanding of the term.

> It is important to note . . . that the term "controlled drinking" has been used in the literature in two different ways. It refers both to

> the use of specific *skills and techniques* designed to teach the individual how to exercise "control" over drinking, and to a *level of drinking* that is considered nonproblematic (drinking that does not eventuate in intoxication or other drinking-related problems). Critics, particularly those identified with the disease model of alcoholism, often overlook this distinction and mistakenly conclude that controlled drinking involves a misguided attempt on the part of the drinker to attempt control by the sheer exercise of willpower or volitional restraint [Marlatt, 1983, p. 1100].

The controlled-drinking controversy also appears to be based on an incorrect framing of the question involved in setting goals. Writers and clinicians concerned about the dangers of setting controlled drinking as a goal tend to ask whether it is "possible for alcoholics." Instead, the question should be, "What outcomes seem to be most appropriate for what clients in what situations?" Clearly, there are individuals for whom controlled drinking is an inappropriate objective, just as some individuals are more likely to relapse when they attempt abstinence. Miller and Munoz (1982, p. xix) suggest to readers of their self-help book that they should not pursue controlled drinking as a goal if any of the following are true for them:

• If you have liver disease, stomach ulcer, or other disease of the gastrointestinal system that will be made worse by drinking. . . .
• If you have a type of heart disease that is made worse by drinking. . . .
• If you have any other physical condition in which your health and well-being would be threatened by even moderate drinking. . . .
• If you are a woman who is pregnant or who is trying to become pregnant, because alcohol is highly dangerous to the fetus from the day of conception and there is *no* known safe level of drinking during pregnancy.
• If you lose control of your behavior every time or almost every time you drink even moderate amounts of alcohol.
• If you are or have been physically addicted to alcohol, so that decreasing or stopping drinking results in . . . physical symptoms. . . .
• If you are taking tranquilizers, sedatives, sleeping pills, antidepressants, or any other drug or medication that is dangerous when combined with alcohol. . . .
• Finally, we *do not* recommend that you try controlled drinking if you are currently abstaining successfully. If you are dry and doing well, it is a definite risk to attempt moderation, particularly if you have a family history of alcoholism or a personal history of serious drinking problems.

Clinicians who are frightened by the concept of controlled drinking tend to believe that, although many people would be harmed by a goal of moderation, none would be put at any particular risk by striving for abstinence. In fact, however, "for nondependent persons the risk of relapse from controlled drinking is, if anything, lower than that from abstinence" (Miller, 1985a, p. 590). If drinkers are young and healthy, if they have not shown signs of physical dependence on alcohol, if their problem drinking is of less than ten years' duration, if they have few life problems associated with alcohol use, and if they object to abstinence, they may do best working toward moderating their drinking. The key to setting goals in this important area is a recognition that differential outcomes are not only possible but also preferable to a rigid insistence that each client fit the counselor's preconceived ideal.

The client's substance abuse must also be considered in the context of other life problems, although not necessarily in terms of causality. Substance abuse tends to be associated with a variety of social, psychological, family, and financial problems. The counselor does not need to determine whether these problems are a cause of or a result of substance abuse. Each of a client's major concerns should be addressed as part of the counseling process under the assumption that a favorable outcome involves rehabilitation across several life domains. Only an assessment process that sets individual goals and takes note of individual deficits can lead to comprehensive treatment. Thus, each client's treatment plan should include long- and short-term goals dealing with both substance use and other issues. Among the general life areas that might be addressed, depending on the individual's concerns, are the following:

- resolving or avoiding legal problems
- attaining financial stability
- attaining marital or family stability
- setting and meeting career development goals
- setting and meeting educational goals
- improving interpersonal or social skills
- improving assertion skills
- enhancing physical health and fitness
- learning more effective methods for coping with stress
- developing more effective problem-solving and decision-making skills
- learning relaxation skills
- learning to recognize and express feelings
- adapting more effectively to work or school situations
- developing social support systems
- increasing involvement in recreational and other social pursuits
- dealing with psychological issues such as depression or anxiety
- increasing general feelings of self-esteem and self-efficacy

Obviously, not every client needs to set goals in each of the areas listed above. The assessment process should identify deficits that can be addressed through treatment, with interventions then tailored to the specific outcomes desired.

The counselor who has worked out a reasonable set of goals with the client can use a number of techniques for reaching those goals. Among the counseling methods most frequently used in the substance abuse field are behavioral self-control training (teaching clients the techniques they need to monitor and change their own behaviors); contingency management (identifying and manipulating environmental factors that reward or punish the substance use behaviors); relaxation, assertion, and social-skills training; marriage and family therapy; vocational counseling; cognitive restructuring (helping clients alter their appraisals of self and environment); assistance with problem solving and decision making; aversive conditioning (coupling substance use with a real or imagined unpleasant experience); stress-management training; group counseling; life-style and recreation planning; provision of information about the effects of psychoactive drugs; and referral to such self-help organizations as Alcoholics Anonymous and Narcotics Anonymous. The counseling process often takes place in the context of an agency also using pharmacological components, such as disulfiram, which acts as an antagonist to alcohol, or methadone, a maintenance drug considered more appropriate than the illegal opiates to which a client had been addicted.

Any combination of the methods listed above may be appropriate for a specific client. It would not be effective, however, to use this entire group of interventions as a package for all substance-abusing clients. What Lazarus (1965) termed a "broad-spectrum" approach, designed to address problems beyond the narrow band of substance use behaviors, can be workable only to the degree that it is adapted to match each client's actual needs.

## Enhancing Self-Efficacy

The substance abuse field's most controversial question involves the degree of responsibility that clients should assume for their recovery. One of the most important contributions of the disease concept of addictions has been its encouragement of the understanding that victims of the disorder should not be blamed or punished for behaviors that are essentially involuntary (Fingarette, 1983). Yet the affected individuals pay a price for social or medical recognition of their inability to establish control over their consuming behaviors. With the assumption of blamelessness may come the attribution of powerlessness.

> It is ironic that the major strength of the disease model, absolving the addict of personal responsibility for the problem behavior, may also be one of its major shortcomings. If alcoholics come to view their drinking as the result of a disease or physiological addiction, they may be more likely to assume the passive role of victim whenever they engage in drinking behavior if they see it as a symptom of their disease. . . . Relapse is the turning point where the disease model is likely to backfire. If an alcoholic has accepted the belief that it is impossible to control his or her drinking (as embodied in the AA slogan that one is always "one drink away from a drunk"), then even a single slip may precipitate a total, uncontrolled relapse. Since drinking under these circumstances is equated with the occurrence of a symptom signifying the reemergence of the disease, one is likely to feel as powerless to control this behavior as one would with any other disease symptom [Marlatt & Gordon, 1985, pp. 7–8].

The notion that some treatment approaches might contribute to clients' feelings of powerlessness is alarming, because such feelings tend to interfere with *any* individual's ability to cope with difficulties or resolve problems. For example, Kobasa (1979) conducted research on factors that differentiated between people who became ill or stayed well in similarly stressful conditions. To describe the individuals who were able to cope with stress and remain healthy, she used the term *hardiness*, which she found to consist of four major elements: vigorousness toward the environment, a sense of meaningfulness, a strong commitment to the self, and an internal locus of control. The people most able to cope with stress were the ones with the strongest belief in their ability to meet the challenges placed on them by their environments!

Similarly, Lazarus (1980) identifies differences between people who see potential stressors as threats to their well-being and those who see the same events as positive challenges.

> A working hypothesis about the causal antecedents of threat and challenge is that the former is more likely when a person assumes that the specific environment is hostile and dangerous and that he or she lacks the resources for mastering it, while challenge arises when the environmental demands are seen as difficult but not impossible to manage, and that drawing upon existing or acquirable skills offers a genuine prospect for mastery [p. 48].

Under the assumption that people can cope more effectively if they believe in their own potential mastery, Stensrud and Stensrud (1983) point out that counselors should help clients "take personal control of their lives, accepting stress as a challenge rather than a harm-loss-threat factor, finding personal meaning within stressful situations" (p. 216).

The unifying concept underlying these notions of competence is what Bandura (1982) terms *self-efficacy*. Efficacy involves a general ability to deal with one's environment, mobilizing whatever cognitive and behavioral skills are needed to manage challenging situations. Perceived self-efficacy entails the individual's judgment about his or her ability to cope with the environment. This judgment affects all aspects of performance; a person who lacks self-efficacy tends to avoid challenges and to give up quickly when obstacles arise.

> In any given activity skills and self-beliefs that ensure optimal use of capabilities are required for successful functioning. If self-efficacy is lacking, people tend to behave ineffectually even though they know what to do. . . . The higher the level of perceived self-efficacy, the greater the performance accomplishments. Strength of efficacy also predicts behavior change. The stronger the perceived efficacy, the more likely are people to persist in their efforts until they succeed [pp. 127–128].

Thus, clients dealing with any pressing life problem are most likely to achieve and maintain behavior changes if they have a positive perception of their self-efficacy. When they are dealing with substance abuse issues, self-efficacy becomes even more important as a means of preventing a relapse.

> When coping skills are underdeveloped and poorly used because of disbelief in one's efficacy, a relapse will occur. Faultless self-control is not easy to come by for pliant activities, let alone for addictive substances. Nevertheless, those who perceive themselves to be inefficacious are more prone to attribute a slip to pervasive self-regulatory inefficacy. Further coping efforts are then abandoned, resulting in a total breakdown in self-control [Bandura, 1982, pp. 129–130].

Given the importance of self-efficacy for the maintenance of positive behaviors and the prevention of relapse, the counselor needs to encourage each client's sense that control is possible. Rollnick and Heather (1982), in applying Bandura's self-efficacy theory to abstinence-oriented alcoholism treatment, point out that both outcome expectations and efficacy expectations have positive and negative forms.

> On the one hand the expectation is created that life-long abstinence (the prescribed behavior) will lead to the resolution of the drinking problem (the desired outcome) while, on the other hand, it is also emphasized that if the alcoholic returns to drinking, this will lead to relapse. Similarly, efficacy expectations also appear in a positive and negative form. Thus, attention is directed at developing the alcoholic's feelings of personal mastery at being able to remain

> abstinent, yet an expectation is also created that stresses the person's weakness and inability to cope with further drinking. . . . For treatment to be successful, the alcoholic would need to endorse the positive form of each expectation; in other words, believe that lifelong abstinence is the desired solution, *and* develop the sense of personal mastery or self-efficacy necessary for achieving this goal [p. 244].

It seems apparent that treatment should focus on enhancing the client's feelings of personal mastery, especially through the provision of opportunities to plan for and practice appropriate coping behaviors. The question that needs to be addressed, however, is whether this focus on personal responsibility brings with it an implication that if substance-abusing clients are responsible for their sobriety, they must also have been responsible (that is, to blame) for the initiation of the problem. Fortunately, "people can learn effective methods of habit change, whether the goal is abstention or moderation, regardless of how the problem initially developed" (Marlatt & Gordon, 1985, p. 12). Clients can learn to take responsibility for resolving their problems without being forced to shoulder the blame for their etiology.

Brickman, Rabinowitz, Karuza, Coates, Cohn, and Kidder (1982) clarify this issue by categorizing models of helping and coping in terms of attribution of responsibility. "Whether or not people are held responsible for causing their problems and whether or not they are held responsible for solving these problems are the factors determining four fundamentally different orientations to the world, each internally coherent, each in some measure incompatible with the other three" (p. 369). Brickman and his colleagues define four models that can inform the helping process:

1. *The moral model:* people are responsible both for creating and for solving their problems.
2. *The medical model:* people are responsible neither for their problems nor for the solutions.
3. *The enlightenment model:* people are responsible for creating their problems but not for solving them.
4. *The compensatory model:* people are not responsible for creating their problems but are responsible for solving them.

Thus, the moral model attributes full responsibility for each problem to the individual affected; if drinking or drug use is the problem, willpower is the solution. In contrast, the medical model suggests that neither the problem nor the solution is under the control of the client; substance-dependent clients should not accept blame for their addictions but should recognize that they cannot resolve their problems without treatment. The enlightenment model suggests that people do bear the responsibility for their past behaviors but can be helped by surrendering personal power to a stronger force outside themselves. Finally, the compensatory model expects individuals to assume responsibility for solving their problems despite the fact that the problems are not of their own making.

> The strength of the compensatory model for coping is that it allows people to direct their energies outward, working on trying to solve problems or transform their environment without berating themselves for their role in creating these problems, or permitting others to create them, in the first place. The compensatory model also allows help recipients to command the maximum possible respect from their social environment. They are not blamed for their problems, but are given credit for coming up with solutions [Brickman et al., 1982, p. 372].

Marlatt and Gordon (1985) exemplify the adaptation of this model to substance abuse issues when they point out that the etiology of an addiction may be governed by totally different factors than the process of recovery and that effective treatment requires "a sense of detachment between the problem behavior and the person's identity and self-concept" (p. 17), rather than an equation of the person and the disorder. The substance-abusing client can become an active master of his or her behavior change. In fact, this sense of mastery — of self-efficacy — may be the most important determinant of the individual's recovery if Peele (1985a) is correct in saying that "people recover to the extent that they (1) believe an addiction is hurting them and wish to overcome it, (2) feel enough efficacy to manage their withdrawal and life without the addiction, and (3) find sufficient alternative rewards to make life without the addiction worthwhile" (p. 156).

## Multidimensional Treatment

Washton (1984) has pointed out that abstinence is a prerequisite to therapeutic progress, not an end point. When a client begins to abstain from or control drug use, not all of his or her problems will automatically fade away. Some remain in effect, either because their etiology was independent of substance abuse or because years of heavy drinking or drug use have created multiple life problems too serious to be ignored.

> Problems in all life areas undoubtedly have multiple determinants, and reduction in drinking cannot be expected to result invariably in across-the-board improvement. A recovered alcoholic who was unemployed while drinking abusively may have to overcome other

obstacles (e.g., acquiring needed skills) before becoming employed [Finney, Moos, & Mewborn, 1980, p. 26].

It is for this reason that counseling must be multidimensional, integrating "dynamic and systematic procedures to maximize the individual's . . . emotional, social, vocational, and biopsychological functioning as well as to obtain drinking behavior goals" (Hart, 1982, p. 930).

Counselors who believe in individualized, efficacy-enhancing treatment tend to appreciate the importance of a number of factors beyond the individual's specific substance-abusing behaviors. They realize that, in the long run, their clients' recovery depends not just on their personal qualities but also on the nature of their social environments and on their repertoire of skills for coping with the "real world" in which sobriety must be maintained.

Social, cultural, biological, and psychological factors interact reciprocally in both the etiology and the resolution of substance-related problems. In discussing adolescent drug use, for instance, Pandina and Schuele (1983) point out:

> A major application of this view is that efforts toward prevention and rehabilitation aimed at changing adolescent alcohol and drug use may not be maximally effective if they are limited in focus to the use behavior itself or to an isolated domain of the adolescent's life. Instead, interventions should focus simultaneously on multiple domains. The multidimensional approach is also advisable because alcohol and drug use is intertwined with many issues and problems confronting adolescents, often to the extent that focusing solely on establishing the "cause and effect" relationship between substance abuse and life problems obscures the path to a successful intervention [p. 971].

Any intervention designed to address adolescent substance abuse obviously needs to take peer and parental influences into account. Yet, if adolescent initiation into drug use is a "group phenomenon" (Polich et al., 1984), so is the maintenance of substance-abusing life-styles among adults. Stephens (1985) describes a "street addict subculture" with an accompanying role that may be highly valued by heroin-dependent individuals. "The role is highly prominent (almost to the exclusion of all other roles), has a very great level of social support from other junkies, provides both intrinsic and extrinsic social and psychological rewards and can be enacted successfully in most social situations" (p. 437). As the addiction process continues, the salience of the street-addict role increases, so that the individual spends an ever-greater percentage of his or her time with other addicts and is increasingly avoided by nonaddict friends and relatives. Stephens hypothesizes that "the greater the role strain felt by the street addict, the greater the likelihood of abstinence" (p. 441) and, conversely, "the greater the extent to which the person is cast into the role of street addict, the more likely the person is to relapse" (p. 442).

Social and environmental factors are important in the recovery of any substance-abusing client, regardless of age or drug of choice.

> It may be that cultural factors exert their greatest influence on the initial decision to experiment with a particular substance. Biological factors may be seen to account for relatively more variance in determining continuation of use and in the transition from use to abuse. Here is where genetic differences in drug sensitivity and metabolism, the development of tolerance, conditioned or otherwise, abstinence phenomena, and the reinforcing properties of the drug may play a critical role. Finally, psychosocial and environmental factors may be most critical in the determination of cessation and relapse [Galizio & Maisto, 1985, p. 428].

The multidimensional nature of recovery has major implications for the counseling process. As Finney, Moos, and Mewborn (1980) point out, "Therapeutic efforts must go beyond the patient to deal with the contexts in which the patient functions after treatment" (p. 28). First, treatment goals need to take into account not just substance use but also rehabilitation in such areas as occupational functioning, psychological well-being, and social involvement. Second, levels of functioning in these aspects of life may have strong influences on the likelihood of relapse.

> The occurrence of stressful events may trigger a relapse, whereas the use of positive coping mechanisms may facilitate the recovery process. This delicate interplay between a patient's functioning and such posttreatment factors points to the importance of offering treatment aimed at (a) helping patients minimize the likelihood of stressful situations where possible and (b) developing coping skills for effectively dealing with problematic situations [Cronkite & Moos, 1980, p. 313].

The negative effects of stressful life events can be lessened if clients learn more effective coping responses, increase their feelings of self-efficacy, and purposefully build the environmental resources available to them. Among the most important social support systems affecting recovery are family and marital resources, positive work environments, and community support networks (Moos, Cronkite, & Finney, 1982). Counselors are most likely to be effective if they help their clients identify and enhance both the personal and the environmental resources at their disposal. Peele (1985b, p. 226) suggests that treatment will succeed if it

1. enhances self-esteem and esteem-gathering opportunities

2. enhances the skills that enable people to control their situations and directs people to more manageable environments
3. enhances interpersonal skills and helps people become involved in more fruitful environments
4. enhances work habits and encourages people to find manageable tasks and satisfying endeavors
5. increases people's tolerance for imperfection and discomfort while removing them from painful circumstances inimical to life

It is a rare counseling setting that successfully addresses these issues and prepares clients to face the social and economic realities of the posttreatment environment. Such treatment programs do exist, however, with one of the best documented examples provided by the Community Reinforcement Program (Azrin, 1976), a state hospital inpatient program for male alcoholics. This program is unusual in its comprehensiveness, providing treatment that includes the following components:

*job counseling:* helping clients find permanent, full-time, well-paying jobs that would interfere with a return to drinking

*marital counseling:* providing counseling for all married couples and arranging "synthetic families" for unmarried alcoholics

*resocialization and recreation:* arranging alcohol-free social and recreational activities in addition to making Alcoholics Anonymous referrals

*problem-prevention rehearsal:* teaching clients how to handle situations that might otherwise lead to drinking

*early warning system:* providing a mail-in Happiness Scale to be used daily by clients

*disulfiram:* developing positive, supportive mechanisms for clients to use Antabuse for impulse control

*group counseling:* providing supportive group sessions that can develop into social or recreational groups after release

*buddy procedure:* selecting recovering peer advisers to work closely with each client

*contracting:* using written contracts to formalize the agreements between counselors and clients regarding the program's procedures and the client's responsibilities

A multidimensional approach like the Community Reinforcement Program is built on a recognition of the very real pressures faced by clients when they return to their familiar social and work environments.

Newly acquired social skills are subject to multiple environmental influences. For example, the physical environment (mass media, advertising, sensory cues for drinking) is structured to increase the likelihood of drinking, and drinking is associated with such social activities as conversation, recreation and dating. Under these environmental influences recovering alcoholics may not only lose existing support, but receive negative sanctions from former drinking associates. Finally, many recovering alcoholics do not have the personal resources (e.g., transportation, family, friends, employment) necessary to engage in new social situations. . . . An alternative approach is to create a new social system in the alcoholics' natural environment that provides wide varieties of social and recreational activities and reinforces the acquisition of appropriate social behaviors [Mallams, Godley, Hall, & Meyers, 1982, p. 1116].

## Choosing the Least Intrusive Alternative

Clients can be helped most effectively if their treatment is based on the least intrusive possible alternative, given any special health, safety, and support needs they may have. Thus, if an individual's physical, emotional, and social resources are adequate, he or she should be referred for self-help in preference to professional treatment. If treatment is needed, outpatient counseling is preferable to inpatient, nonmedical to medical, and short-term to long-term.

> The advantages for outpatient treatment are basically much lower economic and social cost. The patient being treated on an outpatient basis can expect a continued enmeshment in his or her community roles and benefit from community supports—job and family, to name the most important. . . . Outpatient treatment is inherently more flexible and accessible, thus giving it greater probability of being individualized [Brandsma & Welsh, 1982, p. 886].

Outpatient clients may have the greatest likelihood of maintaining effective social ties; of having individualized, multidimensional treatment; and of retaining a sense of responsiblity for themselves and their own recovery. Personal perceptions of self-efficacy are even further enhanced if the individual's recovery involves participation in a self-help organization.

> When people have the opportunity to participate with others. . . their ties to the community are strengthened. When helping becomes a *mutual* occupation, each participant becomes aware of his or her value to others. In "self-help" organizations, people with common bonds have the opportunity to make contact with one another, to provide mutual support, to request or provide active assistance, and to deal with common problems in an understanding but realistic group. . . . The fact that each member of a self-help group becomes a *care giver* is the key to the efficacy of this approach [Lewis & Lewis, 1983, pp. 124–125].

Clients who begin the recovery process in the context of their own communities and who have the opportunity to give help as well

as to receive it can "acquire a new sense of independence and em-
powerment as a consequence of dealing effectively with their own
problems" (Gartner, 1982, p. 64). In contrast, people who have had
long stays in the hospital may achieve abstinence but lose some
personal power in the process. An interesting example is provided
by Longabough, McCrady, Fink, Stout, McAuley, Doyle, and McNeill
(1983), who compared long-term inpatients with a group who lived
at home and commuted to the hospital for day or evening sessions.
A follow-up found no difference between the two groups in drinking
behavior, life tasks, or use of subsequent treatment; both groups had
improved in their average number of days abstinent. But there were
differences between the groups in interpersonal functioning and in
psychological well-being. The partial-hospitalization group improved more in both of these areas, leading the researchers to consider the notion that the stigmatizing and dependency associated
with institutionalization might interfere with personal well-being.

Certainly, some clients will always need more intensive treatment, especially if they have medical problems or lack stable support systems in their own communities. In general, however, it is
the responsibility of practitioners to consider closely the efficacy of
less disruptive choices for clients, rather than assuming that more
acute care is the safest alternative. Giuliani and Schnoll (1985) suggest a set of carefully designed criteria that should inform admissions decisions, as shown in Exhibit 1.1.

As Exhibit 1.1 demonstrates, a number of factors beyond the nature of the client's chemical dependency must be considered in the
choice of treatment modality.

> Traditionally, patients have been slotted into treatment modalities
> and programs based on preconceived assumptions concerning
> what "all alcoholics" or "all heroin addicts" needed. Frequently,
> alcoholics have been hospitalized in 21- or 28-day programs with
> some form of "aftercare" following inpatient treatment. "Drug
> addicts" have either been channeled into long-term (6 months to
> 2 years or more) residential treatment (therapeutic communities)
> or into outpatient methadone treatment (withdrawal or mainte-
> nance) for opiate addicts and outpatient "drug-free" counseling for
> polydrug abusers. . . . As patients are more carefully assessed based
> on specific characteristics, it becomes apparent that not all pa-
> tients require the same level of care [Giuliani & Schnoll, 1985,
> pp. 204–205].

Any decision regarding the intensity of care should take into account both the client's personal resources and supports and the
likelihood that detoxification might become a medical emergency.
"Ideally, an assessment process should take into account all aspects
of the client's functioning, should pave the way for a treatment alternative involving the least possible disruption for the individual,

## ▌Exhibit 1.1

### Admission Criteria for Substance Abusers

#### I. Criteria for Acute Hospital Care

1. failure to make progress in less intense levels of care
2. high-risk chemical withdrawal (seizures, delirium tremens)
3. high tolerance to one or multiple substances
4. acute exacerbation of medical or psychiatric problems related to chemical dependence (cardiomyopathy, hepatitis, depression)
5. concomitant medical or psychiatric problem that could complicate treatment (diabetes, bipolar disorder, hypertension)
6. severely impaired social, familial, or occupational functioning

#### II. Criteria for Nonhospital Residential Care

1. failure to make progress in less intensive levels of care
2. ability to undergo chemical withdrawal without close medical supervision
3. stable medical or psychiatric problems that require monitoring
4. impairment of social, familial, or occupational functioning requiring separation from environment
5. sufficiently developed interpersonal and daily living skills to permit a satisfactory level of functioning

#### III. Criteria for Partial Hospital Care

1. no need for 24-hour medically supervised chemical withdrawal
2. stable psychiatric or medical problems
3. sufficiently developed interpersonal and daily living skills to permit a satisfactory level of functioning in this setting
4. no need for intensive psychiatric care
5. freedom from drugs that alter the state of consciousness, other than prescribed medication approved by the program
6. need for daily support rather than weekly or biweekly sessions
7. social system — that is, family, friends, or employment — capable of providing support

#### IV. Criteria for Outpatient Care

1. ability to function autonomously in present social environment
2. stable psychiatric or medical problems
3. sufficient capacity to function in individual, group, or family therapy sessions
4. no need for 24-hour medically supervised chemical withdrawal
5. willingness to work toward goal of abstinence from harmful drug use

*Source*: Adapted from "Clinical Decision Making in Chemical Dependence Treatment: A Programmatic Model" by D. Giuliani and S. H. Schnoll, 1985, *Journal of Substance Abuse Treatment, 2,* 203–208. Copyright 1986 by Pergamon Press, Ltd. Reprinted by permission.

and should safeguard the client's physical well-being" (Lewis, Fussell, & Dana, 1982).

All substance abuse counselors need to exercise caution in assessments and treatment plans. Clients can, in fact, be harmed if they are coerced into treatment that is more life-disrupting than necessary. Beyond this, there is little evidence that long-term hospital care brings the results that its high costs would warrant, at least where alcoholism treatment is concerned. "The absolutely consistent testimony of . . . controlled studies . . . is that heroic interventions—those in longer, more intensive residential settings—produce no more favorable outcomes overall than treatment in much simpler, shorter, and less expensive settings" (Miller, 1985b, p. 2).

## Openness to New Methods

One of the major shortcomings of substance abuse treatment in recent years has been a rigid tendency to rely too heavily on familiar practices at the expense of fresh possibilities. Although some parts of the United States offer a number of options, treatment alternatives in many areas are severely limited, and clients who find themselves unable to fit into mainstream approaches have few options available.

Many treatment providers seem to be caught in what Odiorne (1974) calls the "activity trap," meaning that they "become so enmeshed in activity they lose sight of why they are doing it, and the activity becomes a false goal, an end in itself" (p. 28). Especially in alcoholism treatment, certain practices have become so common that care-givers, managers, community members, and even clients tend to accept them without question. Yet these methods are grounded neither in theory nor in behavioral research. Many counselors assume, for instance, that "educating clients about alcoholism" is a necessary and possibly even sufficient means to engender sobriety; yet one would be hard pressed to find real support for the generalization that the provision of factual information can be counted on to bring about desired changes in attitude or behavior.

Miller and Hester (1985) describe two thorough reviews of the literature regarding alcoholism treatment. They were seeking to discover what treatment methods had shown promise in controlled research studies. Their first review, culminating in 1979, brought results that the authors saw as disturbing.

> As we constructed a list of treatment approaches most clearly supported as effective, based on current research, it was apparent that they all had one thing in common as of 1979: they were very rarely used in American treatment programs. The list of elements that *are* typically included in alcoholism treatment within the

> United States likewise evidenced a commonality: virtually all of
> them lacked adequate scientific evidence of effectiveness. We were
> shocked. The problem, it seemed, was not that "we know not what
> we do," but rather that in the alcoholism field we are not applying
> in treatment what is already known from research [pp. 526–527].

When the authors updated their review in 1985, they found little
change. The list of methods supported by research and the list of
methods in common use in treatment programs still *did not overlap.*

Among the treatment methods supported by research, Miller and
Hester listed aversion therapies, behavioral self-control training, the
community reinforcement approach, marital and family therapy,
social-skills training, and stress management. The standard treatment methods in American alcoholism programs included Alcoholics Anonymous, alcoholism education, confrontation, disulfiram,
group therapy, and individual counseling.

These findings should not be interpreted to mean that Miller and
Hester believe that the standard treatment approaches are necessarily ineffective. What they are saying is that the treatment methods supported by research have been found to be effective in a
reasonable number of controlled studies, whereas the standard
approaches have not been tested through experimental design.
Some of these poorly documented but commonly used methods
might prove, in time, to have been effective, but they are not at this
time supported by any body of behavioral research. Alcoholics
Anonymous, for instance, has simply not been subjected to enough
controlled research to make any data-based generalizations possible. (It should be noted that Alcoholics Anonymous was never meant
to be considered as a "treatment." In reality, however, most standard treatment programs do utilize AA principles as an important
component; many even require attendance at AA meetings as part of
the treatment protocol or as the basis for aftercare.)

Miller and Hester do not suggest that the treatment interventions listed as supported by research become the new "standard
program." In contrast, they suggest the following:

> We offer three basic principles as prudent guidelines in designing
> future alcoholism treatment programs: (1) Treatment programs,
> both voluntary and involuntary, should be composed of modalities
> supported by current research as having specific effectiveness, and
> consideration should be given to preferential funding of programs
> so constituted. (2) The first interventions offered should be the least
> intensive and intrusive, with more heroic and expensive treatments
> employed only after others have failed. (3) As research warrants,
> clients should be matched to optimal interventions based on pre-
> dictors of differential outcome. Clients should be informed partici-
> pants in their own treatment planning process, and should be
> offered a range of plausible alternatives along with fair and accu-
> rate information upon which to base a choice [1985, p. 562].

## Diversity in Client Populations

Until recently the bulk of information about substance abuse treatment was based on research carried out with White male subjects (Mejta, 1986). Many of the generalizations accepted by substance abuse counselors were therefore severely limited. Most counselors have now come to accept the fact that their clients may be members of highly diverse groups with widely varying goals, needs, and social pressures.

Axelson (1985), in a discussion of groups that are "culturally distinguishable from the mainstream," mentions racial, ethnic, and religious groups; women; the elderly; single-parent families; the divorced; the handicapped; homosexuals; the poor; and young adults (p. 13). These categories represent a cultural pluralism that cannot be overlooked by any counselor. In the substance abuse field the recognition of differing group concerns becomes especially complex because of the need to consider the cultural norms and pressures specifically affecting drug and alcohol use. The counseling process has to take into account the effects of clients' cultural identity on their development of substance abuse problems, as well as on their access to services, likelihood of completing treatment, and ability to maintain long-term recovery.

When considering the service needs of any group or client population, one can usually identify a number of special factors that might influence treatment success. An excellent example of such an effort is provided by a project completed by the Prevention/Treatment Committee of the Illinois Women's Substance Abuse Coalition. In 1985 this committee identified a number of concerns that would be likely to affect the success of substance abuse treatment for women. These concerns, as shown in Exhibit 1.2, were categorized in terms of their importance *before* treatment (hindering access to treatment), *during* treatment, and *after* treatment (affecting the likelihood of a relapse).

Clearly, treatment designed to meet the needs of men cannot hope to succeed with women unless the special concerns identified in Exhibit 1.2 are addressed. Permeating every stage of treatment, from access through relapse prevention, are a host of issues unique to women. The barriers to effective treatment for women run the gamut from practical concerns, such as the lack of child care, to social and psychological issues, such as the culture's contribution to the individual woman's feelings of powerlessness. Appropriate treatment for women depends on the development of programs that increase their options and their feelings of control over their lives. The Illinois Women's Substance Abuse Coalition (1985) suggests a new focus of treatment: "This focus is a shift from dependency to autonomy, from powerlessness to control over one's future, from confrontation to support. While addressing this is not easy or sim-

# ▌ Exhibit 1.2

## Factors Affecting Substance Abuse Treatment for Women

| Factors Important in Seeking Treatment | Factors Important in Completing Treatment | Factors Important in Maintaining Recovery |
|---|---|---|
| lack of child care | availability of specialized medical services | complete follow-up plan with appropriate linkages |
| "stigma" of treatment | housing arrangements | overcoming of cultural and social barriers that contribute to a woman's feeling of helplessness |
| lack of awareness of services | child-care arrangements | |
| legal referrals | children's programming | |
| cost of treatment | appropriate assessment of other needs: sexual abuse, incest, prostitution, eating disorders, mental illness, and so on | establishment of healthy relationships |
| specialized medical and diagnostic services | | counselor attitude that allows women to make choices about their own future |
| support for women seeking treatment | | |
| socialization barriers— always thinking of herself last | programming available to address those needs | reinterpretation of 12-step philosophy* that contributes to recovery for women |
| cultural barriers | training and opportunity to practice coping skills, parenting skills, and the like | |
| unhealthy relationship | | degree of indoctrination with "middle-class" values without recognizing the desires and options of women |
| sexuality issues | vocational assessment and training | |
| | health education, including birth control and sexuality | |
| | legal assistance | |
| | programs designed to empower women, help them look at options and choices; and discourage dependency | |
| | women-only support groups | |
| | positive female and male role models | |
| | cooperation among agencies | |
| | a supportive and trusting environment, with little emphasis on confrontation | |

*The Twelve Steps of Alcoholics Anonymous have been adapted by many other self-help groups. See Chapter 4 for a discussion of this approach.

*Source*: The factors listed here were identified by the Prevention/Treatment Committee of the Illinois Women's Substance Abuse Coalition in January 1985 as part of an effort to improve women's services in the state.

ple, to ignore it is to perpetuate the non-responsive system we have had all along" (p. 4).

Just as women require a more responsive approach, so do other identifiable groups and subcultures. Increasing attention is being paid in the literature to the needs of such groups as the elderly, Native Americans, Hispanics, Blacks, and Asian Americans (Bennett & Ames, 1985; National Institute on Alcohol Abuse and Alcoholism, 1982). Real effectiveness depends, however, on adaptations not just in programs and their components but also in counselor attitudes. Axelson's (1985, p. 385) summary of the competencies recommended by the Education and Training Committee of the American Psychological Association's Division of Counseling Psychology includes the following:

1. awareness of his or her own cultural characteristics
2. awareness of how his or her cultural values and biases may affect minority clients
3. understanding of the American sociopolitical system in relation to minorities
4. the ability to resolve differences of race and beliefs between the counselor and his or her client
5. the ability to know when a culturally different client should be referred to a counselor of the client's own race or culture
6. knowledge and information about the particular group of clients with whom the counselor is working
7. clear and explicit knowledge and understanding of counseling and therapy
8. a wide range of verbal and nonverbal response skills
9. the skill to send and receive both accurate and appropriate verbal and nonverbal messages

Counselors who have developed sensitivity to the sociocultural differences among their clients are likely to work better with either mainstream or minority clients. Ultimately, effective counseling depends on an appreciation of the individuality of each client being served.

# Counselor Roles and Settings

The guidelines just discussed have in common an emphasis on choice, the notion that treatment must be individualized and multidimensional if clients' diverse needs are to be met. We have recommended that counselors address the immediate needs of people whose problems might not require heroic interventions, limit the intrusiveness of their treatments to a level appropriate for the severity of each client's dysfunction, and deal with social and psychological issues beyond substance use behaviors. Pattison (1982, p. 225) suggests that "just on the face validity of clinical logic, it does not seem plausible that treatment efficacy can be optimized by generic, global, diffuse, and nonspecific treatment of such singularly different dimensions of change as drinking behavior, psychological function, social interaction, physical function, and vocational competency." Substance abuse counseling that follows our guidelines will, in fact, tend to be differentiated rather than diffuse, targeted rather than global, and individualized rather than generic.

It is readily apparent that the approach we are suggesting cannot be limited to any one setting or counseling specialization. In fact, providing for each client's special needs actually requires the existence of a number of alternative settings and forms of treatment. Thinking of drug and alcohol use as one aspect of a client's unique constellation of behaviors and characteristics also has two major implications concerning counselors' roles. First, *generalist counselors* must be expected to assess substance abuse issues routinely, just as they would be expected to identify any other behaviors affecting client well-being. Second, *addiction specialists* should recognize their responsibility for dealing with psychological, social, and vocational issues that might interact with drug use, rather than assuming that they can limit the scope of their assessments and interventions to drinking or drug-taking behaviors alone. Counselors' work settings have substantial effects on the issues they face and the day-to-day roles they must perform.

## General Community Settings

Counselors in community agencies and educational settings play a major role in recognizing and confronting substance abuse issues among members of their general client population. Appropriate identification and referral of clients with alcohol or drug problems can mean the difference between timely treatment for the real problem or wasted hours on therapy that fails to address a primary concern.

Pattison (1982), in a discussion of decision strategies in alcoholism treatment, lists seven phases, each of which involves selecting treatments:

*Phase 1: community identification:* In agencies that serve as community ports of entry, alcoholics are identified. If an individual is defined as an alcoholic, decisions concerning the need for treatment or referral are also made.

*Phase 2: triage:* Referral from the entry agency to a treatment facility is made. The referral process may be "desultory or definitive," with the quality of decision making varying widely among agencies.

*Phase 3: entry:* The individual is taken into the specialized treatment facility, with the process now focused on enhancing the client's readiness and motivation for treatment.

*Phase 4: initial treatment:* The client's immediate problems and impairments are identified.

*Phase 5: selection of goals and methods:* Deficits and potential for change in target behaviors are identified, and interventions are planned.

*Phase 6: treatment maintenance and monitoring:* Treatment involvement and goal attainment are assessed and evaluated.

*Phase 7: termination and follow-up:* Evaluation focuses on any remaining deficits, on assessment of potential community functioning, and on planning for community reentry.

Pattison's model also emphasizes three types of decision process: definitional, procedural, and evaluative. Phases 1 and 2 involve definitional decisions, or deciding on diagnostic criteria and defining treatment needs. Phases 3, 4, and 5 involve procedural decisions, or deciding on appropriate clinical interventions. Phases 6 and 7 are evaluative, involving reviews of the client's progress. This model, which would almost certainly be as suitable for drug addiction as for alcoholism, makes it clear that primary definitional decisions take place not in specialized substance abuse facilities but in community agencies dealing with a general client population. Counselors who see themselves as generalists, rather than as substance abuse specialists, bear the bulk of the responsibility both for making initial diagnoses and for helping their clients choose the most appropriate possible treatment strategies for addressing their problems.

## Specialized Substance Abuse Settings

Substance abuse counselors are employed in a variety of settings, each of which meets distinct client needs and tends to raise different concerns regarding the quality of care being offered. Among these organizations are detoxification centers, inpatient rehabilitation programs, therapeutic communities, methadone maintenance programs, drug-free outpatient counseling agencies, and industrial substance abuse programs.

**Detoxification centers**   Detoxification is short-term treatment designed to oversee the client's safe withdrawal from the substance to which he or she is addicted. Whether the abused substance is alcohol or another drug, the initial period of abstinence may bring a high degree of discomfort and may, in fact, constitute a medical emergency for some. In a discussion of detoxification from narcotics, Kleber (1981, pp. 317–318) describes the following general purposes:

1. ridding the body of the acute physiological dependence associated with the chronic daily use of narcotics
2. relieving the pain and discomfort that can occur during withdrawal, especially if it is abrupt
3. providing a safe and humane treatment that can help the individual over the initial hurdle of stopping narcotic use
4. providing an environment that encourages a more long-range commitment to treatment and making appropriate referrals to such other modalities

The goals that Kleber outlines are equally applicable to alcohol detoxification programs, which normally last from three to five days and which also tend to culminate in a referral for additional treatment.

Although detoxification is a physiological phenomenon through which the individual's body becomes free of the abused substance, it also has psychological and social implications that call for a counselor's best efforts. In the context of a detoxification center, the counselor's important role involves

• monitoring the client's progress and referring for medical assistance as needed
• providing emotional support to the client
• encouraging the client and his or her family to use the crisis of detoxification as an opportunity for change
• assessing the client's needs and potential for futher treatment
• working with the client to develop an appropriate plan for treatment
• linking the client to appropriate community and agency resources

Counselors who work in detoxification centers do need to be aware of some pressing issues concerning the well-being of clients seen in such settings. Perhaps most important is the question of the type of client who should be detoxified under the close supervision that these facilities offer. Detoxification centers may be *medical*, in that supervision is provided by medically trained personnel, frequently within a hospital. In these centers physicians may routinely offer medications to enhance the client's safety and comfort. In contrast, *nonmedical*, or *social*, detoxification centers provide counseling, support, and supervision in freestanding, non-hospital settings. Medical personnel are on call in such facilities but are not necessarily present on a regular basis. Many social detoxification centers eschew the use of medications and depend instead on nonpharmacological withdrawal.

Clearly, then, an individual client has at least three choices concerning detoxification: remaining at home, entering a nonmedical detoxification center, or seeking treatment in a medical setting. A number of factors need to be taken into account in the decision-making process, including the stability of the client's home situation and the personal and social support available to him or her. Especially important is the question of the seriousness of the client's physical condition and the likelihood that withdrawal will involve major health risks. Many substance-abusing clients are routinely placed in inpatient detoxification facilities before being provided with additional treatment. In fact, only those clients who demonstrate *physical dependence* on a drug should need supervised detoxification. Even these clients, if medically stable, can be treated effectively in a nonmedical setting. Thus, the principle that treatment should be as unintrusive as possible becomes especially important when we consider the role of the detoxification facility in the general continuum of care.

Individual care is another important issue for counselors working in this milieu. Detoxification can never be more than a first step in treatment and recovery. The counselor at this stage needs to conduct very complete assessments and to work with clients to develop individual treatment plans that include both long- and short-term goals.

**Inpatient rehabilitation** Like detoxification facilities, rehabilitation programs may be housed either in hospitals or in nonmedical settings. In fact, the number of treatment alternatives is increasing as providers experiment with partial hospitalization (providing a full rehabilitation program in the daytime but allowing patients to go home at night) and variable lengths of stay. In general, however, rehabilitation programs tend to have a great deal in common. Whether the facility is run by a general hospital, a freestanding medical treatment unit, or a social agency, the primary emphasis tends to be on psychological rather than physiological factors and on education rather than medicine.

The general purpose of a rehabilitation program is to help individuals gain understanding of their problems and to prepare them for long-term recovery. Ideally, the time spent in the rehabilitation setting should allow clients the opportunity to develop personal recovery goals, to learn the skills needed to prevent a relapse, to prepare for resocialization into the community, and to plan and rehearse an abstinent life-style. An example of such a program is provided by McCrady, Dean, Dubreuil, and Swanson (1985, p. 422) in their discussion of the abstinence-oriented Problem Drinkers Program. The six major goals are as follows:

1. provide clients a social learning framework within which to understand their drinking, and help decrease the guilt and shame about their drinking behavior that many problem drinkers experience
2. assist clients to make a realistic assessment of the extent and severity of their drinking problems, to label their drinking as a problem behavior, and to recognize the necessity of abstaining from the use of alcohol
3. help clients to identify environmental, cognitive, and affective antecedents to their drinking
4. teach clients skills to facilitate maintaining abstinence, such as problem solving, environmental restructuring, social-interpersonal skills, cognitive restructuring, methods of dealing with urges to drink, and relaxation
5. rearrange consequences of drinking by (a) helping clients to change their positive expectancies about the effects of alcohol and to access reinforcers without drinking, and (b) developing social systems to support and reinforce abstinence
6. teach clients about relapses and relapse management

Unfortunately, some rehabilitation programs lack this kind of attention to individual assessment, skill development, and relapse prevention. All too often, inpatients are forced to fit into pre-determined and nondifferentiated activities that may not have any relationship to their unique personal needs. Such programs are especially problematic when they focus almost exclusively on didactic methods, assuming that if clients are "educated" about their disease, rehabilitation will follow. In fact, clients need more than to be sold on the idea of abstinence. They also need help in developing the skills and resources that can increase their control over their lives. They need to know not just why abstinence is desir-able but also how it can be attained.

Another vital issue in any inpatient setting involves the question of its appropriateness for individual clients. In general, outpatient or partial hospital treatment is preferable to hospitalization because of the opportunities clients have to try out their learning in a real-life environment. Clients who have been isolated for weeks from work, family, and social ties may not be accurate in their assess-ments of their own progress and in their expectations regarding their coping skills. If clients are socially stable, physically healthy, and reasonably motivated, a hospital stay should be avoided. If indi-viduals do need inpatient treatment, every effort should be made to ease their transition back to the community at large.

**Therapeutic communities**    Unlike the three- or four-week rehabilitation setting, which has its roots in alcoholism treatment, the therapeutic community has become most prevalent as an intervention for drug abusers, particularly those addicted to opiates. Although the earliest therapeutic communities were staffed by recovering addicts, professional counselors have become increasingly involved with them over the years. Mutual help, however, remains a core value.

> A therapeutic community is a residential center in which the drug user lives, sheltered from the pressures of the outside world and from drugs, and in which he can learn to lead a new, drug-free life. The goal of therapeutic communities is to resocialize the drug abuser by creating a structured isolated mutual-help environment in which the individual can develop and learn to function as a mature participant [Polich et al., 1984, p. 96].

Members have been expected to remain in these isolated residential environments for extremely long stays of a year or more. (In the case of Synanon, an early prototype, the participation of each member was expected to be permanent.) This model depends for its efficacy on a high degree of individual commitment to the community as a whole.

Cohen (1985, p. 281) summarizes the 12 characteristics that therapeutic communities tend to have in common:

1. an arduous admission policy
2. charismatic leadership
3. emphasis on the primacy of personal responsibility
4. mutual assistance
5. self-examination and confession
6. structure and discipline
7. a system of rewards and punishments
8. serving as an "extended family or tribal collective"
9. separation from society
10. staff members not seen as authority figures
11. fostering of physical nonviolence, self-reliance, honesty, and responsibility
12. emphasis on work

Some of the greatest concerns about therapeutic communities are based on these characteristics. The shortcomings of the model lie in the core values of separation from society, long-term isolation, and insistence on conformity to the collective unit.

> Among the criticisms frequently leveled against these facilities have been their use of abrasive and hostile "encounters" (that is, encounter groups) as their central mode of therapy; their inability to attract large numbers of clients, especially minority members, who would be willing to commit themselves to remain for one or more years in a residential setting; the mingling of young users with "hardened" older heroin addicts so that treatment often be-

came an education and incentive toward more serious involvement with drugs and the drug life; the failure to differentiate between different categories of users, such as heroin and marijuana users; the failure to provide for careful record-keeping and for effective follow-up treatment and research; and, finally, the fact that only a small portion of the residents remained in treatment, relapsing in large numbers once they left the facility [Brill, 1981, p. 11].

As in other treatment settings, the key factor in effectiveness remains the appropriateness of the approach for the individual client.

**Methadone maintenance programs**    The use of methadone to treat heroin addiction was pioneerred by Dole and Nyswander in New York in the 1960s. Their goal in using this synthetic opiate was to focus on rehabilitation rather than on abstinence and to help addicts live productive, if not drug-free, lives.

Methadone maintenance has grown in importance as a treatment approach over the last 20 years, at least in part because it is seen as a way to separate the client from the dangers and instability of a life-style devoted to obtaining and using an illegal drug. Ideally, methadone "frees the client from the pressures of obtaining illegal heroin, from the dangers of injection, and from the emotional roller coaster that most opiates produce" (Polich et al., 1984, p. 95). The treatment requires that the client come to a clinic regularly to receive methadone and submit to a urine check to ensure that other drugs are not being used. Methadone is seen as a positive alternative to heroin because it is legal; because it is administered orally, rather than by injection; because it does not produce the level of euphoria of heroin; and because it blocks both the effects and the withdrawal symptoms of the abused opiates. Thus, its use allows for a level of physical, social, and emotional stability that might not be possible if heroin use were continued. This stability is enhanced by the fact that methadone is longer acting than heroin, allowing all doses to be given under clinical observation.

Over the years questions have arisen not so much about the use of methadone but about the context within which it is used. Originally, many agencies provided methadone maintenance in a vacuum, with no other treatment deemed necessary. Now, treatment providers recognize the need to place this method in the context of a treatment plan including counseling and other efforts at rehabilitation. They also recognize that more attention must be paid to the question of whether methadone maintenance is a short-term solution or a long-term panacea.

The primary problem is how to define appropriate treatment goals. Methadone can clearly be used in several alternative treatment models, such as:

1. Brief detoxification. . . .

2. Methadone maintenance as prolonged detoxification lasting months, if not several years. . . . In such cases, the clients could also be placed on high doses of methadone until they had successfully completed other treatment, and then gradually detoxified. This model requires counseling and other ancillary services in association with methadone treatment itself.

3. Methadone maintenance as a "holding device." In this case it is assumed that clients are not motivated to get off drugs but would be willing to be maintained on methadone and reduce the use of illegal narcotics. The assumption is that this would remove the clients from further engagement in a destructive drug-oriented life-style and would keep them out of difficulty until the time when they are motivated to make more substantial changes and perhaps shift to an alternative treatment approach.

4. Methadone maintenance as an indefinite treatment for narcotic addition that perhaps requires life-long continuation of methadone [Renner, 1984, pp. 81–82].

A number of issues thus remain unresolved with regard to methadone maintenance. Most important, substance abuse counselors need to consider the alternative models presented by Renner and to question whether some have more general desirability than others or whether each alternative might have applicability to different subgroups of clients.

**Outpatient counseling agencies**    Substance abuse counseling is offered to outpatients in a number of settings, running the gamut from comprehensive community mental-health centers to the offices of private practitioners, from highly intensive nightly group meetings to biweekly individual sessions, from brief interventions to long-term therapy. Although outpatient counseling varies among counselors and agencies, its positive aspects seem fairly consistent.

First, outpatient counseling allows for a high degree of individualization. Of course, inpatient counselors always attempt to individualize treatment plans as much as possible. In reality, however, the constraints of group-oriented treatment and the need for daily structure often make true differentiation unmanageable. Outpatient counseling, in contrast, is based entirely on the notion that each intervention can be planned with the unique needs of the specific client in mind.

Second, outpatient counseling encourages the development of treatment plans based on both long- and short-term goals. Again, it is difficult for counselors and inpatients working together to think far into the future. Distal goals are seen as ideals, but because only immediate objectives can be met within the context of the typical rehabilitation program, both counselors and clients tend to focus on concrete, readily achievable ends. The outpatient counselor, in contrast, can work with the client one issue at a time until all his or her needs have been addressed. Short-term objectives may still be given priority, but the counselor and client can evaluate each achievement as one step in the direction of the ultimate goal.

Third, outpatient counseling gives the client an opportunity to try out new behaviors in ordinary environments. Much of the potency of substance abuse treatment comes from the client's opportunity to reexamine habitual behaviors, to study the environmental cues that tend to affect drinking or drug use, and to develop a broader repertoire of coping behaviors. Outpatient counseling enhances this process by giving the individual a chance to try new behaviors and attitudes, knowing that the results of each experiment can be discussed at the next counseling session. Furthermore, outpatient counseling allows for easy alteration of the treatment plan in response to any unforeseen difficulties the client may encounter.

Although outpatient counseling should be preferred, it is not appropriate for all clients. The most suitable candidate for an outpatient intervention is one who can function independently on a day-to-day basis, who has sources of social support for a sober or straight life-style, who is medically stable, and who has the ability and motivation to abstain from substance use until a new life-style has been established. As earlier recognition of substance abuse problems becomes the norm, an ever-larger proportion of the clients seen by addiction specialists can be expected to exhibit this profile.

**Occupational substance abuse programs** One of the reasons that substance abuse problems are being identified earlier than previously is the growth of drug and alcohol programs in business and industry. Counseling programs designed for work settings are now known as "employee assistance programs" and deal not just with substance abuse but with a variety of mental- and physical-health issues that might affect job performance. But the employee assistance concept has its roots in the industrial alcoholism programs of the 1940s, and alcohol and drug issues remain central among the concerns of employee assistance counselors, if for no other reason than that the connection between substance abuse and deteriorating work standards is clear. Counselors who work in an employee assistance program (EAP) are expected to be knowledgeable and skilled in assessing and dealing with substance abuse problems. Their primary role involves assessment and referral, not the forming of long-term counseling relationships.

> In the context of an employee assistance program, clients with major health problems, whether physical or psychological, are linked with treatment resources outside of the employing organization. Thus, EAP counselors are not expected to provide treatment or long-term therapy. When they counsel employees, their goal is to give temporary support and assistance so that clients can gain or regain self-responsibility. Employee assistance professionals engage in counseling in the true sense of the word: helping individuals gain skills and mobilize resources so that they can manage problem situations and achieve the highest possible degree of mastery over their environments. The help provided by the employee assistance counselor is short-term, pragmatic, and oriented toward problem solving [Lewis & Lewis, 1986, p. 88].

An employee assistance program is not a treatment modality in itself. Rather, it is a method for helping work organizations to resolve, efficiently and humanely, problems relating to productivity. Thus, an EAP counselor is both a human resource consultant to the organization and a service provider to the employee.

Perhaps the most difficult challenge faced by substance abuse counselors in business and industry involves their ability to wear these two hats, using their clinical skills while working to ensure that the organization as a whole accepts the employee assistance concept as a viable way of solving difficulties. Potential value conflicts are avoided if the employee assistance program is seen as an organizationally based system that includes the following components:

- written policy statements that demonstrate the organization's commitment to referral and treatment for troubled employees
- training for supervisors that encourages them to refer employees to the assistance program on the basis of job-performance criteria
- information for employees that clarifies the nature, purpose, and confidentiality of the services provided
- provision of confidential counseling, assessment, and referral that is easily accessible to all employees
- educational and preventive efforts focused on the organization as a whole

Employee assistance practitioners, like all effective substance abuse counselors, recognize the importance of adapting their methods to the needs of the individuals they serve.

## ▌Summary

Counselors can consider a client's problem as relating to "substance abuse" if continual use of alcohol or another drug affects his or her social or occupational functioning. In dealing with substance abuse issues, counselors should take into account the individual differences among their clients. Among the general principles that can help substance abuse counselors be effective are the following: (1) Conceptualize substance abuse problems as occurring on a continuum, rather than in terms of dichotomous diagnoses. (2) Provide treatment that is individualized, both in goals and in methods. (3) Use methods that enhance the client's sense of self-efficacy. (4) Provide multidimensional treatment that focuses on the social and environmental aspects of recovery. (5) Select the least intrusive treatment possible for each client. (6) Remain open to new methods as research findings become available. (7) Become sensitive to the varying needs of diverse client populations.

These guidelines lead in the direction of treatment that is individualized rather than diffuse and that focuses on other areas of life functioning beyond the specific drinking or drug-use behaviors. Among the contexts in which such counseling might take place are general community settings, detoxification centers, inpatient rehabilitation programs, therapeutic communities, methadone maintenance programs, outpatient counseling agencies, and employee assistance programs. Whether practitioners view themselves as counseling generalists or as substance abuse specialists, they can adapt the methods described in this text to the special needs of their clients. Our general purpose in this book is to describe the approaches best supported by current research and to encourage an individualized, multidimensional approach to the complex problems of substance abuse.

# ▌References

American Psychiatric Association (1980). *Diagnostic and statistical manual of mental disorders* (3rd ed.). Washington, DC: Author.

Axelson, J. A. (1985). *Counseling and development in a multicultural society.* Pacific Grove, CA: Brooks/Cole.

Azrin, H. (1976). Improvements in the community-reinforcement approach to alcoholism. *Behavior Research and Therapy, 14,* 339–348.

Bandura, A. (1982). Self-efficacy mechanism in human agency. *American Psychologist, 37,* 122–147.

Bennett, L., & Ames, G. (1985). *The American experience with alcohol: Contrasting cultural perspectives.* New York: Plenum.

Brandsma, J. M., & Welsh, R. J. (1982). Alcoholism outpatient treatment. In E. M. Pattison & E. Kaufman (Eds.), *Encyclopedic handbook of alcoholism* (pp. 885–893). New York: Gardner Press.

Brickman, P., Rabinowitz, V. C., Karuza, J., Jr., Coates, D., Cohn, E., & Kidder, L. (1982). Models of helping and coping. *American Psychologist, 37,* 368–384.

Brill, L. (1981). *The clinical treatment of substance abusers.* New York: Free Press.

Cahalan, D. (1970). *Problem drinkers: A national survey.* San Francisco: Jossey-Bass.

Cohen, S. (1985). *The substance abuse problems: Vol. 2. New issues for the 1980s.* New York: Haworth Press.

Cronkite, R. C., and Moos, R. H. (1980). Determinants of the posttreatment functioning of alcoholic patients: A conceptual framework. *Journal of Consulting and Clinical Psychology, 48,* 305–316.

Fingarette, H. (1983). Philosophical and legal aspects of the disease concept of alcoholism. In R. G. Smart, F. B. Glaser, Y. Israel, H. Kalant, R. E. Popham, & W. Schmidt (Eds.), *Research advances in alcohol and drug problems.* New York: Plenum.

Finney, J. W., Moos, R. H., & Mewborn, C. R. (1980). Posttreatment experiences and treatment outcome of alcoholic patients six months and two years after hospitalization. *Journal of Consulting and Clinical Psychology, 48,* (1), 17–29.

Fisher, K. (1982, November). Debate rages on 1973 Sobell study. *APA Monitor,* pp. 8, 9.

Galizio, M., & Maisto, S. A. (1985). Toward a biopsychosocial theory of substance abuse. In M. Galizio & S. A. Maisto (Eds.), *Determinants of substance abuse: Biological, psychological, and environmental factors* (pp. 425–429). New York: Plenum.

Gartner, A. (1982). Self-help/self-care: A cost-effective health strategy. *Social Policy, 12,* (4), 64.

Giuliani, D., & Schnoll, S. H. (1985). Clinical decision making in chemical dependence treatment: A programmatic model. *Journal of Substance Abuse Treatment, 2,* 203–208.

Hart, L. S. (1982). Multidimensional rehabilitation of the alcoholic. In E. M. Pattison & E. Kaufman (Eds.), *Encyclopedic handbook of alcoholism* (pp. 930–937). New York: Gardner Press.

Heather, N., & Robertson, I. (1981). *Controlled drinking.* London: Methuen.

Illinois Women's Substance Abuse Coalition (1985). *Report of the Prevention/ Treatment Committee.* Unpublished manuscript.

Kleber, H. D. (1981). Detoxification from narcotics. In J. H. Lowinson & P. Ruiz (Eds.), *Substance abuse: Clinical problems and perspectives* (pp. 317–338). Baltimore: Williams & Wilkins.

Kobasa, S. C. (1979). Stressful life events, personality, and health: An inquiry into hardiness. *Journal of Personality and Social Psychology, 37,* 1–11.

Lazarus, A. A. (1965). Towards the understanding and treatment of alcoholism. *South African Medical Journal, 11,* 736–740.

Lazarus, R. (1980). The stress and coping paradigm. In L. A. Bond & J. C. Rosen (Eds.), *Competence and coping in adulthood* (pp. 28–74). Hanover, NH: University Press of New England.

Lewis, J. A., Fussell, J. J., & Dana, R. Q. (1982). *A three-stage assessment process for alcoholism.* Unpublished manuscript.

Lewis, J. A., & Lewis, M. D. (1983). *Community counseling: A human services approach* (2nd ed). New York: Wiley.

Lewis, J. A., & Lewis, M. D. (1986). *Counseling programs for employees in the workplace.* Pacific Grove, CA: Brooks/Cole.

Longabough, R., McCrady, B., Fink, E., Stout, R., McAuley, T., Doyle, C., & McNeill, D. (1983). Cost-effectiveness of alcohol treatment in partial versus inpatient setting. *Journal of Studies on Alcohol, 44*, 1049–1071.

Mallams, J. H., Godley, M. D., Hall, G. M., & Meyers, R. J. (1982). A social-systems approach to resocializing alcoholics in the community. *Journal of Studies on Alcohol, 43*, 1115–1123.

Marlatt, G. A. (1983). The controlled drinking controversy: A commentary. *American Psychologist, 38*, 1097–1110.

Marlatt, G. A., & Gordon, J. R. (1985). *Relapse prevention: Maintenance strategies in the treatment of addictive behaviors.* New York: Guilford Press.

McCrady, B. S., Dean, L., Dubreuil, E., & Swanson, S. (1985). The problem drinkers' project: A programmatic application of social-learning-based treatment. In G. A. Marlatt & J. R. Gordon (Eds.), *Relapse prevention: Maintenance strategies in the treatment of addictive behaviors* (pp. 417–471). New York: Guilford Press.

Mejta, C. L. (1986). *Study guide: Alcohol and subcultures.* University Park, IL: Governors State University.

Miller, W. R. (1985a). Controlled drinking: A history and critical review. In W. R. Miller (Ed.), *Alcoholism: Theory, research, and treatment* (pp. 583–595). Lexington, MA: Ginn Press.

Miller, W. R. (1985b). *Perspectives on treatment.* Paper presented at the 34th International Congress on Alcoholism and Drug Dependence, Calgary, Alberta.

Miller, W. R., & Hester, R. K. (1985). The effectiveness of treatment techniques: What works and what doesn't. In W. R. Miller (Ed.), *Alcoholism: Theory, research, and treatment* (pp. 526–574). Lexington, MA: Ginn Press.

Miller, W. R., & Munoz, R. F. (1982). *How to control your drinking.* Albuquerque: University of New Mexico Press.

Moos, R. H., Cronkite, R. C., & Finney, J. W. (1982). A conceptual framework for alcoholism treatment evaluation. In E. M. Pattison & E. Kaufman (Eds.), *Encyclopedic handbook of alcoholism* (pp. 1120–1139). New York: Gardner Press.

National Institute on Alcohol Abuse and Alcoholism (1982). *Alcohol and health monograph 4: Special population issues* (DHHS Publication No. ADM 82-1193). Washington, DC: U. S. Government Printing Office.

Odiorne, G. (1974). *Management and the activity trap.* New York: Harper & Row.

Pandina, R. J., & Schuele, J. A. (1983). Psychosocial correlates of alcohol and drug use of adolescent students and adolescents in treatment. *Journal of Studies on Alcohol, 44*, 950–973.

Pattison, E. M. (1982). Decision strategies in the path of alcoholism treatment. In W. M. Hay & P. E. Nathan (Eds.), *Clinical case studies in the behavioral treatment of alcoholism* (pp. 251–274). New York: Plenum.

Pattison, E. M. (1985). The selection of treatment modalities for the alcoholic patient. In J. H. Mendelson & N. K. Mello (Eds.), *The diagnosis and treatment of alcoholism* (2nd ed.) (pp. 189–294). New York: McGraw-Hill.

Pattison, E. M., & Kaufman, E. (1982). The alcoholism syndrome: Definitions and models. In E. M. Pattison & E. Kaufman (Eds.), *Encyclopedic handbook of alcoholism* (pp. 3–30). New York: Gardner Press.

Peele, S. (1985a). *The meaning of addiction: Compulsive experience and its interpretation*. Lexington, MA: D. C. Heath.

Peele, S. (1985b). What treatment for addiction can do and what it can't; what treatment for addiction should do and what it shouldn't. *Journal of Substance Abuse Treatment, 2*, 225–228.

Pendery, M. L., Maltzman, I. M., & West, L. J. (1982). Controlled drinking by alcoholics? New findings and a reevaluation of a major affirmative study. *Science, 217*, 169–174.

Polich, J. M., Ellickson, P. L., Reuter, P., & Kahan, J. P. (1984). *Strategies for controlling adolescent drug use*. Santa Monica, CA: Rand Corp.

Renner, J. A. (1984). Methadone maintenance: Past, present, and future. *Advances in Alcohol and Substance Abuse, 3*, (1,2), 75–90.

Rollnick, S., & Heather, N. (1982). The application of Bandura's self-efficacy theory to abstinence-oriented alcoholism treatment. *Addictive Behaviors, 7*, 243–250.

Sobell, M. B., & Sobell, L. C. (1984). The aftermath of heresy: A response to Pendery et al.'s (1982) critique of "Individualized Behavior Therapy for Alcoholics." *Behavior Research and Therapy, 22*, 413–447.

Stensrud, R., & Stensrud, K. (1983). Coping skills training: A systematic approach to stress management counseling. *The Personnel and Guidance Journal, 62*, 214–218.

Stephens, R. C. (1985). The sociocultural view of heroin abuse: Toward a role-theoretic model. *Journal of Drug Issues, 15*, 433–446.

Vaillant, G. E. (1983). *The natural history of alcoholism*. Cambridge, MA: Harvard University Press.

Washton, A. (1984, October 5). *Cocaine in the workplace*. Paper presented at the national conference of the Association of Labor Management Administrators and Consultants on Alcoholism, Denver.

Willoughby, A. (1979). *The alcohol-troubled person: Known and unknown*. Chicago: Nelson-Hall.

2 | CHAPTER

# Drugs and Their Effects

There is a great deal of ambiguity in our society regarding drug use (Blum, 1984). Only a decade or so ago a drug was something one used to relieve pain, misery, and disease. Today it is frequently viewed in a negative sense, as in the term *drug user* (L. P. Clark, personal communication, 1986). Clearly, drugs offer a number of benefits, including the control of pain and anxiety, the enhancement of feelings of energy and strength, and the achievement of altered states of consciousness. However, drugs can also induce compulsive, bizarre, and irrational behaviors. As a result of this duality of effects, these benefits and risks, we are often uncertain how to approach the topics of drug use, misuse, and abuse.

The purpose of this chapter is to familiarize you with the basic concepts in the study of drugs and drug effects. As members of a drug-using society, we all need to understand better the effects that substances can produce and how they produce them (Leavitt, 1982). As students and counselors we can better understand behavior by understanding how drugs change behaviors. Finally, as substance abuse professionals we will often find ourselves called on by both the community and our clients to explain the effects of drugs.

Drug effects can best be understood as the results of complex interactions among four groups of variables (Blum, 1984): (1) characteristics of the substance itself (Gringauz, 1978), (2) the physiological functioning of the user, (3) the psychological state of the user, and (4) the sociocultural environment in which the drug is used. For simplicity we will discuss each of these variable groups independently.

# Characteristics of Drugs

Let us begin by defining a drug as any substance that alters the structure or function of some aspect of the user. Such a definition is wide-ranging (Kakis, 1982); conceivably, it would include not only the abusable drugs, which will be the focus of this chapter, but also antibiotics, antitoxins, vitamins, minerals, and even water and air.

Water, air, and food are considered to be essential to the survival of organisms and are therefore not generally conceived of as drugs. However, consider the use of oxygen to revitalize a fatigued athlete or the effects of spices and food additives on blood pressure, cardiac function, water retention, and allergic reactions. Similarly, while vitamins and minerals are generally thought of as nutritional supplements, they can produce toxic reactions and other alterations in physiological structure and function. On a different level, numerous drugs used to restore and maintain health are generally not considered to be abusable substances. But there are risks in the use or overuse of such drugs by susceptible individuals.

Thus, drugs, even abusable drugs, are not good or bad per se. Rather, the benefits and risks of substance use depend on how much, how often, in what manner, and with what other drugs a particular substance is used.

## Drug Dosage

Generally, drugs can produce multiple effects. Which effects are produced and how strong those effects are depend partly on the amount of drug ingested. At low doses, for example, alcohol can relax and disinhibit and also stimulate hunger; at higher doses it can cause one to become fatigued and nauseous. The connection between a drug's dose and its effects is called a dose/response relationship. As Figure 2.1 illustrates, below a certain dosage (called the threshold) there is no noticeable effect. As the dosage increases, the effect becomes increasingly strong until it reaches some maximum value. The maximum effect attainable is determined by physiological capabilities (you can only become so relaxed or sedated without falling asleep).

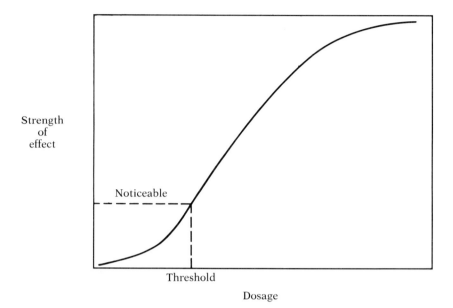

**Figure 2.1**   Dose/response curve

As Figure 2.2 illustrates, the threshold dose may vary with the effect being studied. We see that effect A has a low threshold dosage and also maximizes at a relatively low dose. Effects B and C require higher dosages to initiate. Notice also that effect B terminates well before effect C. Thus, the dosage of a drug affects both what responses will be produced and the strength of the responses. In practical terms this means that users experience quantitatively and qualitatively different effects when they use different dosages of the same drugs.

**Categories of drug effects**   The multiple effects of drugs can be usefully categorized as follows. The desired effect of a drug, or the reason it is used, is the therapeutic effect. All other effects of the drug are collectively referred to as adverse drug reactions (ADRs). Reliable, anticipated, and frequently encountered ADRs are generally referred to as side effects. It should be noted that side effects need not be adverse or undersirable from the client's perspective. In fact, many drugs are used precisely because they contribute to two or more simultaneous effects; for example, acetaminophen and aspirin reduce both pain and fever. Allergic effects differ from side effects in the frequency of occurrence and the ability to anticipate their occurrence. Idiosyncratic reactions are highly unusual effects that are unanticipated and unreliable. Toxic effects result from ingesting lethal or near-lethal doses of a drug (commonly referred to as overdoses). For example, the therapeutic effect of morphine is pain re-

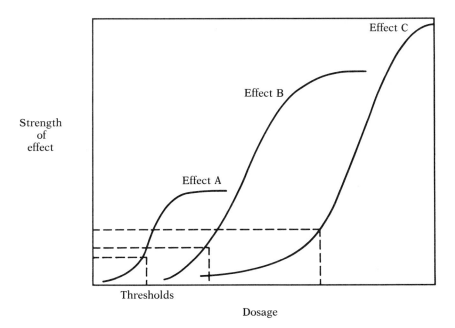

**Figure 2.2**   Multiple dose/response curve

lief; the side effects include pinpoint pupils (miosis) and nausea; the allergic effect might be a mild skin rash; idiosyncratic reactions might include excitation and stimulation; and the toxic effects could include respiratory depression, coma, and death.

**Potency**   The amount of drug necessary to produce a certain effect is determined by the potency of the substance. The more potent a drug is, the smaller the required dosage to produce the desired effect. Alcohol is a relatively impotent drug, since ounces or grams of the drug are required to produce noticeable effects. LSD, on the other hand, is very potent, with dosages measured in micrograms or millionths of a gram.

The potency of a drug is determined by two factors, affinity and efficacy (Goth, 1978). Affinity refers to the drug's ability to attach itself or bind with a receptor, or site of action. Receptors are "slots" on the neural membrane that accept and respond to particular chemical structures, much as a lock will accept and respond to particular keys. Drugs with high affinity bind or attach well with receptors. Efficacy refers to the stimulatory power of the drug on the receptor. Drugs with high efficacy strongly stimulate receptors. To have an effect, a drug must have both affinity and efficacy, and the higher the affinity and efficacy, the more potent the drug is (that is, the smaller the dosage required to produce an effect).

**Therapeutic ratio, or safety margin**    Two dosages of a drug are of particular importance in the study of effects. One of these is the effective dose, or ED. This is the dose required to produce a particular effect in a certain proportion of the population. For example, $ED_{50}$ refers to the effective dose for 50% of the population. The second dosage of importance is the lethal dose, or LD. Again, this is generally specified as $LD_{50}$, referring to the lethal dose for 50% of the population. The ratio of the ED to the LD allows us to compare the relative safety of various drugs as well as giving us some sense of the safety of a particular dose of a drug. This relationship is known as the therapeutic ratio, or safety margin, of a drug. Unfortunately, the lethal dose for many psychoactive drugs is not well established, so we often cannot compute a therapeutic ratio.

## Composition

Pharmaceutical preparations are composed of several ingredients. In addition to the active ingredient a capsule or tablet may also contain binders, fillers, dissolving agents, coloring compounds, coatings, and perhaps even a taste ingredient (Leavitt, 1982). Although these "inactive" ingredients generally do not affect users, some people can react adversely to one or more of them (perhaps because of an allergy or a genetic predisposition). Thus, two apparently identical compounds can have different effects on a user because of sensitivity to the "inactive" ingredients.

Street drugs are not generally subjected to the same quality controls as are prescription and over-the-counter drugs (Cox, Jacobs, LeBlanc, & Marshman, 1983). Street drugs vary in quality, quantity, and purity. By quality, we simply mean that the actual composition of a drug may be different from what it is alleged to be; common mushrooms dusted with phencyclidine can be sold as psilocybin. Quantity and purity refer to the fact that street drugs often vary in the proportions of active ingredients and adulterants. Street cocaine, for example, is from 10% to 90% (averaging about 50%) cocaine, with the remainder consisting of almost anything that is white, flaky, or sparkly (talc, strychnine, phencyclidine, boric acid, and various sugars).

**Drug equivalence**    There are three separate ways of assessing the equivalence of two or more drug compounds. Chemical equivalence means simply that the active ingredients of the compounds are identical. More broadly, chemical equivalence can be used to compare both the active and inactive ingredients of compounds.

The second measure of equivalence is biological equivalence, or bioavailability. Drug compounds that are biologically equivalent provide the same amount of the active ingredient to the user.

The third measure is clinical equivalence, which is based on the observable effects of compounds. Thus, two preparations are said to be clinically equivalent if they produce identical effects.

It is important to realize that these are separate measures of equivalence. In comparing two chemically equivalent drugs, one of them may not dissolve or may dissolve incompletely; hence, the bioavailability and clinical effects will be different. Likewise, the same clinical effects can be produced by two or more related but chemically different drugs with differing bioavailabilities.

## Frequency of Use

How frequently an individual uses a drug has important implications for the effects the drug produces. First, as will be discussed in more detail later, frequent use of a drug increases the likelihood of both physiological and psychological changes in the user. Thus, the user is different from one drug-using episode to the next, and a different user experiences different effects. Second, if a drug is used frequently enough, it or its metabolic by-products can accumulate in the body. Such drug accumulation, in effect, changes the dosage available at any given time and is referred to as a cumulative effect. Figure 2.3 depicts a cumulative-effect curve for four successive doses of a drug.

As Figure 2.3 indicates, the first dose of the drug is administered at $t_0$, when there is none of the drug in the user. The second dose, at $t_1$, is administered before all of the first dose has left the user. Thus, the second dose greatly increases the amount of drug in the body. Likewise, the third and fourth doses are administered before previous doses can be excreted. The overall effect of this series of doses is to produce a much greater effect (and probably more different kinds of effects) than any one dose.

Figure 2.4 depicts a different type of cumulative-effect curve. The doses are spaced in such a way as to establish and maintain a particular drug effect.

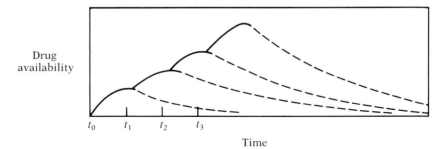

**Figure 2.3**    Enhanced cumulative-effect curve

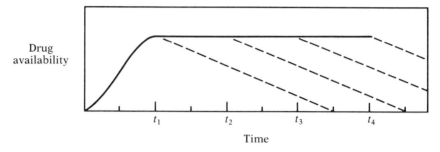

Time

**Figure 2.4**   Maintenance cumulative-effect curve

Figure 2.3 typifies a drinking episode in which the user consumes alcohol faster than the body can excrete it and therefore becomes increasingly intoxicated. Figure 2.4, on the other hand, is typical of a prescription-use pattern designed to achieve and maintain a particular level of the drug in the bloodstream. Figure 2.4 may also be typical of a "speed run," in which the user spaces dosages in such a way as to achieve and maintain a desired "high."

## Route of Administration

There are a number of ways of administering a drug. The three most common methods are oral, injection, and inhalation. However, drugs can also be administered by buccal, sublingual, otic, optic, nasal, rectal, vaginal, and topical routes. We will focus primarily on the swallowing, injection, and inhalation routes.

How a drug is administered affects the onset of effects, the peak effects, and the duration of effects. Drugs administered orally typically take at least 15 minutes to produce an effect and can take much longer, depending on the contents of the stomach and the composition of the drug. Swallowed drugs produce a lower peak, or maximum, effect but typically have a longer duration of effect than either injected or inhaled drugs. Injected drugs typically have quick onsets (a few seconds to a few minutes), very high peaks, and relatively short durations. Inhalation of a drug is, in most respects, very similar to injecting the drug; that is, there is a quick onset, high peak effect, and relatively short duration.

In addition to onset, peak, and duration, several other factors should be taken into consideration in the administration of drugs. Some of these factors are identified in the accompanying box.

## Drug Interactions

In examining the frequency of use, we noted that doses of a drug can be administered in close proximity to one another so as to increase

### Benefits and Risks of Drug-Administration Methods

**Oral**
> *Convenience:* tablets and liquids are very convenient for most people.
> *Cost:* they are generally less expensive to purchase than drugs designed for injection or inhalation.
> *Safety:* they can sometimes be removed by gastric lavage or diluted in the event of an overdose.
> *Gastric irritation:* they can cause stomach or intestinal distress.
> *Dose precision:* part or all of the drug may not be well absorbed or may be chemically altered by stomach, intestine, or liver action before it can affect the individual.

**Injection**
> *Efficiency:* all of the drug dose enters the bloodstream directly.
> *Pain:* many people avoid injections because of the pain involved.
> *Overdose:* it is difficult, if not impossible, to remove, dilute, or neutralize an injected drug.
> *Disease:* unclean needles and improper techniques can result in infections, abscesses, collapsed veins, or scarring.

**Inhalation**
> *Dosage regulation:* rapid onset allows for relatively accurate dose titration.
> *Efficiency:* unless carefully controlled, part of the drug is lost or is diluted by air.
> *Damage:* injury to nose, mouth, trachea, and lungs may occur.

the intensity of the effects and to prolong their duration. The result was referred to as a cumulative effect. Similarly, two or more drugs can be administered in close enough proximity to one another that they alter the type or strength of the effects.

Such drug interactions are categorized into three basic types: additive, synergistic, and antagonistic. Additive interactions occur when the various drugs combine to increase the intensity, number, or duration of the separate drug effects. These additive interactions can be predicted if we know the separate drug effects. For example, Tuinal is a combination of secobarbital and amobarbital designed to achieve the more rapid sedative/hypnotic onset of the secobarbital in combination with the longer effects found with amobarbital. On the street, alcohol or marijuana is sometimes used in conjunction with another drug to enhance the effects of the second substance.

Synergistic interactions are unexpected drug interactions. That is, a knowledge of the separate drug effects does not accurately predict the resultant combined effects. It is not always easy to distinguish additive from synergistic effects. For example, combining alcohol (a depressant) with Seconal (a depressant) may result in severe central nervous system depression, including coma and death, rather than relaxation or sleep, but this effect is partially predictable from a knowledge of both drugs. On the other hand, taking "T's" with "blues" or Tagamet with Valium results in a clearer example of synergistic effects. Combining T's (Talwin, a synthetic opiate) with blues (pyribenzamine, an antihistamine) greatly enhances the narcotic effects of the Talwin, or pentazocine. Likewise, combining Tagamet with Valium greatly enhances the sedative/hypnotic properties of the Valium.

In antagonistic interactions, the drugs counter each other's effects (Goth, 1978). Antagonistic interactions can occur when separate drugs compete for the same receptor (pharmacological antagonism), stimulate opposing physiological reactions (physiological antagonism), or chemically combine to neutralize each other (chemical antagonism). The classic example of pharmacologic antagonism occurs with the combination of morphine and naltrexone. Naltrexone has greater binding power (affinity) than morphine but has no apparent efficacy (stimulator power). Thus, naltrexone occupies the receptor sites, blocks the morphine, and produces no effects of its own. Dexamyl, "speedballs," and "goofballs" are examples of physiological antagonism. Dexamyl is a combination of dextroamphetamine (a stimulant) and amobarbital (a depressant). Speedballs and goofballs are combinations of a stimulant and an opiate or depressant. The purpose of these combinations is to "take the edge off" the drugs—that is, to avoid too much stimulation or depression. These drugs work by stimulating opposing physiological reactions rather than by competing for the same receptor sites. An example of chemical antagonism is the combining of dairy products rich in calcium with tetracycline (an antibiotic), which neutralizes the antibiotic.

Clearly, the effects of a drug depend on several factors, including the dose, composition, frequency of use, route of administration, and presence of other drugs. Once the drug is administered, the physiological characteristics of the user become important in determining what effects the drug will produce.

## Physiological Functioning of the User

The dynamic physiology of the user often influences a drug's effects. Thus, it is important to understand the ways in which people's bodies respond to and process a drug. No two users will experience exactly the same effects from a drug, and one user may have different experiences with the same drug.

Drugs, in turn, often produce direct and indirect changes in the physiological functioning of users. Direct changes occur as a result of chemical actions on the cells, tissues, organs, and systems of the user. Such direct changes occur through irritation, alteration, or destruction of biological constituents. Similarly, drug use may indirectly influence physiological processes through the induction of disease, damage, or malnutrition in the user. However, these direct and indirect changes in physiological processes can often be desirable, as when a drug enhances immune-system activity, reduces irritation or pain, or improves the utilization of nutrients. Thus, physiological processes both affect and are affected by the characteristics of the substances being used.

This section is organized into two parts. The first part focuses on what can be called the pharmacokinetics of drugs. Pharmacokinetics is concerned with the physiological processes involved in the body's absorption, distribution, metabolism, and excretion of a drug (Mayer, Melmon, & Gilman, 1980). The second part focuses generally on pharmacodynamic considerations. Pharmacodynamics is concerned with the study of where and how a drug produces its effects (Gilman, Mayer, & Melmon, 1980). Thus pharmacodynamics involves, for our purposes, the neurological functioning of the user.

## Pharmacokinetics

**Absorption**    Before a substance can have an effect, it must be absorbed by the user. The three principal methods of administering drugs on the street have already been discussed. It is also important to understand that conditions at the site of administration affect the user's absorption of the substance.

The main consideration with injections is the volume of blood flow in the area of the injection. Intravenous (IV) and intra-arterial (IA) injections are generally most rapidly absorbed, since the substance, or bolus, is deposited directly in the blood. The speed of absorption for intramuscular (IM) and subcutaneous (SQ) injections depends on the blood flow in the area of the injection. Similarly, the absorption of inhaled substances varies with disease or damage to the nasal and oral cavities, trachea, and lungs.

Absorption of swallowed drugs is somewhat more complicated. First, the drug must be placed in solution. Liquids are more readily absorbed than tablets or capsules, and the latter can be enhanced by the use of disintegrating agents or retarded through special coatings to delay disintegration. Second, swallowed drugs are generally absorbed more readily in the intestines than in the stomach. Thus, the presence of food may delay absorption. Third, the acidity/alkalinity of the stomach and intestines affects solubility. The acidity of the stomach and the alkalinity of the intestines can be altered by a number of factors, including foods, other drugs, and disease or damage. Fourth, higher doses produce higher concentrations of the drug, and high concentrations are absorbed more readily than low concentrations. Finally, lipid, or fat-soluble, drugs pass through the membrane walls of the digestive system and enter the bloodstream faster than water-soluble drugs.

**Distribution**   Unless it is directly injected into the site of action, a substance must travel there from the site of administration. This transportation depends on the cardiovascular functioning of the user. Several variables affect a substance's distribution in the body.

First, the distribution of a substance is systemic. That is, the drug is distributed throughout the body as it travels with the blood. Second, in order to travel in the bloodstream, the drug must have an affinity for (must attach itself to) some element of the blood chemistry or move by hydraulic pressure. Third, the speed at which a drug is distributed depends on the efficiency of the heart. Cardiac efficiency, in turn, depends on the health and stimulation of the heart muscle. Finally, whether enough drug reaches the site of action depends on both the dose (since it will be diluted throughout the entire body) and the affinity of the drug for various biological components of the organism (the drug may be stored in inactive or nonresponsive areas of the body).

**Metabolism**   As a drug is distributed throughout the body, it eventually arrives at the liver, the primary chemical detoxification system of the body. The liver is capable of chemically altering the original substance to form a new and often inactive drug. The liver may perform any of four chemical alterations on the initial drug: oxidation, hydrolysis, reduction, or conjugation (combining the drug molecule with a biological compound). These chemical alterations produce metabolic by-products, which are generally deactivated forms of the original substance that can be excreted from the body.

One of the disadvantages of swallowed drugs is that significant proportions of them are transported from the digestive system to the liver and metabolized before having any effect on the user's behavior (first-pass metabolism). In addition, although metabolic by-products are generally less active than the original substance, occasionally (as with chloral hydrate) the liver produces an active drug from an inactive one. Finally, we need to be aware that small amounts of the drug may be metabolized outside the liver and that small amounts of most drugs are excreted unmetabolized.

The rate at which a drug is metabolized depends on several factors. Disease or damage to the liver can retard metabolization. Malnutrition can alter metabolism, since vitamins, minerals, and other compounds essential for the production of enzymes and catalysts are unavailable. Cardiovascular functioning is important, since the slower the distribution of the drug to the liver, the slower the rate of metabolism will be. Sequestration, or storage, of the drug in body tissues also inhibits metabolism. One factor that can enhance metabolism is the user's previous use of a substance or related drug. Use of a drug often stimulates the production of the enzymes and catalysts essential to its metabolism. Thus, the liver becomes more efficient at metabolizing the substance because of the increased availability of these chemicals. This efficiency, or metabolic tolerance, is one reason that users develop a tolerance to drugs.

Metabolism of a substance is the primary method by which a drug's actions are terminated. After absorption and during the initial stages of distribution, the relative concentration of the drug is higher in blood plasma than in other tissues. As distribution progresses, a relative balance of the drug in blood plasma and in other tissues is established through homeostatic equilibration. As the liver metabolizes the drug, it is redistributed from other tissue sites back into the bloodstream in order to maintain a relative equilibrium. This redistribution means that the substance leaves the site of action, and the effects terminate.

**Excretion**  The final stage in the pharmacokinetics of a drug is the excretion of the drug and its metabolic by-products. For most drugs the primary method of excretion is through urination. However, some of the drug or its derivatives can also be excreted in defecation, respiration, or perspiration.

Since urination is the principal method of drug excretion, kidney and bladder functioning become important considerations. The ability of the kidneys to remove drugs and their metabolic by-products is dependent on cardiovascular and hepatic (liver) functions. Second, disease or damage to the kidneys or bladder can impair the rate of excretion. Finally, pure drugs and their by-products can be reabsorbed into the bloodstream from the urinary system. Thus, impairment of excretory functions can prolong the duration of a drug's effects or produce different effects. For example, significant amounts of pure phenobarbital and mescaline are found in the urine of users. Delay in the excretion of these drugs once removed from the bloodstream can result in significant reabsorption of the active drug.

The *half-life* of a drug is the amount of time required to metabolize and excrete one-half of the original dose (Lader, 1980). The half-life is therefore a measure of the drug's duration of action. Half-life measures assume "normal" cardiovascular, metabolic, and excretory functioning. If these functions are enhanced or (more likely) impaired, the duration of action for a particular user is decreased or increased.

## Pharmacodynamics

Pharmacodynamics is the study of where and how a drug produces its effects. Generally speaking, the major effects of psychoactive substances are produced through their action on the central nervous system. Thus, to understand better the site of action and mechanism of action for various drugs, we begin with a general review of human neurobiology.

**Review of neurobiological principles**   The neurological system has three parts. The peripheral nervous system (PNS) fans out in all directions over the surface of the body. It carries messages (such as touch, warmth, cold, and pain) from throughout the body to the central nervous system and carries reflex voluntary action messages back to muscles. The autonomic nervous system (ANS) is responsible for the more or less automatic functions of the body. It governs heart rate, respiration, digestion, and similar functions. The ANS is divided into two parts, the parasympathetic nervous system (PSNS) and the sympathetic nervous system (SNS). These two systems complement each other, so that when the PSNS is active, the SNS is inactive, and vice versa. The PSNS is the "normal" operating state of the autonomic system and is energy efficient. The SNS is the aroused state of the ANS and prepares for high energy use as in a fright/fight/flight condition. The effects of PSNS and SNS activation on various physiological functions are summarized in the accompanying box.

The third and probably most significant part of the nervous system for understanding psychoactive substances is the central ner-

---

### Effects of parasympathetic and sympathetic control

| Organ System | Parasympathetic | Sympathetic |
|---|---|---|
| Heart | Normal rate and volume | Increased rate and volume |
| Vascular | Dilated | Constricted |
| Gastrointestinal | Increased tone and motility; facilitated excretion | Decreased tone and motility; inhibited excretion |
| Liver | Glycogenesis | Glycogenolysis |
| Skin | None | Stimulated sweat secretion and piloerection (gooseflesh) |
| Respiratory | Normal rate and efficiency | Increased rate and efficiency |
| Eye | Constricted iris and lens (near vision, or myopia) | Dilated iris and lens (far vision, or hyperopia) |

vous system (CNS). The CNS consists of the brain and spinal cord. Although many PNS and ANS actions take place below the level of awareness, they are all reflected in the CNS and can be modified by CNS activation.

The neuron, or nerve cell, is the basic building block of the nervous system. The neural system contains approximately 20 billion neurons, with about 14 billion within the brain. These neurons vary in length from a few millimeters to about one meter. The basic components of a neuron are represented in Figure 2.5.

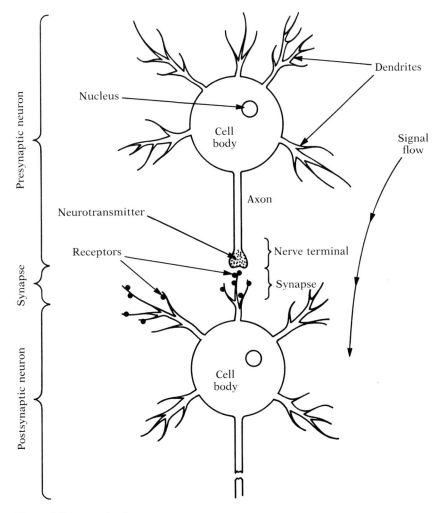

**Figure 2.5**  A typical neuron

Reproduced from *Fifth Special Report to the U.S. Congress on Alcohol and Health*, December 1983.

Messages are conducted throughout the nervous system by electrochemical processes (see Figure 2.5). A message travels along the neuron from the dendrites to the cell body, axon, and terminals by an electrochemical process involving the exchange of chemical ions through the membrane of the neuron. The chemical ion exchange creates an electrical force along the neuron. However, this electrical current is insufficient to jump the synaptic cleft, or gap, between the terminals of one neuron and the dendrites or axons of successive neurons.

In order for a message to transverse the synapse, the electrochemical force is converted into a chemical. This conversion occurs when the chemicals, known as neurotransmitters, are released from storage areas, known as vesicles. The neurotransmitters flood the synapse and stimulate a receptor site on the next neuron. This receptor stimulation alters the electrochemical characteristics of the successor neuron. The change in electrochemical characteristics may be either excitatory or inhibitory. That is, by stimulating a receptor, the neurotransmitter may initiate a corresponding electrochemical flow in the successor neuron, or the neurotransmitter may act to impede the transmission of a signal that would otherwise occur in the neuron. These electrochemical processes occur so fast that impulses travel in the neurological system at about 240 miles per hour, or 350 feet per second. In general, psychoactive substances act by disrupting these electrochemical processes.

There are approximately 40 known neurotransmitters, with some estimates ranging as high as 200 (Leavitt, 1982). Each neuroterminal releases only one neurotransmitter, and dendritic receptors are responsive to only one neurotransmitter. Thus, neurological impulses follow relatively predetermined pathways in the neurological system. Interconnections within the neural systems, particularly the brain, are accomplished when a neuron responds to one neurotransmitter but releases a different neurotransmitter, thus stimulating a collateral pathway.

**Neurotransmitters**    Of the 40 to 200 postulated neurotransmitters, only a few are of special concern in the study of psychoactive drugs.

*Acetylcholine:* Probably the most widely distributed neurotransmitter. It is found in the peripheral, autonomic, and central nervous systems. Acetylcholine sometimes excites and sometimes inhibits impulses. It is involved in such diverse processes as motor activity, sleep and arousal, food and water intake, and learning and memory.

*Catecholamines:* A group of neurotransmitters with similar chemical composition. Dopamine is involved in motor activity. Adrenaline is involved in autonomic neural activity, where it plays a major role in the fright/flight/fight arousal reaction. Noradrenaline is involved in arousal, body temperature, and food-and-water-intake mechanisms.

*Serotonin:* Also referred to as 5-hydroxytriptamine, it is involved in arousal and mood-modification processes.

*Gamma-aminobutyric acid:* GABA is the major inhibitory neurotransmitter of the brain.

*Endorphins:* Naturally occurring morphinelike compounds with considerable analgesic (pain-relief) action.

The remaining neurotransmitters are less clearly involved in the use and abuse of psychoactive substances and are generally not of concern here.

**Drug effects on neurotransmission**   A drug or externally administered chemical can alter neurotransmission pathways in several ways (Leavitt, 1982):

*Destruction of neurons:* The chemical may be toxic, destroying neurons and thereby interrupting the neurotransmission pathways. Chemical-warfare agents are sometimes designed to have this effect.

*Alteration of neuron membranes:* By altering the permeability of the neuron membrane, a drug can inhibit or stimulate the ion exchange that carries out impulses along the neuron.

*Effects of enzymes:* Neurotransmitters are synthesized by enzymes. If those enzymes are affected by a substance, the synthesis of neurotransmitters will also be affected.

*Release of neurotransmitters:* Once synthesized, neurotransmitters are stored in tiny vesicles. A drug may cause the release of a neurotransmitter from these sacs, thus simulating neural stimulation.

*Destruction of neurotransmitters:* One way in which neurotransmitter action is terminated is by enzymatic, or chemical, destruction of the neurotransmitter. A drug may facilitate or retard this breakdown, thereby reducing or enhancing stimulation of the postsynaptic neuron.

*Uptake inhibition:* A second method of terminating a neurotransmitter's activity is through reabsorption (uptake) of the transmitter substance. A drug can facilitate or inhibit this reabsorption, thereby reducing or enhancing the action of the transmitter.

*Mimicking of neurotransmitters:* A drug can have both receptor affinity and efficacy, thereby creating a false neurotransmission.

*Production of a false neurotransmitter:* A drug can be absorbed by the neuron and used to produce a neurotransmitter that lacks either affinity or efficacy.

*Blockade of the receptor:* A drug can have receptor affinity without efficacy, which would allow the drug to occupy the receptor and block neurotransmission.

*Change in receptor sensitivity:* By attaching to the postsynaptic receptor, a drug can alter the sensitivity of the receptor, thereby enhancing or retarding the neurotransmitter's action on the receptor.

Drugs disrupt neural transmission by acting in one or a combination of the foregoing methods. For some drugs this mechanism of action is well understood; for other drugs it is a matter of speculation.

**Homeostasis** One of the fundamental principles of physiological functioning is that the organism and its various systems strive to maintain a homeostatic balance. This means there is a dynamic, or changing, equilibrium, such that every change in some element of the organism is compensated for by a change in some other part. For example, increases in internal body temperature are compensated for by increases in cardiovascular volume, peripheral vascular dilation, and perspiration in an effort to return the body temperature to normal limits. Similarly, the neurological system operates through such compensatory processes. Drug-induced changes in neural transmission can stimulate homeostatic changes in other neurological processes. Such compensatory changes can result in tolerance to the effects of a drug, referred to as neurological, or psychodynamic, tolerance.

**Rebound and withdrawal** The compensatory physiological changes in response to the ingestion of a substance account at least partly for the phenomena of rebound and withdrawal. In response to the ingestion of a drug, the body compensates through homeostatic processes for that drug's effects. The individual is now functioning on a new homeostatic plane, which requires the presence of the drug in order that it be maintained. As the drug is metabolized and excreted, a disequilibrium is created, and physiological adjustments must occur once again. In occasional or periodic usage this compensation results in rebound, as the individual goes from normal to intoxicated to a state opposite from intoxication. For example, stimulant use is often followed by a period of depression, lethargy, and fatigue. In long-term, repeated usage of a drug, the compensatory processes in response to the absence of the drug can require more time and be more difficult to achieve physiologically. Thus, withdrawal can be viewed as a protracted rebound effect. For example, tolerance to depressants and narcotics generally requires frequent use of the drugs. The withdrawal from these drugs equally requires a fairly lengthy period to achieve (or reachieve) a normal state.

**Age**   For several reasons, the age of the user is an important variable in determining drug dosages and effects (Levitt, 1975). First, body weight varies with age, with infants and senior citizens typically weighing less than adolescents, young adults, and middle-agers. Second, physiological functions vary by age, with a gradual slowing of cardiovascular, metabolic, and excretory functions over time. Third, neurological development and functions vary with age. Fourth, the proportions of body fat, protein, and water vary with age. Finally, a number of psychosocial factors vary with age. Thus, there are recommended pediatric doses for many drugs, and geriatric standard doses have been established for some drugs.

**Sex**   The sex, like the age, of the user is a summary factor representing several variables. First, body weight is generally greater among males than females. Second, there are male/female differences in the proportions of body fat and muscle. Third, hormonal differences between males and females can affect drug effects. Fourth, there are differences between females and males in physiological functioning, particularly as those differences relate to hormone variations. Finally, the psychosocial matrix for males and females is often different. Thus, a drug may affect a male differently than it does a female (Levitt, 1975).

**Weight**   The weight, or body mass, of a patient is perhaps the most frequently used variable in adjusting drug dosages in medical practice. Like age and sex, weight is actually an indicator of several variables, including fat and protein proportions, volume of blood, and cardiovascular function. Thus, the more a user weighs, the more drug he or she can typically consume without experiencing undesirable drug effects.

**Race**   The user's race may directly and indirectly influence the effects of a drug. Directly, racial variations in blood chemistry and other physiological characteristics can determine the results a drug produces. Indirectly, the psychosocial matrix of an individual is often partly determined by racial characteristics. Thus, how one is expected to act both when drug-free and when under the influence of a drug, often varies along racial lines.

**Nutrition**   The body requires a variety of proteins, carbohydrates, vitamins, and minerals for normal physiological functioning. Likewise, the enzymes necessary for the metabolism of drugs are built from nutritional sources. Hence, a mildly or severely imbalanced diet can alter the course of a drug's effects.

**Food and drug interactions**   Just as two drugs may interact with each other to potentiate or counter the effects of either or both, various foods and nutrients may interact with drugs to alter the effects of the drugs. Most commonly, the presence of food in the stomach delays the onset of swallowed drugs by interfering with absorption. However, food products also contain natural and added chemicals that can inactivate a drug (for example, calcium-rich foods with tetracycline or acidic foods with penicillin) or stimulate a dangerous reaction (for example, monoamine oxidase inhibitors with tyramine-rich foods).

**Disease and damage**   Clearly, disease or damage to various organs can alter the absorption, distribution, metabolism, or excretion of a drug. Similarly, disease or damage to the neural system can alter both the extent and types of effects a drug produces. Since disease and injury are often corollaries of drug use, chronic users may react very differently to a drug than naive users. This same principle applies as well to individuals who experience disease or injury that is not drug related. For example, both the type and amount of analgesic required to alleviate pain depend on the source and the intensity of the pain (for example, headaches versus postoperative pain).

**Genetics**   Both professionals and the public have shown considerable interest in recent years in the role genetics plays in the effects of drugs (Crabbe, McSwigan, & Belknap, 1985). Allergic reactions by some individuals to certain substances have long been noted. Recent research has begun to explore more systematically the role of heredity in individual susceptibility and immunity to various drugs. Of particular note is the research on sensitivity to alcohol among Asians and the proclivity to alcohol abuse or alcoholism among children of alcoholic parents.

**Biorhythms**   Many physiological processes are cyclic. These cycles may be monthly (as in menstrual cycles); may be daily, or circadian (as in periods of alertness or sleep); or may occur several times within a 24-hour period (as in hunger). Research suggests that a drug's effects may depend on the time of day or month it is administered. For example, stimulants should have less impact on a well-rested and alert individual than on one who is fatigued.

We have reviewed a number of physiological principles and individual characteristics that can affect the way a user responds to a drug. Clearly, there is considerable variation among users. We should not be surprised to learn that different users or the same user on different occasions experience somewhat different effects from the same drug administered in the same way at identical doses. Even in medical situations it is difficult to predict exactly what effects a drug will have, and "street-use" conditions are hardly ideal environments for predicting drug effects. However, it is easier in many respects to understand how physiological factors influence a drug's effects than it is to predict the influence of psychological and sociocultural factors on drug reactions (Zinberg, 1984).

# Psychological Characteristics of the User

The effects of a drug that have been demonstrated by double-blind placebo studies to be related to the chemistry of the drug are referred to as specific effects. Those effects that depend on psychological and sociocultural variables are nonspecific effects. Often, a drug's nonspecific effects are more powerful than its specific effects. In this section we discuss some of the psychological variables that alter a drug's effects; in the next section, we will look at some of the sociocultural variations that contribute to a drug's effects. There are four major psychological variables: previous drug experience; expectations, or set; mood; and task.

## Previous Drug Experience

Experience with a substance similar to the one about to be ingested is clearly an important determinant of the drug's effects. Of primary importance is the fact that previous usage has a major impact on our expectations about the drug's effects (discussed in more detail below).

For some drugs (for example, marijuana) the effects can be so subtle that one has to learn what to look for and to define those effects as pleasurable. In addition, with exposure to a substance we learn how to adjust our behavior to compensate for drug-induced changes in sensations, voluntary behavior control, cognitions, and moods. We also learn that the effects are transient — they will wear off — and thus an experienced user is less likely to panic and less likely to experience "bad trips." This learning process is extremely important in maintaining some semblance of control over one's state of intoxication, and it accounts for a significant proportion of the tolerance that experienced users show for a substance. That is, tolerance is in part a learned response to a drug (McKim, 1986).

Cross-tolerance, reverse tolerance, and rapid tolerance (tachyphlaxis) can be explained at least partially through learning mechanisms. Cross-tolerance occurs when previous experience with one drug or class of drugs increases the user's tolerance to a second substance or class of drugs. For example, the various sedative/hypnotic drugs show considerable cross-tolerance, as do some hallucinogens. Reverse tolerance is said to occur when smaller successive doses are required to produce the same effects. The classic example of reverse tolerance occurs with marijuana, as experienced users find that it requires less to get high than when they began using the drug. Acute, or rapid, tolerance (tachyphlaxis) occurs with several drugs, the most notable being alcohol. For the same blood alcohol level (BAL), intoxication is often more noticeable when the BAL is rising than when it is falling, thereby illustrating a rapid tolerance to the effects of alcohol.

## Expectations, or Set

A user's expectations about a drug's effects are derived from several sources, including experience with the substance, friends' accounts, the mass media, education and training, and professional descriptions. These expectations have a considerable impact on the effects one obtains from a drug.

Placebo studies using inactive materials provide clear information on the effects of expectations on drug reactions. Depending on the manner in whch the placebo is administered, the information provided, and even the physical characteristics of the placebo itself (size, color, taste), significant proportions of users have reported cognitive, sensory, and emotional changes related to the use of the placebo. Similarly, the user's behaviors are generally consistent with the reported subjective changes. Thus, the effects a user experiences are often determined by the user's beliefs about a substance rather than the drug's chemistry.

## Mood

The effects that a substance can have depend on the user's initial mood relative to his or her maximum capabilities. This principle is known as Wilder's Law of Initial Value (Leavitt, 1982). Basically, Wilder's Law states that a drug cannot make a user exceed his or her capabilities behaviorally, emotionally, or cognitively. Further, it notes that a drug's effect depends on the user's predrug state: the further one is from one's maximum, the greater the potential effect. Thus, if you are already highly stimulated, a stimulant will have relatively little effect, but when you are fatigued, that same drug at the same dose can have considerable impact. Wilder's Law also suggests that paradoxical effects (effects opposite to those expected) occur when users are already at or near their maximum and ingest a drug to further enhance their state; for example, methylphenidate, a stimulant, is effective in controlling hyperkinetic children.

## Task

The final psychological characteristic to be discussed is the nature of the tasks a user attempts while under the influence of a drug. Tasks can vary along at least four dimensions: complexity, abstractness, recency of acquisition, and performance motivation. Substances impair complex, abstract, recently acquired, or low-motivation tasks more than they impair simple, concrete, well-learned, or highly motivated behaviors. Thus, it requires a very high dose to keep you from tying your shoes or performing a similar task, but it requires a very small dose to interfere with studying for an examination.

Clearly, users' drug-using experiences, their expectations regarding the effects of a drug, their mood and behavior before taking the drug, and the tasks or behaviors they attempt after ingesting it influence the effect the drug has on them. To some degree the tasks, predrug state, and expectations are determined by the sociocultural environment of the user, to which we now turn.

# Sociocultural Environment

The sociocultural environment of drug use can be separated into physical and social aspects. We must not forget, however, that each influences the other (McCarty, 1985). That is, the physical environment prescribes and proscribes both the types of individuals found there and the types of interactions. Likewise, people and their interactions help define the physical environment and may be the most important characteristic of the environment.

## Physical Environment

It is difficult, if not impossible, to engage in certain behaviors when appropriate props are absent. Thus, one cannot play pool without a pool table. Similarly, the physical environment both constrains and facilitates various behaviors for a drug user. A drug will result in very different behavior when used in a hospital or other medical setting than when used at a party. Thus, the physical environment becomes an important determinant of a drug's effects and a user's behaviors.

## Social Environment

Other people and their behavior influence the relationship between an individual and a drug in several ways. First, others provide a milieu that defines the environment as happy or sad and thereby establishes a general mood, or emotional tone. Second, it is from others that we learn the rules and rituals regarding the use of a substance. Third, the behavior of others becomes a reference point or standard of comparison according to which we judge our own behavior and against which our behavior is judged. Fourth, others act as guides and interpreters to help us identify, define, and assess the effects of a substance. Finally, throughout all of the foregoing, others provide social support and sanctions for appropriate and inappropriate behavior regarding substance use and abuse.

Our actions, whether we are drug-free or high, are likely to be very different in the presence of friends at a party than in the presence of strangers at a formal dinner. Likewise, preparing a fix, rolling a joint, and freebasing require skills and techniques acquired from others. We quickly learn that it is acceptable to say and do under the influence of a drug some things that are not permissible when we are drug-free. Often, especially with novices, one person stays "straight" to help the users understand and interpret a drug's effects and thereby help alleviate panic, tension, and other factors that can contribute to a bad trip. Finally, through their encouragement, acceptance, and support, our peers, friends, family, and associates provide important rewards and punishments for the use or nonuse of substances.

The sociocultural environment, consisting of physical objects and social beings, can either facilitate or hinder the effects of a drug. The resulting drug-related experiences play an important role in shaping our attitudes, values, and beliefs regarding the general use of drugs in society and our own personal use of substances. Thus, the physical and social environments have a considerable impact on both the present and future effects of drugs on behavior.

We have reviewed four groups of variables that contribute to the effects that substance users experience. Clearly, different users or even the same user on different occasions can experience considerable variation in response. Thus, drug effects are generally discussed in terms of the proportion of users who experience a particular effect at a given dosage. For example, a 10-milligram dose of morphine will induce analgesia among most nontolerant users.

Nevertheless, in both medical practice and on the street, relatively consistent effects can be achieved. These effects, including analgesia, hallucinations, hypnosis, sedation, and stimulation are possible even among drug-tolerant individuals if the dosage is increased to obtain the desired or expected effect. We now turn to a discussion of these commonly experienced drug effects.

## Drug-Classification Systems

There are several ways of classifying drugs, according to the needs of the classifier. Drugs can be classified by chemical structure, a system useful to biochemists since common chemical structures often, but not always, imply similar effects. Substances are also classified acording to their origin or source (for example, cannabinoids derived from marijuana). Drug-classification systems have also been developed that rely on the site of action or mechanism of action because of the rather obvious utility in understanding where or how a drug produces physiological changes. Finally, and most usefully for our present purposes, drugs can be classified on the basis of their effects, such as prototype (amphetaminelike), therapeutic use (sedative/hypnotic), or street use (as "uppers"). The end result of each classification is the same: to facilitate the search for commonalities and differences among drugs and their interactions with physiological systems.

## Common Drug-Related Effects

Table 2.1 summarizes some of the more frequently encountered drug-related effects. These effects are classified by drug categories as follows:

*opioids:* natural, semisynthetic, and synthetic narcotic analgesics

*depressants:* barbiturates, minor tranquilizers, and other sedative/hypnotic drugs including alcohol

*stimulants:* amphetamines, cocaine, amphetaminelike drugs, and caffeine

*hallucinogens:* LSD, psilocybin, mescaline, and stimulant-related substances

*phencyclidine:* categorized by itself because it possesses analgesic, depressant, and hallucinogenic properties

*cannabinoids:* marijuana derivatives categorized separately because of their combined depressant and hallucinogenic properties

*inhalants:* a diverse group of volatile chemicals whose effects are largely related to anoxia or hypoxia

For each group of drugs the effects of acute intoxication, overdose, and withdrawal are presented.

Table 2.1 identifies various signs and symptoms that can occur with substance use. These effects are sorted into three broad categories: autonomic, sensorimotor, and psychological. Autonomic effects are those related to the autonomic nervous system and include involuntary muscle control, cardiovascular, respiratory, digestive, and related effects. Sensorimotor effects refer to voluntary muscle control and sensory changes. The psychological category includes perceptual, emotional, and cognitive effects. It should be clear from a review of Table 2.1 that, in general, no single effect is sufficient to determine either the class of drug or the level of dosage that has been used. Unless one has access to body fluid (blood, urine) or tissue (brain, liver) samples and chromatography

**Table 2.1**  Common effects of drugs

| Condition | Drug | Autonomic: Abdominal cramps | Angina | Arrhythmia | Chest pain | Chills | Circulatory collapse | Coryza | Diarrhea | Flushing | Hypertension | Hyperthermia |
|---|---|---|---|---|---|---|---|---|---|---|---|---|
| **Withdrawal** | Stimulants | | | | | | X | | | | | |
| | Depressants | X | | | | | X | | X | | | |
| | Opioids | X | | | | X | | X | X | | | |
| **Overdose** | Inhalants | | | | | | | | | | | |
| | Cannabinoids | | | | | | | | | | | |
| | Phencyclidine | | | | | | | | | | X | |
| | Hallucinogens | X | | | | | X | | X | | X | X |
| | Stimulants | | X | X | X | | X | | X | | X | X |
| | Depressants | | | | | | | | | | | |
| | Opioids | | | | | | X | | | | | |
| **Intoxication** | Inhalants | | | | | | | | | | | |
| | Cannabinoids | | | | | | | | | | | |
| | Phencyclidine | | | | | | | | | | X | |
| | Hallucinogens | | | | | | | | | X | X | X |
| | Stimulants | | | X | | | | | | | X | X |
| | Depressants | | | | | | | | | | | |
| | Opioids | | | | | | | | | X | | |

| | | | | | | | | | | | | | | |
|---|---|---|---|---|---|---|---|---|---|---|---|---|---|---|
| Hypotension (orthostatic) | | X | | | | | | | X | | | | | | X |
| Hypotonia | X | | | | | | | | X | X | | | | | X | X |
| Lacrimation | | | X | | | | | | | | X | | | | | |
| Mouth, dry | | | | | | X | X | | | | | | | X | | |
| Nystagmus | | | X | | X | | | X | | | | | X | | | |
| Piloerection (gooseflesh) | | | X | | | | | | | | | | | | | |
| Pupils, dilated | | | X | | | X | X | | | | | X | | | | |
| Pupils, pinpointed | | | | | | | | | | X | | | | | | X |
| Reflexes, hyperactive | | X | | | | X | X | | | | | | X | X | | |
| Respiration, slow and shallow | | | | X | | | | | X | X | | | | | | |
| Rhinorrhea | X | | X | | | | | | | | X | | | | | |
| Sweating | | | X | | | | X | | | | | | | | | |
| Tachycardia | | X | X | | X | X | X | | | | | | X | X | | |
| Vomiting | | | X | | | X | X | | | | | | | X | | |
| Yawning | | | X | | | | | | | | | | | | X | |
| **Sensorimotor** | | | | | | | | | | | | | | | | |
| Aches, muscle | | | | | | | | | | | | | | | | |
| Analgesia | | | X | | X | | X | X | X | | | X | | X | |
| Ataxia | | | | | X | | | X | X | | | X | | | X |
| Coma | | | | | X | | | X | X | | | | | | |

**Table 2.1** Common effects of drugs *(continued)*

| Condition | Drug | Convulsions | Diplopia | Dysmetria | Facial grimacing | Headaches | Motor seizures (grand mal) | Muscle spasm (rigidity) | Nausea | Paresthesia | Skin pricking |
|---|---|---|---|---|---|---|---|---|---|---|---|
| Withdrawal | Stimulants | X | | | | | | | | | |
| Withdrawal | Depressants | | | | | X | X | | X | | |
| Withdrawal | Opioids | | | | | | | X | X | X | |
| Overdose | Inhalants | | | | | | | | | | |
| Overdose | Cannabinoids | | | | | | | | | | |
| Overdose | Phencyclidine | X | | | | | X | X | X | | |
| Overdose | Hallucinogens | | | | | | X | | X | | |
| Overdose | Stimulants | X | | | X | | X | | X | X | X |
| Overdose | Depressants | | | | | | | | | | |
| Overdose | Opioids | | | | | | | | | | |
| Intoxication | Inhalants | | | | | X | | | | | |
| Intoxication | Cannabinoids | | | | | | | | | | |
| Intoxication | Phencyclidine | | | X | X | | | X | X | | |
| Intoxication | Hallucinogens | | | | | | | | X | X | |
| Intoxication | Stimulants | | | | | | | | X | X | X |
| Intoxication | Depressants | X | X | X | | | | | | | |
| Intoxication | Opioids | | | | | | | | | | X |

| | | | | | | | | | | | | | | | | | |
|---|---|---|---|---|---|---|---|---|---|---|---|---|---|---|---|---|---|
| Sleep disturbance | | | X | X | | | | | | X | | | | | X | X | X |
| Sleepiness | X | X | | | | X | X | | | | | | | | | | X |
| Speech, slurred | | X | | | X | | X | | | | | | | | | | |
| Stare, blank | | | | | X | | | | | | | X | | | | | |
| Tremor | | | X | X | | | | | | X | X | | | | | X | |
| Violent behavior | | X | | | X | | | | | | | X | | | | | |
| **Psychological**<br>Affect, labile | | | X | X | X | | | | | | | X | | | | | |
| Anorexia | | X | X | X | X | | | | | X | X | | | | | | |
| Anxiety | X | X | X | X | | | | | | X | X | X | | | X | X | |
| Body-image changes | | | | X | X | | | | | X | X | X | | | | | |
| Comprehension, slow | X | X | | | X | | | X | X | | | X | | | | | X |
| Delirium | | X | X | | X | | | X | X | X | X | X | | X | | X | X |
| Depressed mood | | X | | | X | | | | | | | | | | | | X |
| Dizziness | | X | X | X | X | | X | | | | X | | | | | | |
| Euphoria | X | X | X | X | X | | | | | | | | | | | | |
| Fatigue | | X | | | | | | | | X | | | | | | | X |
| Floating feeling | X | X | | X | X | | | | | | | | | | | | |
| Hallucinations | | | X | X | X | X | | | | X | X | X | | | | X | |
| Hyperphagia | | | | | | | | | | | | | | | | | X |
| Irritability | | X | X | | X | | | | X | X | X | | | | X | X | |

**Table 2.1** Common effects of drugs *(continued)*

| | Intoxication | | | | | | | Overdose | | | | | | | Withdrawal | | |
|---|---|---|---|---|---|---|---|---|---|---|---|---|---|---|---|---|---|
| | Opioids | Depressants | Stimulants | Hallucinogens | Phencyclidine | Cannabinoids | Inhalants | Opioids | Depressants | Stimulants | Hallucinogens | Phencyclidine | Cannabinoids | Inhalants | Opioids | Depressants | Stimulants |
| Memory, poor | | X | | | | | | | | | | | | | | | |
| Psychosis (toxic) | | X | | X | X | | | | | X | X | X | | | | X | |
| Restlessness | | | X | X | X | | | | | | | | | | X | | |
| Suspiciousness | | | X | X | X | | | | | X | X | X | | | | | |
| Talkativeness | | | X | | | X | | | | X | | | | | | | |

*Source:* Adapted from *Drug Abuse: A Guide for the Primary Care Physician* by B. B. Wilford, 1981, Chicago: American Medical Association.

techniques, identifying the type of drug used and the approximate dosage administered requires one to look for and determine a pattern of signs and symptoms (Cox et al., 1983).

### Alcohol and Other Drugs: A Caveat

We can see in the preceding table that there are a number of similarities among diverse classes of drugs, as well as significant differences. Alcohol, as a drug, is generally classed as a depressant on the basis of its pharmacological actions and behavioral effects. However, alcohol abuse and alcoholism have been considered throughout much of the 20th century to constitute a separate entity from other forms of drug abuse.

The basis for the distinction between alcohol abuse and other types of drug abuse is primarily sociocultural. With repeal of Prohibition in the United States in 1933, alcohol use was legalized subject to various state and local restrictions (for example, drinking age, hours of sale, outlets). Since the use of alcohol has been socially acceptable and beverage alcohol has been widely available, definitions of what constitutes abuse of alcohol have been developed that focus on the pattern of use (for example, more than 3 ounces of absolute alcohol per day or a blood alcohol level in excess of .10) or on the consequences of use (poor work or school performance and marital or family problems). Definitions of drug abuse, on the other hand, have relied on legal considerations regarding the manufacture, distribution, sale, possession, or use of controlled substances. Any use of a controlled drug other than under the direction of a doctor is considered to be drug misuse or abuse by the general public and by many professionals (compare Jaffe, 1980).

We have taken the position in this text that the pharmacological and behavioral similarities between alcohol and other drugs are more important than the differences. Thus, unless otherwise noted, we prefer the term *substance abuse* to the distinction between alcohol abuse (or alcoholism) and drug abuse.

## ▋ Summary

Substance abuse professionals are often expected to explain the effects of drugs, both to their clients and to the community. A wide variety of pharmacological, physiological, psychological, and sociocultural factors contribute in complex ways to the effects experienced by substance users.

The pharmacological variables that influence the effects of a drug include its dosage and composition, the frequency or pattern of use, the method of administration, and its interaction with other drugs. Physiological factors include those processes that are involved in the absorption, distribution, metabolism, and excretion of the drug. In addition, a drug user's sensations, emotions, cognitions, and behaviors change in response to alterations in neurotransmission processes. Psychological influences include the user's previous drug experience, expectations, and mood, as well as the task the user is attempting. Finally, we must consider the influence of physical and social environments on drug effects.

Given the large number of variables and the complexity of the interactions, among them, it should be clear that there can be considerable heterogeneity in the effects of drugs. However, there is also considerable consistency in users' experiences. Recognition of the diversity as well as the commonality of drug effects is important in the assessment, treatment, and aftercare of clients.

# ▌References

Blum, K. (1984). *Handbook of abusable drugs.* New York: Gardner Press.

Cox, T. C., Jacobs, M. R., LeBlanc, A. E., & Marshman, J. A. (1983). *Drugs and drug abuse—a reference text.* Toronto: Addiction Research Foundation.

Crabbe, J. C., McSwigan, J. D., & Belknap, J. K. (1985). The role of genetics in substance abuse. In M. Galizio & S. A. Maisto (Eds.), *Determinants of substance abuse.* New York: Plenum.

Gilman, A. G., Mayer, S. E., & Melmon, K. L. (1980). Pharmacodynamics: Mechanisms of drug action and the relationship between drug concentration and effect. In A. G. Gilman, L. S. Goodman, & A. Gilman (Eds.), *Goodman and Gilman's the pharmacological basis of therapeutics* (6th ed.). New York: Macmillan.

Goth, A. (1978). *Medical pharmacology* (9th ed.). St. Louis: C. V. Mosby.

Gringauz, A. (1978). *Drugs—how they act and why.* St. Louis: C. V. Mosby.

Jaffe, J. H. (1980). Drug addiction and drug abuse. In A. G. Gilman, L. S. Goodman, & A. Gilman (Eds.), *Goodman and Gilman's the pharmacological basis of therapeutics* (6th ed.). New York: Macmillan.

Kakis, F. J. (1982). *Drugs—facts and fictions.* New York: Franklin Watts.

Lader, M. (1980). *Introduction to psychopharmacology.* Kalamazoo, MI: Upjohn Co.

Leavitt, F. (1982). *Drugs and behavior* (2nd ed.). New York: Wiley.

Levitt, R. A. (1975). *Psychopharmacology—a biological approach.* New York: Wiley.

Mayer, S. E., Melmon, K. L., & Gilman, A. G. (1980). Introduction: The dynamics of drug absorption, distribution, and elimination. In A. G. Gilman, L. S. Goodman, & A. Gilman (Eds.), *Goodman and Gilman's the pharmacological basis of therapeutics* (6th ed.). New York: Macmillan.

McCarty, D. (1985). Environmental factors in substance abuse. In M. Galizo & S. A. Maisto (Eds.), *Determinants of substance abuse.* New York: Plenum.

McKim, W. A. (1986). *Drugs and behavior—an introduction to behavioral pharmacology.* Englewood Cliffs, NJ: Prentice-Hall.

Wilford, B. B. (1981). *Drug abuse: A guide for the primary care physician.* Chicago: American Medical Association.

Zinberg, N. E. (1984). *Drug, set, and setting.* New Haven, CT: Yale University Press.

**CHAPTER**

# Assessment and Diagnosis of Substance Use Disorders

Accurate diagnosis and assessment are critical components of effective treatment programs for substance abusers. Incomplete assessments and misdiagnoses lead to poor treatment outcomes and fail to meet the needs of clients. Without comprehensive assessments and consequent correct diagnoses, our clients are unlikely to achieve and maintain positive changes.

Frequently, substance abuse practitioners oversimplify the problems presented by their clients (Lawson, Ellis, & Rivers, 1984). This reductionism ignores critical scientific and clinical distinctions and fails to recognize substance abuse problems as complex and multiply determined. When this complexity is not acknowledged, treatment proceeds on a very simplistic level, abstinence being equated with health and nonabstinence with illness. Unfortunately, this either/or view does not allow for changes in other areas of life function and maintains the myth that substance abuse and dependence are unitary, well-defined, and predictable disorders that are best treated simply by stopping the client from ingesting his or her drug of choice. It is increasingly clear, however, that abstinence is not the sine qua non of successful treatment (Hay & Nathan, 1982;

Miller, 1985; Miller & Munoz, 1982). Rather, it is important to view substance abuse problems as multivariate syndromes that should be individually and differentially treated because they cause different problems for different people (Barrett, 1985; Caddy & Block, 1985; Maisto, Galizio, & Carey, 1985).

In this respect, Pattison, Sobell, and Sobell (1977) articulated several emerging concepts of alcohol dependence. These concepts have been refined by Pattison and Kaufman (1982) and then adapted by Lawson and his colleagues (1984) to address substances other than alcohol, as follows:

1. Multiple patterns of use, misuse, and abuse can be denoted as chemical dependency.
2. Multiple causal variables combine to produce a pattern of chemical dependency.
3. Everyone is vulnerable to some type of chemical dependency.
4. Treatment must be multimodal to correspond to a client's particular pattern of chemical dependency.
5. Treatment outcomes will vary in accord with specific users, patterns, and social contexts.
6. Preventive interventions must be multiple and diverse to address diverse causes of dependence.

Based on this broader view, it is now possible for us to better understand substance abuse problems and to diagnose and treat them less dogmatically. This process begins with assessment.

# ▌ Assessment

Assessment is the act of determining the nature and causes of a client's problem. During the early sessions of treatment, counselors gather data and increase their understanding of the client. At the same time, the client can ask questions and clarify his or her role in counseling. At this point the counselor should fully address confidentiality and other therapy expectations.

To understand our clients' substance abuse problems, we must try to understand our clients. This involves interviewing, taking a history, and administering psychological tests. It is vital that clinicians have no preconceived notions about the client and that they make treatment determinations based only on data collected during the initial evaluation. In this respect, merely walking into a substance abuse treatment facility does not, in and of itself, warrant a diagnosis of "chemical dependency" or "alcoholism" (Hansen & Emrick, 1985). Rather, clinicians must carefully evaluate the client and only then make decisions concerning diagnosis and treatment. These decisions must take into account the client's culture and background. Insensitivity to these critical issues and consequent homogenization of treatment will seriously limit our effectiveness. We must guard against these preventable sources of treatment contamination.

## Initial Interview

Collection of data about the client begins with an interview. This lengthy interview is designed to elicit a great deal of information about the client's background, problems, current functioning, and motivation for treatment. The interview is designed solely to elicit information that will form the basis for a diagnosis and a treatment plan. Counselors must make the client feel welcome and as comfortable as possible (some anxiety is expected and quite appropriate). They must create a situation in which they can elicit all the information they need, which is best done by being slightly directive, in control, and armed with a clear agenda. In essence, then, counselors ask a series of questions and attempt to get the clearest answers possible. To do this effectively, counselors must maintain structure and keep the client calm and on track. This sounds difficult, but with practice, clinical interviewing is a manageable task. To get a clear and broad understanding of the client, the interview should include the following:

1. referral source
2. chief complaint
3. history of present problem (illness)
4. history of substance use and abuse
5. life situation
   a. living arrangements
   b. marriage or cohabitation
   c. children
   d. social life
   e. current functioning
6. family history
   a. siblings
   b. parents or other family
   c. discipline
   d. how and where the client was raised
7. religious history
8. work history of client, siblings, parents, and spouse
9. legal history
10. sexual history
11. mental status
    a. appearance, behavior, and attitude
       1) general appearance
       2) motor status

      3) activity
      4) facial expression
      5) behavior
  b. characteristics of talk
      1) blocking
      2) circumstantiality
      3) perseveration
      4) flight of ideas
      5) mutism
  c. emotional state: affective reactions
      1) mood
      2) affect
      3) depression
      4) mania
  d. content of thought: special preoccupations and experiences
      1) hallucinations
      2) delusions
      3) compulsions
      4) obsessions
      5) ritualistic behaviors
      6) depersonalization
      7) fantasies or daydreams
  e. anxiety
      1) phobia(s)
      2) generalized (diffuse)
      3) specific
  f. orientation
      1) person
      2) place
      3) time
      4) confusion
  g. memory
      1) remote past experiences
      2) recent past experiences
      3) immediate impressions
      4) general grasp and recall
  h. general intellectual evaluation
      1) general information
      2) calculation
      3) reasoning and judgment
  i. insight

Although the above outline is helpful in forming the evaluation agenda and in clarifying the client's condition, it is wise to add substance to each category. In this vein a standardized format is helpful in guiding the interview and providing structure so that all essential information is gained. The history form in Exhibit 3.1, which is based on one used by the South Suburban Council on Alchoholism, in East Hazelcrest, Illinois, is highly structured and enables counselors to begin an effective assessment. More information will be gathered if the counselor gets this information from the client rather than asking the client to fill out the form.

# ▌ Exhibit 3.1

## Psycho-Social and Substance Use History

Client's name ＿＿＿＿＿＿＿＿＿＿＿＿＿＿＿ Date ＿＿＿＿＿＿

Social Security no. ＿＿＿＿＿＿＿ Nationality ＿＿＿＿＿＿

Age ＿＿＿ Birth date ＿＿＿＿＿＿ Sex ＿＿＿

Address ＿＿＿＿＿＿＿＿＿＿＿＿＿ Telephone no. ＿＿＿＿

In your own words, why did you come here? ＿＿＿＿＿＿＿＿

＿＿＿＿＿＿＿＿＿＿＿＿＿＿＿＿＿＿＿＿＿＿＿＿＿＿＿＿＿＿＿

＿＿＿＿＿＿＿＿＿＿＿＿＿＿＿＿＿＿＿＿＿＿＿＿＿＿＿＿＿＿＿

How do you feel about being here? ＿＿＿＿＿＿＿＿＿＿＿＿

＿＿＿＿＿＿＿＿＿＿＿＿＿＿＿＿＿＿＿＿＿＿＿＿＿＿＿＿＿＿＿

＿＿＿＿＿＿＿＿＿＿＿＿＿＿＿＿＿＿＿＿＿＿＿＿＿＿＿＿＿＿＿

A. Marital history (*spouse* refers to husband, wife, girlfriend, or boyfriend)
   1. Marital status (circle the word that best explains your status)
      single          engaged          married
      separated       divorced         widowed
      divorced/remarried      widowed/remarried      common-law
   2. If you have been married, how many times? ＿＿＿＿＿＿
   3. How old were you when you were first married? ＿＿＿＿＿
   4. How many years have you been married to your present spouse? ＿＿＿＿＿＿＿＿＿＿＿＿＿＿＿＿＿＿＿＿
   5. How old is your present spouse? ＿＿＿＿＿＿＿＿＿＿＿

B. Educational history (please circle)
   1. Grade school
   2. High school:  1 yr.  2 yrs.  3 yrs.  4 yrs.  GED
   3. College:  1 yr.  2 yrs.  3 yrs.  4 yrs.  postgraduate
   4. Have you ever been in special education classes?
      ＿＿ yes ＿＿ no
      If so, why were you in these classes? ＿＿＿＿＿＿＿＿

      ＿＿＿＿＿＿＿＿＿＿＿＿＿＿＿＿＿＿＿＿＿＿＿＿＿＿＿＿＿

      ＿＿＿＿＿＿＿＿＿＿＿＿＿＿＿＿＿＿＿＿＿＿＿＿＿＿＿＿＿

   5. Have you ever had tutoring? ＿＿ yes ＿＿ no
      If so, what for? ＿＿＿＿＿＿＿＿＿＿＿＿＿＿＿＿＿＿＿＿

      ＿＿＿＿＿＿＿＿＿＿＿＿＿＿＿＿＿＿＿＿＿＿＿＿＿＿＿＿＿

      ＿＿＿＿＿＿＿＿＿＿＿＿＿＿＿＿＿＿＿＿＿＿＿＿＿＿＿＿＿

C. Drinking and drug history relative to school
   1. Are you still in school? ___ yes ___ no
     Name of school _____
   2. Has your drinking or drug use ever caused problems in school? ___ yes ___ no
   3. Have you ever been sent home from school because of drinking or drug use? ___ yes ___ no
   4. Have you ever been suspended from school? ___ yes ___ no
     Why were you suspended? Please explain: _____
     _____
     _____
   5. Have you ever been expelled from school? ___ yes ___ no
     Why were you expelled? Please explain: _____
     _____
     _____
   6. Are you in danger of being expelled now? ___ yes ___ no
     If so, please explain: _____
     _____
     _____
   7. Have the school authorities suggested that you come here?
     ___ yes ___ no
     If they have, please explain: _____
     _____
     _____
   8. Are you having any other school problems? ___ yes ___ no
     If so, please explain: _____
     _____
     _____
   9. Do you have enough credits to graduate? ___ yes ___ no
     If not, please explain: _____
     _____
     _____

D. Military history
   1. Have you ever been in the armed forces? ___ yes ___ no
     If yes, which branch? _____
   2. What was your rating and rank? _____
   3. How long were you in the service? _____
   4. Date you enlisted _____ Date you entered service _____
     Current status _____
   5. Type of discharge _____

E. Employment history
   1. Are you employed? _____ How long? _____
   2. Name of employer _____
   3. Job title _____ Gross annual income _____

4. What is your occupation? _____

5. How long have you done this type of work? _____

6. What type of work would you like to do, even though you may not have the necessary training or skills? _____

7. Employment history (list most recent jobs first)

    *Job Title     Date Start     Date Finish     Reason for Leaving*

  a. _____

  b. _____

  c. _____

8. Describe any problems on the job (past or present).

_____

_____

9. Do you have medical insurance? ___ yes ___ no
What company? _____

10. Do you have public aid? ___ yes ___ no      Number _____

F. Family history

1. Are your parents still living together? ___ yes ___ no

2. If your parents are separated or divorced, whom do you live with? mother ___ father ___

3. Describe your father: _____

_____

_____

4. Describe your mother: _____

_____

_____

5. List your brothers and sisters and circle any stepbrothers or stepsisters.

| Name | Sex | Year of Birth | Date of Death | Occupation | Education | Marital Status |
|------|-----|---------------|---------------|------------|-----------|----------------|
|      |     |               |               |            |           |                |
|      |     |               |               |            |           |                |
|      |     |               |               |            |           |                |
|      |     |               |               |            |           |                |
|      |     |               |               |            |           |                |
|      |     |               |               |            |           |                |
|      |     |               |               |            |           |                |

6. Where were you in the order of birth (oldest, youngest)?

_____

7. Which brother or sister are you closest to? _____
Please explain: _____

_____

_____

8. Which brother or sister are you the least close to? _____

Please explain: _____
_____
_____

9. Which person in your family makes the decisions? _____
Please explain: _____
_____
_____

10. If you needed to borrow money, which member of the family
would you ask? _____ Please explain: _____
_____
_____

11. Do you eat dinner with your family? ___ yes ___ no
How many nights a week? _____ Please explain: _____
_____
_____

12. What family activities does your family do? _____
Please explain: _____
_____
_____

13. Do you believe in God? ___ yes ___ no
14. Do you go to church regularly? ___ yes ___ no
Which denomination? _____
15. Do you have a girlfriend or boyfriend? ___ yes ___ no
16. Do the two of you spend a lot of time together?
___ yes ___ no
17. Would you say that your girlfriend/boyfriend has a drinking
problem? ___ yes ___ no Please explain: _____
_____
_____

18. Would you say that your girlfriend/boyfriend has a drug
problem? ___ yes ___ no Please explain: _____
_____
_____

19. Did anyone in your family suffer from the following (underline)?
nervous breakdown; fits or convulsions; nervousness; migraine
headaches; visions; stuttering; times when they could not
remember what they were doing; times when they acted
strangely or peculiarly; alcohol problem; drug abuse
If you have underlined any of the choices above, state which
family member and when and how you were affected.
_____
_____
_____

20. Did you ever belong to a gang? ___ yes ___ no

21. What teams or clubs did you belong to as a child? Circle those in which you were an officer. _____
_____

22. What do you do outside of work or school (hobbies, leisure)?
_____

23. About how many close friends do you have? _____
Describe them by name, sex, and age: _____
_____

Has any of them ever had a drinking or drug problem?
____ yes ____ no
If so, please describe: _____
_____
_____
_____

24. List your children and circle those who are adopted or by a previous marriage.

| Name | Living? | Sex | Age | Grade | Occupation |
|------|---------|-----|-----|-------|------------|
|      |         |     |     |       |            |
|      |         |     |     |       |            |
|      |         |     |     |       |            |
|      |         |     |     |       |            |

G. Legal history
  1. Do you have any arrest charges pending? ____ yes ____ no
     If so, what are they?

     | Charge | Court Date | Location |
     |--------|-----------|----------|
     | a. |  |  |
     | b. |  |  |
     | c. |  |  |
     | d. |  |  |

  2. Have you had previous arrests? ____ yes ____ no
     If so, what were the charges and when were they filed?

     | Charge | Date |
     |--------|------|
     | a. |  |
     | b. |  |
     | c. |  |
     | d. |  |

  3. Are you on probation? ____ yes ____ no
     Parole? ____ yes ____ no
     Court supervision? ____ yes ____ no
  4. Have you attended or are you attending an alcohol or drug safety class? ____ yes ____ no
     If so, where? _____

5. Were you referred to treatment by the class?
   ___ yes ___ no
6. Were you referred to treatment by the Social Service Department of the Circuit Court? ___ yes ___ no
   If so, what county? _____
7. Were you ordered to treatment by the Circuit Court?
   ___ yes ___ no
   If so, what county? _____
   Who was the judge? _____
8. Do you have a lawyer or public defender? ___ yes ___ no
   Which? _____
9. Were you referred to treatment by your lawyer?
   ___ yes ___ no
   If so, what is your lawyer's name? _____
   Phone no. _____
10. Would you consent to sign a release of information allowing us to communicate with any of the above agencies or authorities on specific treatment issues? ___ yes ___ no
11. What is your court date? _____
12. If not listed above, who referred you? _____

H. History of drinking, other drug use, and treatment (check all items that apply to you, or give the information requested; if not applicable, mark N/A)
   1. Have you ever been treated for an alcohol problem before?
      ___ yes ___ no If yes, complete the following:

      a. Detoxification only ___ How many times? _____
         Places and dates _____
         _____
         Did you finish treatment?___ yes ___ no
         If no, please explain: _____
         _____
         _____

      b. Rehabilitation ___ How many times? _____
         Places and dates _____
         _____
         Did you finish treatment?___ yes ___ no
         If no, please explain: _____
         _____
         _____

      c. Outpatient therapy ___ How many times? _____
         Places and dates _____
         _____
         Did you finish treatment?___ yes ___ no

If no, please explain: _____

_____

_____

    d. Would you consent to sign a release of confidential information allowing us to communicate with any of these programs on specific treatment issues? ___ yes ___ no

2. Have you been involved with Alcoholics Anonymous?
___ yes ___ no
If so, how often did/do you attend meetings? _____
Was it open or closed? _____
Did/do you have a sponsor? ___ yes ___ no

3. At what age did you first drink? ___ Describe the circumstances and consequences: _____

_____

_____

4. At what age did you first lose control of drinking? _____
(I never lost control of my drinking; I just drank daily.) ___

5. At what age did you have your first blackout? _____
(I never had blackouts.) _____

6. At what age did your blackouts begin to increase? _____

7. When and why did you first become concerned about your drinking? _____

_____

_____

8. What is the average amount of hard liquor you consume (check one)?
___ none                           ___ about 1 quart a day
___ very little                    ___ more than 1 quart a day
___ a couple of "shots" a day      ___ occasional "benders"
___ about 1 pint a day             other _____

9. What is the average number of beers you consume (check one)?
___ none                           ___ close to 20 a day
___ very few                       ___ more than 20 a day
___ several a day                  ___ occasional "benders"
___ about 5 to 10 a day

10. What is the average amount of wine you consume (check one)?
___ none                           ___ about 2 to 4 quarts a day
___ very little                    ___ more than 4 quarts a day
___ about 1 pint a day             ___ occasional "benders"
___ about 1 quart a day

11. Do you ever go on "binges" (periods of uncontrolled drinking)? ___ yes ___ no

___ once a year                          ___ every 1 to 3 months
___ every 6 to 8 months             ___ every weekend
___ every 3 to 6 months             other _____

12. Do you drink daily? ___ yes ___ no How long have you been drinking daily (check one)?
    ___ just this last month          ___ one year
    ___ 1 to 3 months                    ___ two years
    ___ 3 to 6 months                    ___ longer than two years
    ___ 6 to 9 months                    How long? _____

13. Do you notice that you have the "shakes" when you stop drinking? ___ yes ___ no If so, when did this first happen?
_____

Please describe: _____
_____

Have you ever seen or heard things that were not actually there? ___ yes ___ no If so, when? _____
Have you ever had delirium tremens (DTs)?
___ yes ___ no If so, when? _____

Please describe: _____
_____
_____

Have you ever had a seizure? ___ yes ___ no
If so, when? _____

Please describe: _____
_____

14. Has a physician ever told you to stop drinking?
    ___ yes ___ no If so, why? _____
_____

15. With whom do you usually drink (check as many as apply)?
    ___ spouse                              ___ "buddies" on the street
    ___ other relatives                   ___ strangers
    ___ neighbors                           ___ by myself
    ___ people at work                   ___ kids at school
    ___ friends at a bar

16. When drinking, how do you act?
    ___ seldom get angry or violent     ___ get happy
    ___ get mean or surly                    ___ have fun
    ___ get into angry arguments        other _____
    ___ get into physical fights

17. How do your parents, wife/girlfriend, or husband/boyfriend feel about your drinking?

___ don't seem to mind        ___ nag me about it
___ don't say much about it    ___ question doesn't apply
___ threatened to leave because of my drinking

18. Have your family activities changed because of your drink-
ing? ___ yes ___ no
19. Has your sexual life changed because of your drinking?
___ yes ___ no
20. Have you ever quit drinking? ___ yes ___ no
How long did you stay sober? _____
When was the last time (date)? _____
Did this dry period follow any form of treatment?
___ yes ___ no
If so, what type and where? _____
What things do you do to stay sober? _____
Did you have any symptoms when you stopped drinking? ___
_____

21. Have you ever used cough syrup or other medicines containing alcohol as substitutes for liquor or for the purpose of
getting high?
___ yes ___ no ___ prescription ___ nonprescription
Have you used any other alcohol substitutes?
___ yes ___ no If so, please identify: _____
22. What mood-altering drugs have you taken (check as many
as apply)?

|  | *Prescribed by Physician* |
|---|---|
| ___ tranquilizers (Valium, Librium, Miltown, etc.) | ___ yes ___ no |
| type _____ |  |
| ___ psychotropics (Stelazine, Cogentin, Thorazine, etc.) | ___ yes ___ no |
| type _____ |  |
| ___ barbiturates (Quaaludes, phenobar- bital, Nembutal, Tuinal, Seconal) | ___ yes ___ no |
| type _____ |  |
| ___ amphetamines (Dexedrine, Benze- drine, Methedrine, etc.) | ___ yes ___ no |
| type _____ |  |
| ___ sleeping pills | ___ yes ___ no |
| type _____ |  |
| ___ opiates (heroin, morphine, opium, etc.) | ___ yes ___ no |
| type _____ |  |
| ___ pain killers (Darvon, codeine, etc.) | ___ yes ___ no |
| type _____ |  |
| ___ other type _____ |  |

___ hallucinogen (LSD, STP, MDA, PCP,
mescaline, etc.)                                    ___ yes ___ no
type _____
___ cocaine. If so, how often? _____
___ marijuana. If so, how often? _____
___ glue sniffing. If so how often? _____

23. Have you ever received treatment for a drug problem? ___
___ yes ___ no If so, what type of treatment? _____
_____
_____

Where? _____
_____

When? _____
_____

24. Have you ever been involved with Narcotics Anonymous?
___ yes ___ no
If so, how often did/do you attend meetings? _____
Was it open or closed? _____
Do you have a sponsor? ___ yes ___ no

25. When do you usually drink or use drugs (check as many as
apply)?
___ weekends                    ___ long, occasional "benders"
___ after work or evenings      ___ frequent, short "benders"
___ occasionally during the     ___ most of the time
     day
___ regularly during the day

26. Which apply to you (check as many as apply)?
___ I am losing control of      ___ My tolerance is
     my drinking/drug use.           decreasing.
___ I'm an alcoholic/drug        ___ I need a drink when I
     addict.                          wake up.
___ I can't stop by myself.      ___ I'm not eating regularly.
___ I am deteriorating           ___ I'm strictly a social
     rapidly.                         drinker.
___ I know why I drink/use       ___ My tolerance is
     drugs.                           increasing.
___ I hate myself.               ___ I can quit anytime.
___ I have a drinking            ___ I might be an alcoholic/
     problem.                         drug addict.
___ I have accidents or fall     ___ I have been unable to
     while drinking and               complete a task (or begin
     sometimes injure                 a task) because I was
     myself.                          drinking.
___ I'm a problem drinker/       ___ I have a drug problem.
     drug user but not an         ___ I get arrested because of
     addict.                          my drinking or drugging.

27. Which of these apply to you at this time?
  \_\_\_ school problems          \_\_\_ financial problems
  \_\_\_ marital problems         \_\_\_ threat to job
  \_\_\_ physical problems        \_\_\_ loss of job
  \_\_\_ family problems          \_\_\_ legal problems
  \_\_\_ loneliness               other _____

28. What do you expect from treatment? _____
  _____
  _____

  What may we expect from you? _____
  _____

29. In your own words, what is alcoholism/drug dependence?
  _____
  _____
  _____
  _____

30. Is alcoholism/drug dependence a disease, or is it a bad habit?
  _____

31. Have you ever been treated for emotional/psychiatric prob-
  lems? \_\_\_ yes \_\_\_ no If so, complete the following:
  How may times? _____
  Where? _____ When? _____
  Where? _____ When? _____
  Where? _____ When? _____
  Have you ever attempted or considered attempting suicide?
  \_\_\_ yes \_\_\_ no How many times, and when? _____
  _____

32. Describe yourself: _____
  _____
  _____
  _____

33. What are your weaknesses?_____
  _____

  What are your strengths? _____
  _____

34. Are you interested in further treatment or help, and do you
  know what is available? _____

35. Please add any information that you feel could be important
  to your treatment: _____
  _____
  _____
  _____
  _____

36. Do you have any questions? _____
_____

37. Next of kin _____
     Address _____
Client signature _____ Staff signature _____
Date _____ Date _____
DSM III diagnosis: _____

*Note.* Adapted with permission from the South Suburban Council on Alcoholism, East Hazelcrest; IL, N. Haney, executive director.

## Behavioral Assessment

Once the initial interview is completed, the counselor is ready to do a behavioral assessment and functional analysis. A behavioral assessment allows the counselor to discover the antecedents and consequences of the client's substance abuse behaviors and to examine the acquisition of these behaviors (Maisto, 1985). The behavioral assessment (Hersen & Bellack, 1981; Nathan & Lipscomb, 1979) and functional analysis (Sobell, Sobell, & Sheahan, 1976) also let the counselor determine what is reinforcing and punishing for the client and specify the factors correlated with a high probability of substance abuse (Maisto, 1985). The functional analysis, a component of behavioral assessment, clearly shows when and why a client abuses substances, and *the counselor can then use this information to tailor a treatment plan to the unique needs of each client.* The behavioral assessment and functional analysis interview (Exhibit 3.2) is designed to be administered orally by the counselor. An attempt should be made to gather as much information as possible in each content area. The counselor should be sensitive and directive in conducting this interview.

# ▍Assessment Devices

The assessment instruments outlined in this section were chosen because they are readily available, reliable, valid, easily administered, easily scored, and practical. Their results can be applied easily to the clinical setting.

## Comprehensive Drinker Profile

The Comprehensive Drinker Profile (CDP) was initially used in 1971 as a structured intake interview to assess alcohol problems. It was revised by Marlatt in 1976. Since that time the CDP has undergone

## ▌ Exhibit 3.2

### Initial Behavioral Assessment and Functional Analysis

Date _____ Name of counselor _____

    I. Background data
       Name of client _____
       Age _____ Marital status _____ Religion _____
       Address _____
       Who lives with the client? _____
       Previous substance abuse and psychiatric treatment (including
       hospitalizations) _____
       _____
       _____
       _____

    II. Problems (frequency, intensity, inappropriate form, duration,
       inappropriate occasions)
       A. Behavioral excesses _____
       _____
       _____
       _____

       B. Behavioral deficits _____
       _____
       _____
       _____
       _____
       _____

    III. Assets and strengths (indicate current and best past functioning)
       A. Grooming _____
       _____

       B. Self-help skills _____
       _____
       _____

       C. Social (including conversation, recreation, and friendships)
       _____
       _____
       _____

       D. Education and vocational training _____
       _____
       _____

    IV. Functional analysis of problems
       A. What are the consequences (both positive and negative) of
       the client's current problems? _____

_____
_____
_____

1. Who or what persuaded or coerced the client into treatment? _____

2. Who reinforces the client's problems with sympathy, help, attention, or emotional reactions? _____

3. What would happen if the problems were ignored? reduced in frequency? _____
_____
_____

4. What reinforcers would the client gain if the problems were removed? _____

B. What stimulus determinants or conditions and settings serve as occasions for the occurrence of the problems? ___
_____

   1. Where? _____
   2. When? _____
   3. With whom? _____

C. Congruence between client's self-description and that of other observers? _____
_____

V. Reinforcement survey. Be sure to assess the correspondence between the client's verbal report and the observations made by you and significant others.

A. People. With whom does the client spend the most time (family, relatives, friends, coworkers)?

   1. _____  4. _____
   2. _____  5. _____
   3. _____  6. _____

With whom would the client like to spend more time?

   1. _____  3. _____
   2. _____  4. _____

B. Places. Where does the client spend the most time (bedroom, kitchen, yard, car, work, store, church, etc.)?

   1. _____  4. _____
   2. _____  5. _____
   3. _____  6. _____

Where would the client like to spend more time?

   1. _____  3. _____
   2. _____  4. _____

C. Things. What does the client spend most of his or her time with (books, hobbies, tobacco, foods, drinks, clothes, favorite possessions)?

1. _____ 5. _____
2. _____ 6. _____
3. _____ 7. _____
4. _____ 8. _____

What things and foods would the patient like to have greater access to?

1. _____ 3. _____
2. _____ 4. _____

D. Activities. What activities occur with the highest frequency or longest duration (work, smoking, sports, watching television, listening to music, dancing, napping, being alone, driving a car, reading, pacing)?

1. _____ 5. _____
2. _____ 6. _____
3. _____ 7. _____
4. _____ 8. _____

What activities would the client like to increase?

1. _____ 3. _____
2. _____ 4. _____

E. Negative reinforcers. What are relief stimuli and events for the client (people, substances, situations, activities, social isolation)?

1. _____ 4. _____
2. _____ 5. _____
3. _____ 6. _____

F. Punishments. What are aversive stimuli and events for the patient (people, situations, activities, fears, social isolation, etc.)?

1. _____ 4. _____
2. _____ 5. _____
3. _____ 6. _____

G. Natural reinforcers. Who among those that the patient is in daily contact with would make potential mediators in a counseling program?

1. _____ 5. _____
2. _____ 6. _____
3. _____ 7. _____
4. _____ 8. _____

VI. Biological analysis

A. Medical and surgical problems and limitations to activity

1. _____ 3. _____
2. _____ 4. _____

B. Date of last physical exam _____ Name and address of the physician performing the exam _____

_____

_____

C. Current medical treatment and drugs _____

_____

_____

_____

D. Psychotropic drugs

| 1. *Current Drugs* | *Dose* | *Prescribed by* | *Date* |
|---|---|---|---|
| | | | |
| | | | |
| | | | |
| | | | |

| 2. *Past Drugs* | *Dates* | *Response* |
|---|---|---|
| | | |
| | | |

E. Family history. What other family members have significant psychiatric or substance abuse behavioral disturbances?

_____

_____

_____

VII. Sociocultural analysis

A. Recent changes in milieu (migration, intergenerational conflicts in the family, work changes, etc.) _____

_____

_____

_____

_____

B. Recent changes in social relationships (separation, divorce, deaths, etc.) _____

_____

_____

_____

C. Language and values (conflicts between minority group and majority culture) _____

_____

_____

_____

D. Other recent traumas or stresses _____

_____

_____

_____

_____

VIII. Formulation of behavioral goals (be specific)
   A. Increase desirable behaviors (include strengthening assets)
      1. *Short term (3 months)*          2. *Long term (9 months to*
                                             *1 year)*

      _____        _____
      _____        _____
      _____        _____
      _____        _____

   B. Decrease or extinguish undesirable behaviors
      1. *Short term (3 months)*          2. *Long term (9 months to*
                                             *1 year)*

      _____        _____
      _____        _____
      _____        _____
      _____        _____

   C. Treatment techniques and interventions
      1. _____
      2. _____
      3. _____
      4. _____
      5. _____
      6. _____
      7. _____
   D. Recording methods              Behaviors
      1. _____      _____
      2. _____      _____
      3. _____      _____
      4. _____      _____
Diagnosis: _____
_____
_____
_____

*Note.* Compiled from various sources.

extensive revision. It has been used and validated with both clinical and research populations, is appropriate for use with men and women in any type of treatment modality, and is culture sensitive.

The CDP provides an intensive and comprehensive history and status of clients' use and abuse of alcohol. The interview focuses on information that is relevant to the selection, planning, and implementation of treatment. It is also exceptionally useful in creating a data base for clinics and research programs desiring comparable pretreatment and follow-up evaluations (Miller & Marlatt, 1984).

The CDP covers a wide array of important information about the client, including basic demographics, family and employment status, history of drinking problem, pattern of alcohol use, alcohol-related problems, severity of dependence, social aspects of use, associated behaviors, relevant medical history, and motivations for drinking and treatment. The CDP has incorporated the Michigan Alcoholism Screening Test (MAST) (Selzer, 1971). Unlike any other instrument, it yields quantitative indexes of other dimensions, including duration of the problem, family history of alcoholism, alcohol consumption, alcohol dependence, range of drinking situations, quantity and frequency of other drug use, range of beverages used, emotional factors related to drinking, and life problems other than drinking (Miller & Marlatt, 1984).

The interview can be administered, with proper training and practice, by most mental-health or substance abuse workers. It is complex, and counselors should carefully read the manual in the CDP kit before they undertake any interviews. Additionally, Miller and Marlatt suggest that counselors engage in role-played practice interviews before trying client interviews. The CDP kit also contains individual interview forms and eight reusable card sets needed to administer the interview.

The CDP is the most comprehensive empirically derived instrument of this kind. It is carefully constructed and proceeds in a logical order, as outlined by Miller and Marlatt (1984):

A. demographic information
   age and residence
   family status
   employment and income information
   educational history
B. drinking history
   development of the drinking problem
   present drinking pattern
   pattern history
   alcohol-related life history
   drinking settings
   associated behaviors
   beverage preferences
   relevant medical history
C. motivational information
   reasons for drinking
   effects of drinking
   other life problems
   motivation for treatment
   drinker type ratings

Selected elements of the CDP are shown in Exhibit 3.3 to illustrate its format and types of questions.

# ■ Exhibit 3.3

## Comprehensive Drinker Profile

Date _____ Interviewer _____

Full name of client _____
                     First            Middle            Last

Prefers to be called _____ Sex (1) _____ F   (2) _____ M

A. Demographic information
   Age and residence
   A1. Date of birth _____ _____ _____      Present age _____
                     Month   Day    Year
   A2. Present local address
       Street address or box no. _____
       City or town _____
       State _____ Zip code _____
   A3. Local telephone   Area code _____ Number _____
       Best times to reach you at this number _____
   A4. Name and address of a person through whom you can be lo-
       cated if we lose contact with you (must be different from A2)
       Name _____ Relationship _____
       Street address or box no. _____
       City or town _____ State _____ Zip code _____
       Telephone   Area code _____ Number _____
   A5. How did you first hear about this program? _____
       If referred, by whom? _____
                             Name              Agency
   Educational history
   A21. Describe your educational background _____
        _____ degree _____ major _____
   A22. Code highest year of education completed _____
   A23. Are you currently pursuing education or training?
        (1) ___ full time (2) ___ part time (3) ___ no classes now
B. Drinking history
   Development of the drinking problem
   B24. About how old were you when you first took one or more
        drinks? _____
   B25. About how old were you when you first became intoxicated?
        _____
        Do you remember what you were drinking? _____
        Beverage _____

B26. How would you describe the drinking habits of

___ your mother?    0 = client does not know

1 = nondrinker (abstainer)

___ your father?    2 = occasional or light social drinker

3 = moderate or average social

___ spouse/partner?    drinker

4 = frequent or heavy social drinker

5 = problem drinker (at any time in life)

6 = alcoholic (at any time in life)

B27. Do you have any *blood* relatives whom you regard as being or having been a problem drinker or an alcoholic?

|  | Number males | Number females |
|---|---|---|
| parents | ___ × 3 = ___ | ___ × 3 = ___ |
| brothers or sisters | ___ × 3 = ___ | ___ × 3 = ___ |
| grandparents | ___ × 2 = ___ | ___ × 2 = ___ |
| uncles or aunts | ___ × 2 = ___ | ___ × 2 = ___ |
| first cousins | ___ × 1 = ___ | ___ × 1 = ___ |
| Total scores | Males: ___ | Females: ___ |

Were you raised by your biological parents?

___ (1) yes ___ (2) no

If not, who raised you? _____

B28. At what age (how long ago) did drinking begin to have an effect on your life which you did not approve of? When did drinking first begin to be a problem for you?

___ age of first problem    ___ denies that drinking is a problem

___ years of problem duration (age minus age at first problem)

At that particular time in your life when drinking first became a problem, were there any special circumstances or events that occurred which you feel were at least partly responsible for its becoming a problem?

_____

_____

_____

_____

_____

B29. Did you arrive at your present level of drinking:

(1) ___ gradually over a long period of time?

How long? _____

or (2) ___ by a more rapid increase (over several months or less)?

Present drinking pattern

B30. Drinking pattern (check one)
Determine which of the following categories best describes the client's current drinking pattern:

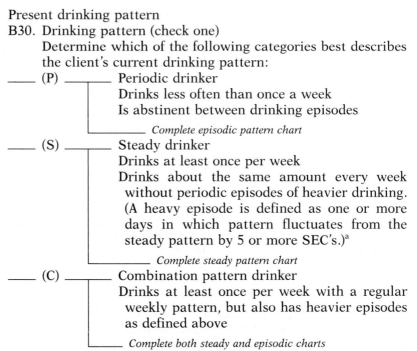

_____ (P) ——— Periodic drinker
Drinks less often than once a week
Is abstinent between drinking episodes

———— _Complete episodic pattern chart_

_____ (S) ——— Steady drinker
Drinks at least once per week
Drinks about the same amount every week without periodic episodes of heavier drinking. (A heavy episode is defined as one or more days in which pattern fluctuates from the steady pattern by 5 or more SEC's.)[a]

———— _Complete steady pattern chart_

_____ (C) ——— Combination pattern drinker
Drinks at least once per week with a regular weekly pattern, but also has heavier episodes as defined above

———— _Complete both steady and episodic charts_

If client used to smoke but does not smoke now, how long has it been since the last cigarette? _____

_____

Indicate any other use of tobacco (cigars, pipe, chewing).

_____


B49. Are you satisfied with your present weight? (If yes, enter 00. If no, indicate the number of pounds client regards self as overweight (+) or underweight (−) using proper arithmetic sign).                                           _____

B50. Describe _all_ medications that you currently use, including vitamins, birth control, aspirin, etc. [Ask specifically about tranquilizers, sedatives, stimulants, diet pills, pain medications — by prescription or otherwise. Indicate name of each drug, dosage, frequency, purpose, and whether taken by prescription (Rx).]

| Medication | Dosage | Frequency | Purpose | Rx? |
|---|---|---|---|---|
| _____ | _____ | _____ | _____ | ___ |
| _____ | _____ | _____ | _____ | ___ |
| _____ | _____ | _____ | _____ | ___ |
| _____ | _____ | _____ | _____ | ___ |
| _____ | _____ | _____ | _____ | ___ |
| _____ | _____ | _____ | _____ | ___ |

[a]SEC = standard ethanol content. 1 SEC = 0.5 oz (15 ml) of pure ethyl alcohol. 1 SEC = 10 oz beer, 4 oz wine, 2.5 oz fortified wine, 1.25 oz 80-proof spirits, 1 oz 100-proof spirits.

B51. Other drugs card sort

| | Specify | Last Use? | Past 3 Mos. Frequency | How? | Dose? |
|---|---|---|---|---|---|
| ___ amphetamines | _____ | ____ | _____ | ____ | ____ |
| ___ barbiturates, etc. | _____ | ____ | _____ | ____ | ____ |
| ___ cannabis | _____ | ____ | _____ | ____ | ____ |
| ___ cocaine | _____ | ____ | _____ | ____ | ____ |
| ___ hallucinogens | _____ | ____ | _____ | ____ | ____ |
| ___ inhalants | _____ | ____ | _____ | ____ | ____ |
| ___ opiates | _____ | ____ | _____ | ____ | ____ |
| ___ phencyclidine | _____ | ____ | _____ | ____ | ____ |
| ___ other drugs | _____ | ____ | _____ | ____ | ____ |

___ Total drug classes used        ___ Total past 3 mos.

B64. Are you currently seeing a counselor, psychologist, or psychiatrist for counseling or therapy? (If yes, specify.)

_____

_____

B65. (Women) Are you pregnant or planning to become pregnant?

_____

C. Motivational information
Reasons for drinking

C66. What are the main reasons why you drink? In other words, when you are *actually drinking,* what for you is the most positive or desirable *effect* of alcohol? What do you like best about alcohol? _____

_____

C67. Are you aware of any inner thoughts or emotional feelings, or things *within* you as a person, which "trigger off" your need or desire to take a drink at a particular moment in time?

_____

C68. Are you aware of any particular situations or set of events, things which happen to you in the *outside world*, which would result in your feeling like having one or more drinks?

_____

C69. In terms of your *life as a whole*, what are the most positive *effects* or consequences of drinking? _____

_____

_____

C70. When you are *actually drinking*, what for you is the most negative or undesirable *effect* of alcohol? In other words, what is the thing you like least about alcohol when you are drinking? _____

_____

_____

C71. In terms of your *life as a whole*, what do you see as the most negative effects or consequences of your drinking? _____

_____

_____

C87. Some people say that alcoholism is a disease or sickness, while others say that it is not a disease, but rather is more like a bad habit that a person has learned. Do you see it as a disease or as a bad habit? (If person says "both" have him or her indicate which they would agree with *more*.)
(1) __ disease     (2) __ bad habit

Drinker type ratings

C88. Now I am going to give you a list of six different types of drinkers and I would like you to tell me which one, in your opinion, best describes you at the present time. (Obtain rating.)
(If applicable): Now I'd like you to tell me the one that you think *your husband/wife* would choose as best describing you. (Obtain rating.)
Which one do you think your *closest friend* would choose as best describing you? (Obtain rating.)
Which one do you think *most people who know you* would choose as best describing you? (Obtain rating.)
Ratings: Self __ Spouse __ Friend __ Most people __
1 = total abstainer            4 = heavy social
2 = light social               (nonproblem) drinker
(nonproblem) drinker           5 = problem drinker
3 = moderate social            6 = alcoholic
(nonproblem) drinker
Compare self-rating with rating for "most people." Is self-rating:
(1) __ higher than "most"        (2) __ equal to "most"
          (3) __ lower than "most"?

Additional comments _____

_____

*Note.* The 20-page Comprehensive Drinker Profile Test Administration Kit and manual are available from Psychological Assessment Resources, Inc., P.O. Box 998, Odessa, FL 33556; (813) 968-3003. Copyright © 1984 by Psychological Assessment Resources, Inc. Reprinted by permission.

## A Priori Method of Assessment

Assessment is a complex procedure. There are no short cuts, and each clinician is responsible for maintaining the integrity and comprehensiveness of his or her assessment procedures. Before we move to more drug and alcohol assessment questionnaires, we will discuss an approach that is likely to improve the integrity and thoroughness of all assessments. This procedure is known as the a priori method of substance abuse assessment (Carey, Flasher, Maisto, & Turkat, 1984). It is quite scientific and much more efficient than standard assessment. It has the clinician develop in the initial interview a specific set of hypotheses about the client that a testing session is designed to evaluate. The counselor looks at the "big picture" that the client represents and then, based on the information gathered, tests hunches about the client. For instance, let's say that a counselor hypothesizes that the client is depressed and that this depression is playing a part in the client's substance abuse. In response to this hunch, then, the counselor administers the Beck Depression Inventory and evaluates the client's mental status vis-à-vis depression. If the interview and the Beck test are both positive, there is convergent validity to substantiate the hypothesis that the client is depressed, and the hypothesis is validated before treatment begins. The a priori method thus has four steps: (1) conduct the initial interview; (2) develop a case formulation or hypothesis (the client drinks abusively because he or she is depressed); (3) validate the hypothesis; and (4) develop a treatment plan based on all proved (validated) hypotheses and on the information gathered in the initial interview.

## Standardized Scales

As an adjunct to the initial interview, behavioral assessment, functional analysis, and the a priori approach, the counselor may choose to use standardized scales and objective assessment techniques to gain information about the client. At this point we will review a number of these tools and present several for examination.

Surprisingly, there are very few well-defined and empirically derived direct measurement tests of alcohol abuse or other drug problems. This reality argues for heavy reliance on techniques previously discussed in this chapter. It is important, though, that the counselor gather as much information as possible before making a diagnosis, and the following measurement devices will prove to be of help in this respect.

**Substance Abuse Problem Checklist**   A relatively new clinical aid for practitioners is the Substance Abuse Problem Checklist (SAPC) (Carroll, 1984). The checklist is a self-administered inventory containing 377 specific problems grouped into eight categories: (1) problems associated with motivation for treatment, (2) health problems, (3) personality problems, (4) problems in social relationships, (5) job-related problems, (6) problems associated with the misuse of leisure time, (7) religious or spiritual problems, and (8) legal problems. The client benefits by assuming the role of an active collaborator in the treatment process. Furthermore, the SAPC aids the clinician in diagnosing and treating drug abusers and also has a potential use in research. The results of a study of 114 SAPC's completed in a Pennsylvania hospital reflect the contribution of suppressed and depressed feelings to the evolution of chemical dependency and also provide a clear indication of the importance of the ecological perspective. One problem with the SAPC is its unsuitability for clients with limited ability in English. In addition, clients may consciously or unconsciously deny or conceal problems when responding.

**Short Michigan Alcoholism Screening Test**    The Short Michigan Alcoholism Screening Test (SMAST) (Pokorny, Miller, & Kaplan, 1972) is a useful and manageable measurement device for the clinician. This test, however, applies only to alcohol. It is composed of 17 yes or no questions chosen as the most discriminating of alcoholism from the original Michigan Alcoholism Screening Test (MAST) (Selzer, 1971). (The original form will be discussed next.) Jacobson (1976) reports that the SMAST does not tend toward false positives, as does the MAST, and that it is more accurate in correctly diagnosing alcohol problems. Pattison and Kaufman (1982) report that the SMAST is a more effective diagnostic instrument than is the National Council on Alcoholism's Major and Minor Symptom Typology.* The SMAST, then, is a simple, quick test with a high degree of reliability and validity. It is useful in targeting all types of alcohol-abusing populations, and it correlates highly (0.83) with the full MAST (Miller, 1976; Selzer, Vinokur, & Van Rooijen, 1974). On the SMAST, weighted scores range from 0 to 53. Scores of 20 or more indicate severe alcoholism.

**Michigan Alcoholism Screening Test**    The MAST, like the SMAST, is used to diagnose alcohol problems. It contains 24 items that ask about drinking habits, and its usefulness has been consistently supported by empirical evaluations (Miller, 1976; Selzer et al., 1974). MAST scores range from 0 to 53. A score of 0 to 4 indicates no problem; a score greater than 20 indicates severe alcoholism. The MAST is included here because it is widely used. The SMAST, however, is highly correlated with the MAST in predictive ability and is much more manageable because it is shorter and thus more quickly and easily administered (see Exhibit 3.4).

*For a further discussion of the council's criteria, see the *American Journal of Psychiatry*, 1972, *129* (2), pp. 127–135.

# ▌ Exhibit 3.4

## Michigan Alcoholism Screening Test

Answer
yes
or no.

1. Do you feel you are a normal drinker? (By normal we mean you drink less than or as much as most other people.)     _____
2. Have you ever awakened the morning after some drinking the night before and found that you could not remember a part of the evening?     _____
3. Does your wife, husband, a parent, or other near relative ever worry or complain about your drinking?     _____
4. Can you stop drinking without a struggle after one or two drinks?     _____
5. Do you ever feel guilty about your drinking?     _____
6. Do friends or relatives think you are a normal drinker?     _____
7. Are you able to stop drinking when you want to?     _____
8. Have you ever attended a meeting of Alcoholics Anonymous?     _____
9. Have you ever gotten into physical fights when drinking?     _____
10. Has drinking ever created problems between you and your wife, husband, a parent, or other near relative?     _____
11. Has your wife, husband, a parent, or other near relative ever gone to anyone for help about your drinking?     _____
12. Have you ever lost friends or girlfriends/boyfriends because of your drinking?     _____
13. Have you ever gotten into trouble at work because of your drinking?     _____
14. Have you ever lost a job because of drinking?     _____
15. Have you ever neglected your obligations, your family, or your work for two or more days in a row because you were drinking?     _____
16. Do you drink before noon fairly often?     _____
17. Have you ever been told you have liver trouble or cirrhosis?     _____
18. After heavy drinking have you ever had delirium tremens (DTs) or severe shaking, heard voices, or seen things that weren't really there?     _____
19. Have you ever gone to anyone for help about your drinking?     _____
20. Have you ever been in a hospital because of drinking?     _____

21. Have you ever been a patient in a psychiatric hospital or on a psychiatric ward of a general hospital where drinking was part of the problem that resulted in hospitalization?    _____
22. Have you ever been seen at a psychiatric or mental-health clinic or gone to any doctor, social worker, or clergyman for help with any emotional problem where drinking was part of the problem?    _____
23. Have you ever been arrested for driving under the influence of alcoholic beverages?    _____
24. Have you ever been arrested, even for a few hours, because of other drunken behavior?    _____

Answer Key

| Question | Appropriate Answer | Points |
|---|---|---|
| 1. | yes | 2 |
| 2. | no | 2 |
| 3. | no | 1 |
| 4. | yes | 2 |
| 5. | no | 1 |
| 6. | yes | 2 |
| 7. | yes | 2 |
| 8. | no | 5 |
| 9. | no | 1 |
| 10. | no | 2 |
| 11. | no | 2 |
| 12. | no | 2 |
| 13. | no | 2 |
| 14. | no | 2 |
| 15. | no | 2 |
| 16. | no | 1 |
| 17. | no | 2 |
| 18. | no | 2 |
| 19. | no | 5 |
| 20. | no | 5 |
| 21. | no | 2 |
| 22. | no | 2 |
| 23. | no | 2 |
| 24. | no | 2 |
| 25. | no | 2 |

Points are scored if the answer is different from that listed. The highest possible score is 55 points:

0–4: nonalcoholic
5–6: suggestive of alcohol problem

greater than 7: alcoholism
10–20: moderate alcoholism
greater than 20: severe alcoholism

*Note.* From "Michigan Alcoholism Screening Test: The Quest for a New Diagnostic Instrument" by M. L. Selzer, 1971, *American Journal of Psychiatry, 127,* pp. 1653–1658. Copyright © 1971 by the American Psychiatric Association. Reprinted by permission.

**Questionnaire on Drinking and Drug Abuse**    Another interesting measurement device, known simply as the Questionnaire on Drinking and Drug Abuse (Heckman, 1983), has been developed solely for use with college students. It looks at the problems caused by drug and alcohol use and realistically assesses problem situations that might arise in a college situation. The questionnaire is easily administered, consisting of 36 questions that are answered yes for alcohol, yes for drugs, or no. Positive outcomes on this test, as on all other tests, demand that the clinician follow up with the client on important issues brought out by the instrument. This device does not assess the amount of a drug consumed or the frequency of consumption. The clinician must clarify these issues and through clarification make a determination of problem severity (see Exhibit 3.5).

# ▌ Exhibit 3.5

## Questionnaire on Drinking and Drug Abuse

For each of the following questions, mark an X in one or two columns, as appropriate. Please answer each question for the past six-month period only.

| During the past six months, have you: | Yes Alcohol | Yes Drugs | No |
|---|---|---|---|
| 1. Felt guilty about your drinking or drug use? | ( ) | ( ) | ( ) |
| 2. Received a poor grade on an exam or paper because you were drinking or using drugs the night before? | ( ) | ( ) | ( ) |
| 3. Used alcohol or drugs before going to a class or before a test? | ( ) | ( ) | ( ) |
| 4. Cut a class or missed work after having several drinks or taking drugs? | ( ) | ( ) | ( ) |
| 5. Turned a class assignment in late because you were drinking or using drugs the day (night) before it was due? | ( ) | ( ) | ( ) |

6.  Heard anyone close to you complain about your drinking or drug use *or* suggest that you cut down on your drinking or drug use?    ( )    ( )    ( )

7.  Engaged in sex after drinking or using drugs that you were later sorry for or embarrassed about?    ( )    ( )    ( )

8.  Gotten "high" on alcohol or drugs *before* going out on a date?    ( )    ( )    ( )

9.  Passed out from drinking or using drugs while on a date or out with friends?    ( )    ( )    ( )

10.  Gotten into conflicts with your friends or acquaintances after drinking or using drugs?    ( )    ( )    ( )

11.  Drunk or used drugs and stayed at home instead of going out to be with others?    ( )    ( )    ( )

12.  Lied to friends about your drinking or drug use?    ( )    ( )    ( )

13.  Acted more quarrelsome or angry after drinking or using drugs?    ( )    ( )    ( )

14.  Had a difficult time being with friends without drinking or using drugs?    ( )    ( )    ( )

15.  Had bad abdominal pain in the morning after drinking or using drugs?    ( )    ( )    ( )

16.  Injured yourself badly enough after drinking or using drugs that you required medical attention?    ( )    ( )    ( )

17.  Found that you could not remember what you did the night before when you were drinking or using drugs?    ( )    ( )    ( )

18.  Missed morning classes because of alcohol or drug hangovers?    ( )    ( )    ( )

19.  Drunk or used drugs when you felt lonely or depressed?    ( )    ( )    ( )

20.  Become more depressed when drinking or using drugs?    ( )    ( )    ( )

21.  Drunk or used drugs after blowing an exam or after other disappointments?    ( )    ( )    ( )

22.  Been scared by your reaction to alcohol or drugs?    ( )    ( )    ( )

23.  Run out of money because you spent too much on alcohol or drugs?    ( )    ( )    ( )

24.  Gotten into trouble with the police or campus officials because of your behavior after drinking or using drugs?    ( )    ( )    ( )

25. Spent more money on alcohol or drugs    ( )    ( )    ( )
    than you think you should have?
26. Damaged personal or university property    ( )    ( )    ( )
    after drinking or using drugs?
27. Driven a car when you knew you had    ( )    ( )    ( )
    had too much alcohol or drugs?
28. Been driving after drinking or using drugs    ( )    ( )    ( )
    and become involved in an accident?
29. Usually gulped the first two or three    ( )    ( )    ( )
    drinks or tried to "get high" quickly?
30. Chosen not to attend a social activity    ( )    ( )    ( )
    because there would have been no
    alcohol or drugs present?
31. Increased the amount of alcohol or    ( )    ( )    ( )
    drugs that you use?
32. Found that you are using more and    ( )    ( )    ( )
    enjoying it less?
33. Gotten "high" with alcohol or drugs    ( )    ( )    ( )
    almost every day?
34. Drunk or used drugs in order to forget    ( )    ( )    ( )
    or feel better about problems?
35. Thought that you might have a drinking    ( )    ( )    ( )
    or drug problem?
36. Has answering the above questions    ( )    ( )    ( )
    caused you to think any differently about
    your drinking or use of drugs?

These assessment instruments, then, are used in conjunction with the clinical interview, formal assessment procedures, and the a priori method. It is unwise to depend solely on one assessment device. Doing so increases the likelihood of a false negative or false positive diagnosis. These incorrect decisions lead to inappropriate treatment and consequent treatment failure. This failure perpetuates the revolving-door syndrome, clients' poor self-esteem, and a mistrust and lack of confidence by clients in themselves and in the treatment community.

# Diagnosis

Once the assessment has been completed, the counselor is in a position to make a diagnostic impression. Diagnosis is critical, because it allows counselors to communicate with other professionals and, more importantly, provides a framework for treatment. If the diagnosis is incorrect or incomplete, the treatment will fail. Counselors should treat their diagnoses as tentative. If they see that the client is not doing well with a certain treatment or if new information is uncovered during counseling, they should feel free to make a new and more accurate diagnosis and, consequently, a new treatment plan. It is perfectly appropriate to admit that an initial impression was incorrect.

## Diagnostic and Statistical Manual of Mental Disorders

The most useful diagnostic approach for substance abuse and mental-health personnel comes from the *Diagnostic and Statistical Manual of Mental Disorders,* third edition (DSM III), (American Psychiatric Association, 1980). Each diagnosis made by DSM III criteria is assigned a number corresponding to the number of the syndrome as listed in the International Classification of Diseases (ICD), so that the two documents will be compatible. Next, each diagnosis is assigned to an axis. DSM III allows coding a client on five different axes. Substance use diagnoses fall on axis I, Clinical Psychiatric Syndromes and Other Conditions. A client who is diagnosed as a substance user can be simultaneously coded on axis II for a personality disorder, on axis III for a physical disorder, on axis IV for psychosocial stress, and on axis V for adaptive functioning in the last year. DSM III also allows an individual to be assigned more than one diagnosis on axis I, although some diagnostic combinations are not allowed. However, no other axis I diagnosis would preclude a diagnosis of a substance use disorder (Robins, 1982).

Diagnoses related to the use or abuse of substances appear in two sections of DSM III. The first section is called Organic Mental Disorders. This section designates a particular organic brain syndrome in which the cause is known or presumed (for example, alcohol intoxication, barbiturate withdrawal, or hallucinogen hallucinosis). The most important feature of these disorders is an abnormality associated with transient or permanent dysfunction of the brain. It is unlikely that this diagnostic category will be used very frequently, but clinicians should be aware of its existence and the signs and symptoms associated with these disorders.

The second section is entitled Substance Use Disorders, and it is this group that substance abuse counselors are likely to use frequently. This category deals with behavioral changes associated with the use of psychoactive substances. These behavioral changes are typically viewed as extremely undesirable. Examples include disturbance in social or occupational functioning as a consequence of substance use, inability to control use of the substance, and the development of serious withdrawal symptoms after cessation of substance use. These conditions are seen as mental disorders and are different from recreational or medical use. This section on substance use disorders applies to the maladaptive behaviors associated with regular use of the substances; the section on organic mental disorders describes the acute or chronic effects of these substances on the central nervous system (American Psychiatric Association, 1980).

The material on diagnosis of substance use disorders presented below is intended as an overview. Before using the DSM III diagnostic schema counselors should read the entire text and be trained in psychodiagnosis. Remember that diagnosis is safe and ethical only if counselors practice within the bounds of their competence.

**Substance abuse**    Three criteria distinguish substance abuse from non-pathological substance use:

1. *A pattern of pathological use*
   Depending on the substance, a pattern of pathological use can be defined by intoxication throughout the day, inability to cut down or stop use, numerous efforts to control use through periods of temporary abstinence or restriction of use to certain times of the day, continuation of substance use despite a serious physical disorder that the individual knows is exacerbated by use of the substance, or a need for daily use of the substance for adequate functioning.
2. *Impairment in social or occupational functioning caused by the pathological use of a substance*
   Social relations can be disturbed by the individual's failure to meet important obligations to friends and family, by display of erratic and impulsive behavior, and by inappropriate expression of aggressive feelings. The individual may have legal difficulties because of complications resulting from intoxication (for example, a car accident) or because of criminal behavior to obtain money to purchase the substance. Occupational functioning is implicated if an individual misses work or school or is unable to function effectively because of being intoxicated.
3. *Duration*
   Use must occur for at least one month.

**Substance dependence**    Substance dependence is a more severe form of substance abuse, and this diagnosis requires that physiological dependence, evidenced by either tolerance or withdrawal, be present. *Tolerance* means that the client needs markedly increased amounts of the substance to achieve the desired effect. In the case of alcohol, there are wide individual variations in the capacity to drink large quantities without intoxication. Since some people can drink large amounts despite limited drinking experience, the distinguishing feature of tolerance is that the client reports that the amount of alcohol he or she can drink before showing signs of intoxication has increased considerably over time. *Withdrawal* means that the client experiences a physiologic syndrome marked by profuse sweating, tremors, heart palpitations, malaise, increased blood pressure and, possibly, delirium when he or she decreases or discontinues drug or alcohol use. Withdrawal demands immediate medical attention.

**Classes of substances**   Five classes of substances are associated with both abuse and dependence: alcohol, barbiturates or similarly acting sedatives or hypnotics, opioids, amphetamines or similarly acting sympathomimetics, and cannabis.

**Use of multiple substances**   Substance abuse and dependence frequently involve several substances. Consequently, when an individual's condition meets the criteria for more than one substance use disorder, multiple diagnoses should generally be made.

**Recording specific diagnoses**   The DSM III diagnostic schema uses a five-digit code. Abuse of a drug or dependence on a drug is always specified by the first three digits. For example, 305.xx designates the abuse of an unspecified drug, whereas 303.xx indicates alcohol intoxication, and 304.xx indicates dependence on a drug other than alcohol. The fourth digit in the diagnostic code indicates the type of substance abuse or dependence. For example, 305.0x indicates alcohol abuse, whereas 305.4x indicates abuse of a barbituratelike drug, 304.1x indicates dependence on a barbituratelike drug, and 304.0x indicates an opioid dependence. The fifth digit in the DSM III system is used to indicate the course of the disorder, as follows:

| Code | Course | Definition |
|------|--------|------------|
| 1 | continuous | regular maladaptive use for over six months |
| 2 | episodic | a fairly circumscribed period of maladaptive use, with one or more similar periods in the past |
| 3 | in remission | previous maladaptive use, but not using substance at present |
| 0 | unspecified | course unknown |

Thus, a code of 304.11 would indicate a continuous barbituratelike dependence, and 304.13 would be used to show a barbituratelike dependence in remission. Hence, DSM III should be used by clinicians to record specific diagnoses that indicate whether the client's problem is abuse or dependence, type of drug(s) being used, and what the current course of the disorder is.

Diagnostic Criteria for Alcohol Abuse (305.0x)

A. *Pattern of pathological alcohol use:* need for daily use of alcohol for adequate functioning; inability to cut down or stop drinking; repeated efforts to control or reduce excess drinking by "going on the wagon" (periods of temporary abstinence) or restricting drinking to certain times of the day; binges (remaining intoxicated throughout the day for at least two days); occasional consumption of a fifth of spirits (or its equivalent in wine or beer); amnesic periods for events occurring while intoxicated (blackouts); continuation of drinking despite a serious physical disorder that the individual knows is exacerbated by alcohol use; drinking of nonbeverage alcohol.

B. *Impairment in social or occupational functioning due to alcohol use:* e.g., violence while intoxicated, absence from work, loss of job, legal difficulties (e.g., arrest for intoxicated behavior, traffic accidents while intoxicated), arguments or difficulties with family or friends because of excessive alcohol use.

C. *Duration of disturbance:* at least one month.

Diagnostic Criteria for Alcohol Dependence (303.9x)

A. Either a pattern of pathological alcohol use or impairment in social or occupational functioning due to alcohol use.

B. Either tolerance or withdrawal:
   *Tolerance:* need for markedly increased amounts of alcohol to achieve the desired effect, or markedly diminished effect with regular use of the same amount.
   *Withdrawal:* development of Alcohol Withdrawal (e.g., morning "shakes" and malaise relieved by drinking) after cessation of or reduction in drinking.

Diagnostic Criteria for Barbiturate or Similarly Acting Sedative or Hypnotic Abuse (305.4x)

A. *Pattern of pathological use:* inability to cut down or stop use; intoxication throughout the day; frequent use of the equivalent of 600 mg or more of secobarbital or 60 mg or more of diazepam; amnesic periods for events that occurred while intoxicated.

B. *Impairment in social or occupational functioning due to substance use:* e.g., fights, loss of friends, absence from work, loss of job, or legal difficulties (other than a single arrest due to possession, purchase, or sale of the substance).

C. *Duration of disturbance:* at least one month.

Diagnostic Criteria for Barbiturate or Similarly Acting Sedative or Hypnotic Dependence (304.1x)

*Tolerance:* need for markedly increased amounts of the substance to achieve the desired effect, or markedly diminished effect with regular use of the same amount.

*Withdrawal:* development of Barbiturate or Similarly Acting Sedative or Hypnotic Withdrawal after cessation of or reduction in substance use.

Diagnostic Criteria for Opioid Abuse (305.5x)

A. *Pattern of pathological use:* inability to reduce or stop use; intoxication throughout the day; use of opioids nearly every day for at least a month; episodes of opioid overdose (intoxication so severe that respiration and consciousness are impaired).
B. *Impairment in social or occupational functioning due to opioid use:* e.g., fights, loss of friends, absence from work, loss of job, or legal dificulties (other than due to a single arrest for possession, purchase, or sale of substance).
C. *Duration of disturbance:* at least one month.

Diagnostic Criteria for Opioid Dependence (304.0x)

*Tolerance:* need for markedly increased amounts of opioid to achieve the desired effect, or markedly diminished effect with regular use of the same amount.

*Withdrawal:* development of Opioid Withdrawal after cessation of or reduction in substance use.

Diagnostic Criteria for Cocaine Abuse (305.6x) (Because no clear withdrawal syndrome or tolerance to this substance has been produced experimentally or observed clinically, a category in dependence is not included.)

A. *Pattern of pathological use:* inability to reduce or stop use; intoxication throughout the day; episodes of cocaine overdose (intoxication so severe that hallucinations and delusions occur in a clear sensorium).
B. *Impairment in social or occupational functioning due to cocaine use:* e.g., fights, loss of friends, absence from work, loss of job, or legal difficulties (other than due to a single arrest for possession, purchase, or sale of the substance).
C. *Duration of disturbance:* at least one month.

Diagnostic Criteria for Amphetamine or Similarly Acting Sympathomimetic Abuse (305.7x)

A. *Pattern of pathological use:* inability to reduce or stop use; intoxication throughout the day; use of substance nearly every day for at least one month; episodes of either Amphetamine or Similarly Acting Sympathomimetic Delusional Disorder or Amphetamine or Similarly Acting Sympathomimetic Delirium.

B. *Impairment in social or occupational functioning due to amphetamine or similarly acting sympathomimetic use:* e.g., fights, loss of friends, absence from work, loss of job, or legal difficulties (other than due to a single arrest for possession, purchase, or sale of the substance).

C. *Duration of disturbance:* at least one month.

Diagnostic Criteria for Amphetamine or Similarly Acting Sympathomimetic Dependence (304.4x)

*Tolerance:* need for markedly increased amounts of substance to achieve the desired effect, or markedly diminished effect with regular use of the same amount.

*Withdrawal:* development of Amphetamine or Similarly Acting Sympathomimetic Withdrawal after cessation of or reduction in substance use.

Diagnostic Criteria for Phencyclidine (PCP) or Similarly Acting Arylcyclohexylamine Abuse (305.9x) (Because no clear withdrawal syndrome or tolerance to this substance has been produced experimentally or observed clinically, a category for dependence is not included.)

A. *Pattern of pathological use:* intoxication throughout the day; episodes of Phencyclidine or Similarly Acting Arylcyclohexylamine Delirium or Mixed Organic Mental Disorder.

B. *Impairment in social or occupational functioning due to substance use:* e.g., fights, loss of friends, absence from work, loss of job, or legal difficulties (other than due to a single arrest for possession, purchase, or sale of the substance).

C. *Duration of disturbance:* at least one month.

Diagnostic Criteria for Hallucinogen Abuse (305.3x) (Because no clear withdrawal syndrome or tolerance to this substance has been produced experimentally or observed clinically, a category for dependence is not included.)

A. *Pattern of pathological use:* inability to reduce or stop use; intoxication throughout the day (possible only with some hallucinogens); episodes of Hallucinogen Delusional Disorder or Hallucinogen Affective Disorder.

B. *Impairment in social or occupational functioning due to hallucinogen use:* e.g., fights, loss of friends, absence from work, loss of job, or legal difficulties (other than due to a single arrest for possession, purchase, or sale of the illegal substance).

C. *Duration of disturbance:* at least one month.

Diagnostic Criteria for Cannabis Abuse (305.2x)

A. *Pattern of pathological use:* intoxication throughout the day; use of cannabis nearly every day for at least a month; episodes of Cannabis Delusional Disorder.

B. *Impairment in social or occupational functioning due to cannabis use:* e.g., marked loss of interest in activities previously engaged in, loss of friends, absence from work, loss of job, or legal difficulties (other than due to a single arrest for possession, purchase, or sale of the substance).

C. *Duration of disturbance:* at least one month.

Diagnostic Criteria for Cannabis Dependence (304.3x)

A. *Pattern of pathological use:* intoxication throughout the day; use of cannabis nearly every day for at least a month; episodes of Cannabis Delusional Disorder.

B. *Impairment in social or occupational functioning due to cannabis use:* e.g., marked loss of interest in activities previously engaged in, loss of friends, absence from work, loss of job, or legal difficulties (other than due to a single arrest for possession, purchase, or sale of an illegal substance).

C. *Tolerance:* need for markedly increased amounts of cannabis to achieve the desired effect or markedly diminished effect with regular use of the same amount.

Diagnostic Criteria for Tobacco Dependence (305.1x)

A. *Continuous use of tobacco for at least one month.*

B. *At least one of the following:*
    1. Serious attempts to stop or significantly reduce the amount of tobacco use on a permanent basis have been unsuccessful.
    2. Attempts to stop smoking have led to the development of tobacco withdrawal.
    3. The individual continues to use tobacco despite a serious physical disorder (e.g., respiratory or cardiovascular disease) that he or she knows is exacerbated by tobacco use.

Other, Mixed, or Unspecified Substance Abuse (305.9x)

*Other Substance Abuse* should be recorded if a substance abused cannot be classified in any of the categories noted above, e.g., glue (inhalants), amyl nitrite.

*Mixed Substance Abuse* should be noted when the substances abused are from more than one nonalcoholic substance category, e.g., amphetamines and barbiturates. This category should be used only when the specific substances cannot be identified or when the abuse involves so many substances that the clinician prefers to indicate a combination of substances rather than list each specific substance. *Unspecified Substance Abuse* should be recorded when a substance abuse is unknown.

Other Specified Substance Dependence (304.6x)

This category should be used when the individual is dependent on a substance that cannot be classified in any of the previous categories, e.g., codeine or corticosteroids.

Unspecified Substance Dependence (304.9x)
This diagnosis can be used as an initial diagnosis in cases in which the specific substance is not yet known.

Dependence on a Combination of Opioid and Other Nonalcoholic Substances (304.7x)
This category should be used when the individual is dependent on both an opioid and a nonopioid nonalcoholic substance. An example might be dependence on both heroin and barbiturates. This category should be used only when the specific substances cannot be identified or when the dependence involves so many substances that the clinician prefers to indicate a combination of substances rather than list each specific substance.

Dependence on a Combination of Substances, Excluding Opioids and Alcohol (304.8x)
This category should be used when the individual is dependent on two or more nonopioid nonalcoholic substances. An example might be dependence on both amphetamines and barbiturates. This category should be used only when the specific substances cannot be identified or when the dependence involves so many substances that the clinician prefers to indicate a combination of substances rather than list each specific substance.

From the *American Psychiatric Association Diagnostic and Statistical Manual of Mental Disorders*, (3rd. ed.), Washington, D.C.. Copyright 1980, APA. Used with permission.

## ▎Summary

In this chapter we have covered the important topics of comprehensive assessment and diagnosis. We began by discussing individual assessment and the concept of initial evaluations, and went on to examine systematic behavioral assessment and the assessment devices that the substance abuse counselor is likely to find most helpful. We then presented an overview of a scientific form of evaluation known as the a priori method of case assessment or formulation: next, we surveyed standardized scales that counselors can use in evaluating their substance abusing clients. Finally, we presented a thorough discussion of diagnosis.

Competent and professional assessment and diagnosis require careful administration of interviews and objective measures. Counselors who fail to build their diagnoses and treatment plans on comprehensive techniques are failing their clients and violating professional standards of practice.

It is important that counselors not become frustrated as they begin this process. Assessment and diagnosis are difficult, but counselors will become much more confident with continued education and practice. Be patient, for the fruits of complete assessment and correct diagnosis are improved treatment outcomes. When our clients succeed, so do we.

# ▌ References

American Psychiatric Association. (1980). *Diagnostic and statistical manual of mental disorders* (3rd ed.). Washington, DC: Author.

Barrett, R. J. (1985). Behavioral approaches to individual differences in substance abuse: Drug-taking behavior. In M. Galizio & S. A. Maisto (Eds.), *Determinants of substance abuse: Biological, psychological, and environmental factors.* New York: Plenum.

Caddy, G. R., & Block, T. (1985). Individual differences in response to treatment. In M. Galizio & S. A. Maisto (Eds.), *Determinants of substance abuse: Biological, psychological, and environmental factors.* New York: Plenum.

Carey, M. P., Flasher, L. V., Maisto, S. A., & Turkat, I. D. (1984). The a priori approach to psychological assessment. *Professional Psychology: Research and Practice, 15,* 515–527.

Carroll, J. F. X. (1984). Substance Abuse Problem Checklist: A new clinical aid for drug and/or alcohol treatment dependency. *Journal of Substance Abuse Treatment, 1,* 31–36.

Hansen, J., & Emrick, C. D. (1985). Whom are we calling alcoholic? In W. R. Miller (Ed.), *Alcoholism: Theory, research, and treatment.* Lexington, MA: Ginn Press.

Hay, W. M., & Nathan, P. E. (1982). *Clinical case studies in the behavioral treatment of alcoholism.* New York: Plenum.

Heckman, B. (1983). *Questionnaire on Drinking and Drug Abuse.* Unpublished instrument, Illinois State University, Normal.

Hersen, M., & Bellack, A. S. (Eds.). (1981). *Behavioral assessment* (2nd ed.). New York: Pergamon Press.

Jacobson, G. R. (1976). *Diagnosis and assessment of alcohol abuse and alcoholism: A report to the National Institute of Alcohol Abuse and Alcoholism* (DHEW Publication No. ADM 76-228). Washington, DC: U. S. Government Printing Office.

Lawson, G. W., Ellis, D. C., & Rivers, P. C. (1984). *Essentials of chemical dependency counseling.* Rockville, MD: Aspen Systems Corp.

Maisto, S. A. (1985). Behavioral formulation of cases involving alcohol abuse. In I. D. Turkat (Ed.), *Behavioral case formulation.* New York: Plenum.

Maisto, S. A., Galizio, M., & Carey, K. B. (1985). Individual differences in substance abuse. In M. Galizio & S. A. Maisto (Eds.), *Determinants of substance abuse: Biological, psychological, and environmental factors.* New York: Plenum.

Miller, W. R. (1976). Alcoholism scales and objective measures. *Psychological Bulletin, 83*, 649–674.

Miller, W. R. (1985). Motivation for treatment: A review with special emphasis on alcoholism. *Psychological Bulletin, 98*, 84–107.

Miller, W. R., & Marlatt, G. A. (1984). *Manual for the comprehensive drinker profile.* Odessa, FL: Psychological Assessment Resources.

Miller, W. R., & Munoz, R. F. (1982). *How to control your drinking.* Albuquerque: University of New Mexico Press.

Nathan, P. E., & Lipscomb, T. R. (1979). Behavior therapy and behavior modification in the treatment of alcoholism. In J. H. Mendelson & N. K. Mello (Eds.), *The diagnosis and treatment of alcoholism.* New York: McGraw-Hill.

Pattison, E. M., & Kaufman, E. (1982). The alcoholism syndrome: Definitions and models. In E. M. Pattison & E. Kaufman (Eds.), *Encyclopedic handbook of alcoholism.* New York: Gardner Press.

Pattison, E. M., Sobell, M. B., & Sobell, L. C. (1977). *Emerging concepts of alcohol dependence.* New York: Springer.

Pokorny, M. D., Miller, B. A., & Kaplan, H. B. (1972). The brief MAST: A shortened version of the Michigan Alcoholism Screening Test. *American Journal of Psychiatry, 129*, 343–345.

Psychological Assessment Resources. (1984). *The Comprehensive Drinker Profile by W. R. Miller and G. A. Marlatt.* Odessa, FL: Psychological Assessment Resources.

Robins, L. N. (1982). The diagnosis of alcoholism after DSM III. In E. M. Pattison & E. Kaufman (Eds.), *Encyclopedic handbook of alcoholism.* New York: Gardner Press.

Selzer, M. L. (1971). The Michigan Alcoholism Screening Test: The quest for a new diagnostic instrument. *American Journal of Psychiatry, 127*, 1653–1658.

Selzer, M. L., Vinokur, A., & Van Rooijen, L. A. (1974). Self-administered Short Michigan Alcoholism Screening Test (SMAST). *Journal of Studies on Alcohol, 15*, 276–280.

Sobell, M. B., Sobell, L. C., & Sheahan, D. B. (1976). Functional analysis of drinking problems as an aid in developing individual treatment strategies. *Addictive Behaviors, 1*, 127–132.

South Suburban Council on Alcoholism. (1986). *Psycho-social/substance abuse history.* East Hazelcrest, IL: Author.

# Counseling Individual Substance Abusers

Once an assessment has been completed and a diagnosis made, the counselor is prepared to meet the needs of the client through treatment. The client's most immediate need is to make changes in substance abuse and other maladaptive behaviors. The counselor can best aid this process by taking what has been learned in the initial evaluation and forming a clear and individualized treatment plan.

## ▌ Developing a Treatment Plan

The treatment plan is the foundation for success, giving both counselor and client a structure in which to function. Expectations become clear, and any misunderstandings are relatively easy to resolve. Treatment plans allow counselors to clearly specify goals and monitor and evaluate progress. With such a plan, counseling can proceed in a straightforward, outcome-oriented fashion. Without it the client/counselor relationship will be poorly defined, rocky, and much less likely to succeed.

A treatment plan can be simple or elaborate as long as it addresses all the problems that must be dealt with in treatment. In this respect the counselor needs to articulate short-term goals (for those problems that can be solved in three to six months) and long-term goals (for those problems that may take up to one year to solve and are likely to involve continuous monitoring for the duration of the client's life).

P. M. Miller and Mastria (1977) have outlined six issues that dictate the setting of long- and short-term goals. They are (1) the extent and seriousness of the client's problem, (2) the client's motivation, (3) the setting, (4) the projected treatment time, (5) the preference of the client and the therapist, and (6) the cooperation of significant others.

In substance abuse counseling, the seriousness of the client's condition sometimes dictates the priorities. For example, a client who is physically dependent on drugs or alcohol must be medically detoxified before other treatment can begin. A suicidal client must have his or her depression treated before the chemical-dependency issue is addressed, and a psychotic individual must be stabilized before chemical-dependency treatment can begin.

The client's motivation also strongly affects goal setting. Clients who appear to have little hope and no faith in treatment should be given small tasks that they can quickly and successfully accomplish. These successes will improve clients' self-esteem and bolster their confidence in the treatment process. This technique, called shaping, is extremely effective in increasing motivation and, consequently, in improving treatment outcomes.

Certain treatments can be used only in an inpatient setting (for example, detoxification). Others (such as *in vivo* desensitization and maintenance of a job) are best completed on an outpatient basis.

The projected treatment time is always of concern to the client. It is often thought that treatment should encompass 28 days (7 days of detoxification and 21 days of intensive inpatient rehabilitation), a lifetime (continuous commitment to Alcoholics Anonymous), or a relatively well-defined period in outpatient therapy in which all salient issues can be dealt with. Based on the initial evaluation and diagnosis, counselors will be able to give their clients a fairly accurate timetable to go by. Certain treatments for certain problems take certain periods of time, and with experience and practice counselors become adept at predicting these times.

Client and counselor preferences are important variables in choosing goals. For example, a client may choose to deal with issues one, two, and three during a course of treatment but not with issues four, five, and six. Similarly, counselors may advise against addressing certain issues in treatment because they perceive them to be too resistant to therapy or believe that their introduction into therapy is contraindicated. Counselor and client must jointly articulate their respective preferences and then, through negotiation, determine treatment goals.

The involvement of significant others is quite important. The family or other people close to the client can be either natural therapists (helping the client, administering contingencies and rewards, providing support, and encouragement) or saboteurs (undermining therapy, disrupting the client, punishing the client). Counselors must set the stage for cooperation and, if they see it is not forthcoming, advise the client on appropriate ways to proceed. Significant others are critical allies, and therapists should struggle to gain their support.

An effective treatment plan need not be complex and can take the form illustrated in Exhibit 4.1. Examples of completed treatment plans are found in Exhibits 4.2 and 4.3.

## ▎ Exhibit 4.1

### Treatment Plan Form

*Name* _____ *Date* _____
*Date entered treatment* _____ *Sex* _____ *Birth date* _____
*Review date (every three months)* _____
*DSM III diagnosis(es)*
   *Axis I* _____
   *Axis II* _____
   *Axis III* _____
   *Axis IV* _____
   *Axis V* _____

A. *Brief history:* _____
   _____
   _____

B. *Case formulation:* _____
   _____
   _____
   _____

| | *Short-Term* | | *Time* | *Measurement* | *Goal Met* |
|---|---|---|---|---|---|
| C. | *Goals* | *Intervention* | *Frame* | *Device* | *(Yes or No)* |
| | 1. ____ | | | | |
| | 2. ____ | | | | |
| | 3. ____ | | | | |
| | 4. ____ | | | | |

| D. | Long-Term Goals | Intervention | Time Frame | Measurement Device | Goal Met (Yes or No) |
|---|---|---|---|---|---|
| | 1. _____ | | | | |
| | 2. _____ | | | | |
| | 3. _____ | | | | |
| | 4. _____ | | | | |

E. *Comments:* _____

F. *Review updates (every three months). Plan redone at one year.*
    *Review 1* _____
    *Review 2* _____
    *Review 3* _____
    *Review 4* _____

# ▌Exhibit 4.2

## Treatment Plan for an Alcohol User

*Name* _____ John Doe _____ *Date* __1-15-88__

*Date entered treatment* __1-10-88__ *Sex* __Male__ *Birth date* __5-20-57__

*Review date (every three months)* __3-15-88, 6-15-88, 9-15-88, 12-15-88__

*DSM III diagnosis(es):*
  *Axis I* 303.91 Alcohol dependence, continuous
     300.02 Generalized anxiety disorder
  *Axis II* 301.60 Dependent personality disorder
  *Axis III* Fatty infiltration of the liver
  *Axis IV* Psychosocial stressors: loss of girlfriend, financial difficulty due to recent loss of job. Severity 5—SEVERE
  *Axis V* Highest level of adaptive functioning past year: 5—POOR

A. *Brief history:* This 30-year-old white male began daily drinking (9 to 18 12-oz. beers per day) about 1 year ago when his girlfriend of 3 years left him for another man. She complained of his "always being nervous" and weak. Client has, in the past year, been arrested 3 times for alcohol-related offenses (1 drunken driving, 2 public intoxications). He claims to drink for anxiety reduction and for a sense of protection afforded by the alcohol. Client recently lost job due to absenteeism and intoxication, and in the last month he was diagnosed as having fatty infiltration of the liver. The client has increased tolerance but no withdrawal symptoms.

B. *Case Formulation:*   30-year-old man with an old dependent personality disorder began drinking excessively and detrimentally when his girlfriend (on whom he was very dependent) left him. Before this heavy drinking period the client typically consumed 3–4 alcoholic drinks per day to calm himself, to facilitate social interaction, and to hasten the onset of sleep.

| Short-Term C. *Goals* | *Intervention* | *Time Frame* | *Measurement Device* | *Goal Met (Yes or No)* |
|---|---|---|---|---|
| 1. Enforced abstinence | 250 mg Antabuse every day | 6 mos. | Biweekly blood screening for Antabuse | |
| 2. Functional analysis of behavior/ anxiety | Functional-analysis protocol | 2 mos. | Standard forms | |
| 3. Decreased anxiety | Progressive muscle-relaxation training | 3 mos. | Client's self-report/self-monitoring of anxiety | |
| 4. Education of client about his current dysfunction | Individualized education | 1 mo. | Posttest on specific dysfunctions | |
| 5. Improved problem-solving and decision-making skills | Training in decision making and problem solving | 2 mos. | Problem-solving inventory and therapist discretion | |
| 6. Engaging of client in therapy; increased treatment alliance | Generic techniques; small-success experiences | 3 mos. | Client compliance | |

| Long-Term D. *Goals* | *Intervention* | *Time Frame* | *Measurement Device* | *Goal Met (Yes or No)* |
|---|---|---|---|---|
| 1. Continued abstinence | Self-monitoring support-group participation | 1 year and then ongoing | Client and collateral report | |
| 2. Decreased dependency | Contingency contracting; individual counseling | 1 year | Client, collateral, and therapist report | |

| | | | |
|---|---|---|---|
| 3. Decreased anxiety | Perfection of relaxation skills; alternatives training; stimulus control and cognitive restructuring | 6 mos. | Client and therapist report; anxiety scale |
| 4. Engaging in productive and fulfilling relationships | Relationship training; communication training; skills training | 1 year | Therapist and client perception |
| 5. Termination of relationship; successful goal accomplishment | Fading out of schedule | 1 year + | ——— |

E. *Comments*: Client seems highly motivated and interested in treatment. His parents are willing to be involved. Client is bright and will do well with a combination of behavioral and insight-oriented psychotherapy. Termination should be designed to ease client out of this relationship. Counseling should proceed from weekly sessions to biweekly to 1 per month to a standard booster schedule.

F. *Review updates (every three months). Plan redone at one year.*
*Review 1* Reviews will be used to add any newly found pertinent information and to comment on new stressors, problems, or successes.

*Review 2* _____

*Review 3* _____

*Review 4* _____

# ▌ Exhibit 4.3

## Treatment Plan for an Dilaudid User

*Name* _____ Jane Doe _____ *Date* __1-8-88__

*Date entered treatment* __1-4-88__ *Sex* __Female__ *Birth date* __6-8-59__

*Review date (every three months)* __4-8-88, 7-8-88, 10-8-88, 1-8-89__

*DSM III* diagnosis(es):

*Axis I* 304.01 Opioid dependency, continuous (Dilaudid)

*Axis II* 301.70 Antisocial personality disorder

*Axis III* Client has elevated serum triglycerides, history of veneral disease.

*Axis IV* Psychosocial stressors: drug addiction, prostitution, unstable living environment, multiple arrests. Severity 5 — SEVERE

*Axis V* Highest level of adaptive functioning past year: 6 — VERY POOR

A. *Brief history:* 28-year-old white female with 7-year history of opioid dependence. Client currently uses 8 to 10 4-mg Dilaudid per day and prostitutes to support this habit. Client was repeatedly raped by her father between the ages of 12 and 16. Client's mother died when she was 3. No prior treatment. No current court involvement. Self-referred. No stable living environment.

B. *Case formulation:* Client began experiencing difficulty early in life. She was repeatedly lying, fighting, and stealing, beginning at age 8. Client began abusing a number of drugs at age 14 in an effort to escape her home reality. Given her mother's death and her father's aberrant behavior, it is evident that this woman has had no stable positive role models and has been unable to form stable relationships. She used drugs initially for symptom relief and escape and now for maintenance of dependence.

| Short-Term C. Goals | Intervention | Time Frame | Measurement Device | Goal Met (Yes or No) |
|---|---|---|---|---|
| 1. End of illicit drug use | Methadone maintenance 40 mg, by mouth, every day | 6 mos. | Random urine tests | |
| 2. Therapeutic treatment alliance | Individual counseling twice a week | 6 mos. | ———— | |

| | | | |
|---|---|---|---|
| 3. Improved social skills | Skill-training group | 6 mos. | Weekly attendance |
| 4. Legitimate employment | Placement in Job Club | 6 mos. | Weekly attendance with contingency for failure to have gainful employment within 6 mos. |

| Long-Term<br>D. Goals | Intervention | Time Frame | Measurement Device | Goal Met (Yes or No) |
|---|---|---|---|---|
| 1. Continued abstinence | Methadone, Narcotics Anonymous; detoxification and contingency management | 1 year | Urine screens | |
| 2. Stable employment | Job Club | 1 year | Work reports | |
| 3. Increased behavioral coping skills | Assertion training; relaxation training | 8 mos. | Assertion scale; biofeedback data | |
| 4. Improved physical condition | Nutrition counseling; exercise regime; M.D. visits | On-going | Physical correlates | |
| 5. End of therapy | Phaseout from weekly to biweekly to monthly to booster schedule | 2 years | ——— | |

E. *Comments*: Client is ambivalent about seeking treatment. She is fully ensconced in a drug-using culture and has no insight into the relationship between drug use and her current problems. Client has antisocial personality disorder, and this makes the treatment prognosis grim.

F. *Review updates (every three months). Plan redone in one year.*
*Review 1* Reviews will be used to add any newly found pertinent information and to comment on new stressors, problems, or successes.

*Review 2* _____

_____

_____

*Review 3* _____

_____

_____

*Review 4* _____

_____

_____

Once the treatment plan is completed, formal counseling can begin. The next section discusses the preparatory phase of counseling.

# ▌Preparing to Counsel

Caring and competent counselors must prepare themselves psychologically. Counseling is an extremely difficult endeavor, and it demands a great deal from practitioners. If counselors do not have their feet on the ground or if they are dealing with difficult psychological or chemical-dependency issues, they should put off doing counseling until they are ready. Such a delay is no disgrace. Rather, it exemplifies a strong degree of professionalism and a well-defined set of ethics. Counselors simply cannot meet the needs of others if their own needs will get in the way. The best way to avoid "contaminating" the therapy relationship is for practitioners to get counseling themselves. All counselors—whether or not they have overwhelming personal problems—should at some point in their training or career be involved in their own personal counseling, if for no other reason than personal growth. We all have issues floating around, and this experience is instructive in showing us what it's like on the other side of "the couch."

Other preparatory concerns are pragmatic, such as how the counselor looks, the appearance of the office, and the overall atmosphere of the counseling agency. Lawson, Ellis, and Rivers (1984) have outlined some advice for counselors before they sit down for their first therapy session:

1. Be genuinely interested in the client. Ensure the sanctity of the appointment hour; do not accept calls during counseling, and hang out the Do Not Disturb sign.
2. Keep your office organized and relatively neat.
3. Have the client's file available, and review it before each session. Do not review it during the session.

4. Keep your client calm. Discuss what is happening and why it is happening. Don't force the client to continue if he or she does not want to.

5. Do not be an inquisitor—"why" questions don't work well. Be open ended, and do not mobilize the defenses of the client. If he or she says no or disagrees with you, simply move on and come back to the issue later.

6. Clearly specify the time limits of your sessions. Do not arbitrarily break these limits.

7. Do not engage in personal or sexual relationships with your clients.

8. Do not act like God.

9. If possible, meet each week at the same time.

10. Explain approximately how long the counseling process is likely to take.

11. Listen to the client carefully. Clients need to be respected, and what they say is not, as it is usually thought to be, a product of denial or rationalization.

12. *Explain confidentiality, and then protect the relationship.*

13. Feel free to say "I don't know, but I'll check into it."

14. Always begin to end the session five minutes before its conclusion. Summarize and answer questions during this period.

These do's and don'ts are not all-inclusive, nor are they set in concrete. Counselors develop their own style and rules as they become more practiced. Being a critical evaluator of one's own behavior and skills and allowing oneself to change are signs of a good counselor.

# General Counseling Techniques and Skills

The basic counseling techniques we discuss in this section are not bound to any theory. All good counselors utilize these skills, which are intended to improve the counseling relationship and, consequently, treatment outcomes. It really doesn't matter whether you are a Skinnerian or a Rogerian, a Freudian or an Adlerian; these techniques are essential to your overall ability as a counselor. We will discuss (1) empathy, (2) genuineness, (3) immediacy, (4) warmth, (5) respect, (6) self-disclosure, (7) confrontation, (8) silence, (9) therapy organization and movement skills, and (10) cognitive restructuring (Lawson et al., 1984; Small, 1983).

## Empathy

We begin with the quintessential counselor quality—empathy, or fellow feeling, translated from the German *Einfühlung* in 1912.

Empathy refers to taking the feelings, sensations, or attitudes of another person or object into oneself. In other words, we have the capacity for experiencing vicariously the feelings, thoughts, or posture of another person. For example, a counselor may listen to a client explain how hopeless and useless, how unable to go on, he or she feels. An empathetic response would be direct and comforting. The response does not indicate that the counselor is experiencing what the client is experiencing but, rather, that the counselor is beginning to develop a very clear picture of what the client is describing. An empathic response to the above situation might be: "I hear you saying that you're useless and that you don't feel hopeful about the future. It's as if you're very sad, very depressed—just feeling overwhelmed. Am I reading the situation correctly?" Thus, empathy is caring, but it is not sympathy. Empathy is an "as if" quality. (It's *as if* I feel what you're feeling.) Obviously, counselors cannot know their client's experience, but they can share with the client their feelings as they perceive that experience. Empathy is a here-and-now quality, and it will occur only if counselors pay very close attention to their clients. They must be "present" with the client. This "present" orientation and appropriate empathy will help the client feel understood, and this feeling is extremely curative for substance-abusing individuals.

## Genuineness

Another important counselor quality is genuineness, which refers to the ability to freely be oneself. Genuine counselors are not phony, are not playing a role, and are not defensive. Their external behavior matches their internal feelings. If they are angry, they say so; if they are happy, they let it be known. This type of behavior improves the alliance between counselor and client and increases treatment compliance (that is, how well the client follows through in therapy). Genuineness is a natural state, but it may need to be practiced; counselors must remember always to be themselves.

## Immediacy

Immediacy, like genuineness, involves real feelings between the therapist and the client in the here and now. Ideally, counselor and client are constantly sharing what is going on between them in an open, honest, way. This technique focuses the client on reality and is very effective at keeping the counseling process moving.

## Warmth

Warmth is also related to genuineness. This quality typically shows up in nonverbal ways. Behaviors such as smiling, touching, crying, or head nodding are warm responses from the counselor to the client. These responses show that the counselor, too, is a human being, and they reinforce the client's humanness. Warmth demonstrates openness and responsivity, and it teaches clients that the counselor, at a bare minimum, will respond positively to them when they need it. A warm counselor improves treatment quality, and therefore treatment outcomes improve, too.

## Respect

Respect refers to the counselor's ability to tell clients that they are capable of surviving in a difficult environment and bright enough and free enough to choose their own alternatives and participate in the therapeutic decision-making process. This orientation empowers clients and begins the process of returning locus of control and responsibility to an internal orientation. ("I am in control and am directly and solely responsible for my well-being and happiness.") This reversal of orientation is a significant achievement, and the giving of respect is no manipulation. Clients are powerful people, but they have been oppressed. Counselors must work, through giving genuine respect, to empower them and move them forward on their important journey.

## Self-Disclosure

Self-disclosure is the sharing of the counselor's personal experiences, feelings, and attitudes with a client — but only for the sake of the client. It is a powerful tool, and it can sometimes be used in a countertherapeutic fashion. Self-disclosure is never to be used to help the counselor. In order for this technique to be of any help, it must be relevant to the situation at hand. Self-disclosure should be utilized only when the client can tolerate the information imparted by the counselor and make use of it. Self-disclosure should not be used just for the sake of maintaining talk or for a counselor's own personal fulfillment.

Appropriate self-disclosure will improve clients' self-esteem by making them feel less alone, less pathological, and more at ease with the ups and downs of life. Additionally, self-disclosure will equalize the relationship the counselor has with clients and consequently strengthen the treatment alliance and improve treatment outcomes.

## Confrontation

Some chemical-dependency counselors feel that confrontation is the only skill they need. Confrontation is an important tool that can be helpful in propelling clients forward, but it definitely does not and cannot independently meet all the needs of a substance abuse client. If a counselor relies too heavily on this technique, he or she probably has a skills deficit. In this case the counselor should step back, assess the situation, and, if necessary, seek additional training. Nothing is simple in chemical dependency. These are complex disorders, and they warrant complex treatment.

Therapeutic confrontation should occur, according to Small (1983), when there is an observed discrepancy between any of the following:

1. what clients say and what the counselor perceives they are experiencing
2. what clients are saying now and what the counselor heard them say earlier
3. what clients are saying now and their behavior in their day-to-day existence

There are five types of confrontation: (1) experiential confrontation, (2) strength confrontation, (3) weakness confrontation, (4) action confrontation, and (5) factual confrontation. An experiential confrontation occurs when clients say one thing and you believe (by virtue of the way the client looks) that they feel a different way. A strength confrontation occurs when clients claim weakness (play dumb), and the counselor empowers them by pointing out the disparity between what they are saying they can't do and what he or she knows they can do. A weakness confrontation, on the other hand, occurs when clients refuse to feel painful feelings. They put up a facade and act as if they can't be hurt. Here the counselor empowers the clients to drop the tough-guy image so that they can experience true feelings. An action confrontation occurs when clients are engaging in helpless behavior. Here the counselor motivates them and pushes them forward to complete certain tasks that are necessary for a successful treatment outcome. Finally, a factual confrontation occurs when the counselor disabuses clients of myths, or, in other words, educates them. This opportunity will present itself frequently in typical clinical practices, and it is advisable to let substance-abusing clients know the facts concerning the substances they are using and the problems they are encountering.

## Silence

It may seem easy to be quiet, or maybe even odd, but this skill is essential if counselors are to foster growth in their clients. Appropriately placed silence facilitates introspection and the creation of therapeutic dissonance (anxiety). This dissonance often serves as a spur in getting a client to take difficult and painful steps in therapy. Counselors feel that silence is taboo and contraindicated in "talking therapies." This is not true, and the adage that silence is golden could easily be revised to say that silence is potent.

Silence is a powerful tool. It should be used to allow for thoughtful reflection, a slowing down of the therapy process, or a reflection of feelings. Counselors should not use silence to intimidate clients or to cover up indecision about how to proceed. If counselors find that they are using silence frequently for no well-defined reason, they should step back, assess their skills, examine their motivation, and, if necessary, discontinue their counseling of chemically dependent clients until they have more skills and are more capable of providing competent treatment.

## Organization and Movement Skills

Skills for organizing therapy and moving it along include lead-ins, restatements, reflection, and questioning. These skills are used after the therapy relationship has been structured. They tend to organize, or systematize, counseling and facilitate therapeutic movement. Counselors must remember that therapy is hard work and that they will need specific techniques to keep it rolling.

**Lead-ins**   The counselor might use a lead-in in an effort to get more information from clients about their problems or to get them to feel more comfortable while talking about their specific situation. A lead-in used in this way is simply a "nudge" given to clients that encourages them to further explore or expand an issue. Simple statements such as "Could you tell me more about that" or "I'm not sure I understand. Can you talk more about that issue" are particularly useful in getting clients to draw a clearer picture for themselves and for the counselor.

**Restatement**   In restatement a counselor takes what a client has said and rephrases it in a clearer and more articulate way. This technique decreases the negative effects of confused or defensive self-statements and strengthens the therapeutic relationship while facilitating the therapy process. Restatement is frequently referred to as paraphrasing, and this process lets the client know that the counselor is paying attention, cares, and thinks that the client is an important person. Additionally, this procedure clarifies issues for the client and facilitates growth. Suppose, for instance, that a client says: "Everyone says my drinking is a problem. Well, I don't think it is, and it's probably a better idea to talk with my family. They're the ones with a problem—not me!" The therapist can facilitate communication and movement by responding: "It seems that you're unhappy with all the pressure that's being put on you and that you're not sure that you have a problem. If I were to speak with your family, how would that help you?" This type of response is nonthreatening and powerfully reinforcing. It is an essential component of the counseling relationship that provides needed organization, and consequently, increased insight and improved treatment outcomes.

**Reflection**    This technique, a parroting of cognitive or emotional statements, facilitates communication, gives the client a feeling of being understood, and allows the counseling relationship to grow. In this regard counselors may find that they have to reflect what the client is feeling or what he or she has said or is thinking. If they choose not to use reflection, they run the risk of prematurely ending the counseling relationship, stalling the therapeutic process, frustrating or confusing the client, or generally wasting the client's time. Use of this tool, conversely, hastens the process, improves the client's self-esteem, deepens the counseling relationship, and generally improves the therapeutic outcome. Here is an example of a counselor's response to a woman with a drinking problem:

> *Client:* Every time I think of my drinking, I want to crawl into a hole and cry. Sometimes it seems easier to keep drinking—maybe I'll die soon.
>
> *Counselor:* It sounds as if you're awfully embarrassed by your drinking. You seem to feel hopeless and very depressed.

Here the therapist has reflected the client's feelings and uncovered her thinking process. This exchange allows the client to be heard and gives her a strong sense of being heard. Therapy is advanced, and the relationship with the client is strengthened. Remember, then, that counselors can reflect either a feeling or a thought. Both forms of reflection serve to move treatment along and provide an impetus for continued progress.

**Questioning**    A final movement and organization technique is questioning. Questioning allows the counselor to clarify the client's needs, feelings, and beliefs. It facilitates the expansion of ideas, therapeutic growth, and self-understanding. Questioning should not be used arbitrarily or solely to fill time. Continual questioning is regressive. Facilitative questioning can effectively enlighten the client, short-circuit maladaptive defense mechanisms, and move the therapy process along to deeper, more meaningful, levels. Questions are typically most useful when they ask "what" or "how." A "why" question implies a right/wrong dichotomy, fosters the use of defense mechanisms such as intellectualization, rationalization, and denial, and generally impedes useful counseling. Compare these three types of question:

> *Counselor:* What is it about your drinking that is important to you?
>
> *Counselor:* How does your drinking make you feel?
>
> *Counselor:* Why do you drink?

It is evident that the "what" and "how" questions are nonjudgmental and likely to facilitate open communication. The "why" question, however, sounds judgmental and almost punitive. It immediately puts the client on guard and is very likely to bear little fruit other than a litany of denial and rationalization.

Questions can also be either direct or, more effectively, open-ended. Open-ended questions expand the therapy process and aid the client in establishing a free-flowing pattern of communication. In this respect counselors will do well to avoid questions like "Do you want to die?" in favor of questions like "What sorts of burdens will be lifted if you kill yourself?" Questioning done in a sensitive and therapeutic way will facilitate growth and begin the process of separating behavior from self. It will encourage discussion while improving self-acceptance, self-disclosure, and honesty.

## Cognitive Restructuring

A final basic counseling technique is known as cognitive restructuring. It allows clients to restate their beliefs and ideas in a fashion that more closely represents reality as opposed to fantasy. For example, a client who says "I can't change my behavior" would be encouraged to say "I won't change my behavior." This type of self-statement more accurately reflects reality and gives clients a spur to initiative, since they will begin to "own" their behavior. Additionally, the statements that clients make will begin to be less overwhelming ("Some people dislike me," as opposed to "Everyone hates me") and consequently easier to deal with in the therapy relationship. In essence, this technique will help ensure that clients' cognitions, emotions, and actions will be rational. To promote cognitive restructuring, counselors should teach their clients to ask the following questions as they evaluate their thoughts and feelings:

1. Is my thinking in this situation based on an obvious fact or on fantasy?
2. Is my thinking in this situation likely to help me protect my life or health?

3. Is my thinking likely to help me or hinder me in achieving my short- and long-term goals?
4. Is my thinking going to help me avoid conflict with others?
5. Is my thinking going to help me feel the emotions I want to feel?

Cognitive restructuring in this way will serve to decrease negative self-statements, negative self-fulfilling prophecies, hopelessness, anxiety, and fear, and to increase realistic cognitions, positive self-image, and self-esteem. It requires consistent attention to what the client is saying and a continuous orientation back to reality.

The use of these very basic skills will improve counseling relationships and improve treatment outcomes. These techniques require practice and cannot be taken for granted. Counselors should not rely exclusively on any one skill. Rather, techniques should be used in concert and only when they will serve the client.

# Behavioral Techniques and Substance Abuse

The specific techniques we discuss in this section for use with substance-abusing clients are designed to interrupt dysfunctional behaviors. To use these techniques effectively, the counselor must refer back to the initial assessment and evaluation. In this way the counselor will be able to choose specific techniques (for example, relaxation training) to treat specific disorders that have been identified during the initial evaluation (for example, anxiety).

All clients are unique and have unique problems that must be individually addressed and treated. The label "alcohol-dependent" or "opioid-dependent" cannot dictate treatment. For example, not all clients with barbiturate problems should receive assertion training, relaxation training, and a referral to Narcotics Anonymous; rather, each should be treated for the specific problems he or she has exhibited. Substance abuse problems are complex, but this complexity is not best addressed by using everything in one's black bag to treat every client.

Some of the behavioral techniques that will be most helpful to counselors and their clients are (1) relaxation training, (2) assertion training, (3) modeling, (4) contingency contracting and management, (5) systematic desensitization, and (6) covert aversion therapy. Additionally, counselors need to be familiar with the concept of controlled drinking and its method of implementation (behavioral self-control training), which will be discusssed in a later section of this chapter. These behavioral techniques have been included for two reasons. First, they have been well tested in research on the treatment of alcohol and drug problems (W. R. Miller, 1985). Second, we feel that, in the case of a substance abuser, dysfunctional life behaviors should be changed before any attempts are made at long-term, insight-oriented therapy. Narcotics Anonymous and Alcoholics Anonymous will also be discussed in this chapter, not because we see them as treatment techniques but because clinicians frequently refer clients to these well-known self-help groups for ongoing support.

## Relaxation Training

Anxiety is very frequently a precipitant to substance use and abuse. This is not to say that anxiety causes excessive alcohol or drug use. Rather, it is an extremely problematic symptom that many substance abusers report. In light of this reality it is wise to have a tool with which we can help our clients reduce their anxiety. This tool is relaxation training. It is vital that counselors understand that anxiety does not occur in a vacuum. There are always a number of social, emotional, and cognitive components from which anxiety (fear) is created. Therefore, one should never solely use relaxation training to "cure" anxiety. Rather, this technique should be used to treat the specific symptom of anxiety, and other techniques should be used to enable clients to deal with the situations that have led to anxiety (that is, assertion deficit, fear of rejection, poor self-esteem).

Relaxation training, as described by Jacobsen (1968), is widely called progressive muscle relaxation. This procedure involves successively tensing and then relaxing muscle groups in the body. The technique is used because relaxation is incompatible with anxiety. It is easy to administer and easy to learn. Substance abusers with anxiety respond well to this technique because it allows them to (1) reduce generalized anxiety and normal tension, (2) reduce anxiety and tension that is generated in highly charged emotional or social situations, (3) relax before sleep, and (4) diminish the intensity of urges and cravings that often precede a relapse to drug or alcohol use. These uses are quite positive for substance abusers, who are used to treating many, if not all, of their symptoms with alcohol or another drug. This relaxation response, once learned, is easy to use, positively reinforcing, and effective in reducing negative outcomes (such as unremitting anxiety or a relapse) in clients' lives.

Learning to use progressive muscle relaxation is relatively simple. It requires that the counselor carefully and fully explain to the client what progressive muscle relaxation is, why it is being used, how it works, and how to make it work. In general a statement such as the following is an acceptable introduction to this technique:

> Today I'm going to begin teaching you a new technique to handle your anxiety. It's called relaxation training, or progressive muscle relaxation. It's a simple technique that

you can use to reduce and eliminate unpleasant anxiety that you carry around with you or that presents itself in specific situations or at specific times. This tool will become an effective deterrent to anxiety, and you can use it to eliminate your urges and cravings for alcohol [or other drugs].

Relaxation works on a simple system. Basically, if you're relaxed, you can't be uptight or anxious. We're going to spend plenty of time seeing to it that you learn this skill and that it becomes a part of you. People will often use relaxation constantly, and by doing this they greatly improve the quality of their life. You'll see when you're first learning this skill that it requires a lot of activity on your part. You'll be required to tense and then relax a lot of muscles throughout your body. You're probably asking yourself, 'How can I possibly use this all day or anywhere but in private?' Well, quite simply, once you learn to do relaxation, it becomes another habit, and relaxation will occur spontaneously in response to signs and signals that your body gives you. No one will ever know you're practicing relaxation.

Now then, in order to learn relaxation and have it become a part of who you are, it's very important that you practice. I can get you to relax here in the office, but with practice you'll begin to "own" the behavior, and you'll find that it becomes easier and easier to relax. With practice, relaxation will become a part of you. Now, do you have any questions?

In order to do relaxation training the counselor will need a comfortable moderately firm recliner or couch. The client should be instructed to remove all jewelry and to loosen restrictive clothing and to assume as comfortable a position as possible. The lights should be dimmed, and the noise level should be kept low. During relaxation one wants to minimize external stimulus intrusions so clients can relax and concentrate on the counselor's voice and on their increasing relaxation. Before relaxation begins the counselor should instruct clients that their level of relaxation will be monitored as the relaxation procedure progresses and that they are to signify persistent tension in a muscle group, when asked, by raising an index finger.

Relaxation should be sequential and should proceed in the following fashion:

1. Relax the muscles in the dominant and nondominant hand.
2. Relax muscles in the dominant and nondominant arm.

 3. Relax muscles in the head.
 4. Relax muscles in the neck.
 5. Relax muscles in the face.
 6. Relax muscles in the jaw.
 7. Relax muscles in the shoulders.
 8. Relax muscles in the back.
 9. Relax muscles in the chest.
10. Relax muscles in the stomach.
11. Relax muscles in the upper legs.
12. Relax muscles in the lower legs.
13. Relax muscles in the feet.

With practice the counselor will probably be able to complete two or three muscle groups per session of 30 to 60 minutes. The client is simply instructed to contract the muscle group being worked on and, during this contraction, to experience as vividly as possible the tense, tight, and uncomfortable feelings that are produced. When the muscle group has been appropriately tensed, the client is instructed to release the tension and to focus on the positive and soothing feelings associated with relaxation. For each muscle group this contraction/relaxation pattern should be executed two or three times so that the client learns the difference between the two feeling states.

When the client is fully able to relax the different muscle groups, full-body relaxation training can begin. In this procedure the counselor still follows the muscle-group sequence but goes through all groups during the training session. It is advisable to tape relaxation-training sessions so the client can use these to practice with at home.

In an effort to get relaxation in all muscle groups, the following instructions to clients will be useful:

 1. *Hands and arms:* Make a very tight fist, and fully extend your arms.
 2. *Head:* Roll your eyes to the back while straining to look up.
 3. *Neck:* (a) Rotate your head fully to the left and hold. (b) Rotate your head fully to the right and hold. (c) Bring your head all the way back and try to touch your back with the back of your head. (d) Move your head forward as far as possible so that your chin makes contact with your chest.
 4. *Face and jaw:* Grit your teeth, furrow your forehead, purse your lips, squeeze your eyes shut, and smile and frown in an exaggerated fashion. After gritting your teeth to tense your jaw, you must allow your mouth to open slightly in order to achieve relaxation.
 5. *Shoulders:* Raise your shoulders in an effort to touch your ears. Rotate your shoulders toward the middle of your chest.

6. *Back:* Arch your back while moving your shoulders in reverse as if you were trying to get them to connect. Hold your head still, and roll your shoulders forward toward the middle of your chest.
7. *Chest:* Puff out your chest, and then inhale deeply. Hold your breath for three to five seconds, and then slowly exhale.
8. *Stomach:* Suck in your belly, and then push it out. Finally, take a deep breath, hold it for 3 to 5 seconds, and then slowly exhale.
9. *Legs:* Elevate your legs slightly off the relaxation chair, and extend them fully.
10. *Feet:* Fully extend or arch your foot and toes in a downward position, and then do this in an upward position.

Each muscle group must be fully relaxed before the client moves to the next group. Remember to have the client indicate continued tension in a muscle group or area by raising an index finger. Muscle groups should be tensed and held for approximately 15 seconds, and relaxation in the muscle group should be slowly phased in over 15 to 20 seconds.

The following case example demonstrates a full-body relaxation procedure.

OK, John, please make yourself comfortable. Get completely relaxed now, and when you're ready to begin, signal me by raising the index finger on your right hand. OK. Now let's begin with your left hand and arm. I'd like you to make a very powerful fist with your left hand. Good, make it tighter now, hold it, hold it, good. Feel the tension, notice how uncomfortable it is, hold it, good. Now slowly begin to open your fist, slowly now, feel the good feelings, and notice the difference between tension and relaxation, good. Now feel the feelings, notice how nice it feels.

OK, John, now let's move to your arm now. Begin to extend your arm, John, feel the tension building, feel it building, notice the discomfort, the pain, feel your arm shaking and recognize that you can control this feeling, hold it, hold it. OK, now let's slowly begin relaxing your arm, feel the bad feelings draining away, feel the tension leaving your body and notice how good your arm is beginning to feel, notice the difference between tension and relaxation, keep relaxing and keep feeling the good feelings. If any tension is left in your hand or arm, please tell me by raising your right index finger. OK, good, continue to relax. [Now move to the right arm and hand using the same procedure and then move to the head.]

OK, John, now we're going to relax your head. Feel the tension there, and know that you can control these feelings.

OK, now let's arch your eyebrows and without moving your head look straight up. OK, good, now hold it, hold it, good, feel the tension, notice the feelings, hold it, hold it, good. Now let the tension slip away and feel it being replaced by good feelings, a sense of relaxation. Good, feel it, . . . good. [Have the client do appropriate neck exercises, always pointing out the positive differences between relaxation and tension. Once the client has fully relaxed the neck, move on to the face and jaw.]

OK, John, let's begin to relax your jaw. I want you to notice the tension and fatigue in your jaw and to understand that through relaxation you can remove these bad feelings. OK now, John, let's grit your teeth, tighter, tighter, OK, hold it, feel the discomfort, notice how it feels, hold it, OK. Now slowly begin to relax your jaw, OK, separate your teeth and open your mouth slightly. Good, now feel the relaxation, relax, relax now. OK, let's relax your face now. [Have the client do facial exercises, and when relaxed, move to the shoulders and then to the back and on to the chest.]

OK, John, feel the tension in your chest, feel the anxiety and all the bad feelings that build up there and know, John, that you can control these feelings. OK, John, let's take a deep, deep breath, good, good, now hold it, hold it, feel that tension, hold it, good, feel the tension, feel the discomfort, OK, slowly now begin to let it come out, and as the air leaves your body, notice how good you feel, notice how the pressure is leaving you, good, feel those good feelings. Now breathe normally. [Move now to the stomach and then to the legs.]

Finally, John, let's see about relaxing your feet and toes. OK, John, feel the tension there, and understand that your body is fully free of tension now and all that remains is to let the tension go from your feet, so let's tense your foot. [Do only one appendage at a time.] Now, make it tense, feel the tension, more tense, more, hold it, hold it, feel the discomfort. OK, now, let's start shaking that tension loose, let it go, let it go, feel the relaxation, feel the difference and know that you can control these feelings.

OK, good, good, are you completely relaxed? If not, raise the index finger on your right hand. Good, feel the relaxation and now relax even more deeply, good, good, rest now, relax, let it all go, good, and now just keep relaxing and enjoy these feelings for a moment. [Silence for one minute.]

And now we're slowly going to begin to move about, stay relaxed now, and I'd like you to keep your eyes closed and wiggle your toes, arch your feet, and stretch your legs. OK, now take a deep breath, good, let it out and move your stomach and chest, and now begin to flex your hand and fingers and stretch out your arms. Stay relaxed now, good, and let's move your shoulders and rotate your neck and scrunch up your face, lift your eyebrows, and close your eyes tightly. Good. Now I'd like you to continue to be relaxed, and as I count backward from five, slowly open your eyes, 5—4—3—2—1—0. Good, very good, you did a great job today.

These sessions should last from 30 to 60 minutes. The therapist's voice should be low, smooth, and comforting. Be relaxed, and encourage the client to maintain the relaxation response throughout the day, and to ask any questions that he or she may have.

After five to eight one-hour sessions and two 15-minute practice periods per day throughout the treatment period, the relaxation response should be well learned. The client will be better equipped to handle both underlying anxiety and the tension evoked when he or she is placed in certain highly charged social or emotional situations.

## Assertion Training

A common concern of substance-abusing clients is the difficulty they have in asserting themselves. Assertion is the behavior or trait that allows people to appropriately express their personal rights and feelings. In this respect assertion may be an expression of positive feelings ("I love you") or negative feelings ("I'm angry because you're insensitive"). Assertion, too, can be as simple as saying yes or no or even expressing an opinion that runs counter to the group opinion. The appropriateness of the assertive response, or the indicator that a response is assertive, is judged by three criteria.

1. Does the assertion result in a desired outcome; that is, does something change, in the direction you want it to change, as a result of your being assertive?
2. Is the assertive response acceptable to you; that is, do you feel good about your style and good about the way you handled and resolved the situation?
3. Is your assertion acceptable to and good for the person you are asserting yourself to? Aggression, which might effect a behavior change and make you feel more powerful, is inappropriate, since it is unacceptable for the other person.

Assertion is best understood when compared with three other behavioral responses: (1) aggression, (2) passive/aggression, and (3) passivity. A short vignette will clarify the differences.

Joe was a polydrug abuser who had recently discontinued all substance use. He was feeling pretty good about this accomplishment and had not had any urges to use substances. To celebrate his victory, Joe asked his wife to join him for a special dinner at a local restaurant. The sky was the limit, and Joe ordered his favorite meal — very rare prime rib of beef. When his meal came, Joe quickly realized that his beef was overcooked. He had been given assertion training in his therapy, and he chose to make the following response to the waiter who had brought his dinner.

> *Waiter:* Is everything OK here?
> *Joe:* No. I ordered very rare prime rib, and this meat is over-cooked. Would you please take it back to the kitchen and get me a rare one.
> *Waiter:* I'm very sorry, sir. Certainly.
> *Joe:* Thank you.

After this discussion Joe felt very good. He had had a slight amount of anxiety but recognized that it was his right to ask for and receive exactly what he had ordered. He discussed the situation with his wife and recounted to her three other ways he might have responded in the past. When he was intoxicated, for example, the situation might have gone as follows:

> *Waiter:* Is everything OK here?
> *Joe:* This damn steak is a piece of crap, and I'm not going to put up with this. Get this away from me and get the manager, you idiot.

Here Joe was being aggressive. He upset his wife, angered the waiter, and was forced to leave without eating. This response was not appropriate, since Joe's response was not acceptable to him, his wife, the waiter, or the manager.

When he was angry with himself and everybody else but not intoxicated, this might have been the result:

> *Waiter:* Is everything OK here?
> *Joe:* Yes, thank you.
> *Joe (to wife):* Can you believe this crap? Look at this lousy prime rib. I'm never coming back here. (Throughout the course of the meal Joe makes a mess with bread crumbs and spills water, but he never voices his discontent to the waiter. He leaves a very small tip.)

This response was passive/aggressive. Joe felt slighted and angry but was fearful of expressing his feelings or of demanding his rights. This response upset Joe's wife, made Joe feel weak and powerless, and confused the waiter, who wondered why such a small tip was left and why Joe had made such a mess. Clearly this response was not appropriate.

When everything seemed to be going all right and Joe was not intoxicated, this might have happened:

> *Waiter:* Is everything OK here?
>
> *Joe:* Yes, thank you—everything is lovely. (Joe feels a slow burn in his stomach and becomes very anxious. He does not like the prime rib but is afraid to say anything for fear that the waiter will retaliate and his wife will be upset.)

Joe convinced himself that it was no big deal and tried to enjoy himself. He left a big tip. Joe felt very weak, very powerless, and very overwhelmed. He got angry later that evening and drank to overcome his negative emotional state. This passive response diminished Joe's self-esteem. Despite being perfectly acceptable to the waiter and Joe's wife, this response was also inappropriate.

Clearly, the assertive response is most acceptable for all involved. It improves one's self-image, self-esteem, and self-confidence, and it does not injure anyone in the process. Joe had a long history of nonassertion followed by decreased self-esteem, feelings of self-pity, and consequent intoxication. With assertion training Joe felt that he had much more personal power, his self-esteem improved, and he had far fewer episodes of self-pity and drinking. Thus, the use of assertion training with Joe, as with other substance abusers, is justified by the fact that by teaching new ways of coping with difficult social and emotional situations, we effectively eliminate many cues (anxiety due to nonassertion) to excessive drinking. In essence, assertion training provides substance abusers with a healthy alternative to substance use.

Assertion consists of both verbal and behavioral components. These components should be melded together to form an appropriate response that, after practice, is comfortable for the client, appears rational, and is not too anxiety provoking.

1. *The assertive statement:* The appropriate assertive response should include the following components—I feel——(emotion) because you——(action). Would you please——(change statement).
2. *Duration:* Assertive responses should be slightly longer than nonassertive responses.
3. *Voice tone:* Assertive responses should be made in a firm, slightly loud (not yelling, whining, or shrieking) voice.
4. *Request for a behavior change:* Requests to change behavior can be framed in the present ("Please leave now") or in the future ("Next time please call before you visit").
5. *Eye contact:* During assertive responses clients should maintain a steady (not glaring) eye contact.

6. *Gesticulation:* During assertive responses clients should use their hands to effectively accentuate what they are saying.
7. *Posture:* During assertive responses the client should sit or stand up straight, with shoulders squared and trunk slightly forward.
8. *Affect:* During assertive responses the client's affect must be appropriate to the situation. If the situation is serious, look serious, if it is humorous, look humorous.

These components are taught to clients in assertion training. Some clients need work in all areas, others in only a few. The initial evaluation will enable the counselor to clearly understand what type of training is needed. Before assertion training can be done, the client must be prepared for the treatment. The counselor should spend time discussing assertion as a behavior, its utility in people's lives, and the client's lack of assertion. This should not be a punitive exercise but rather an exploratory process in which clients are enlightened about behavioral patterns. Once clients have explored their fears and myths concerning assertion and are fully prepared, training can begin. The most frequently used treatment components in assertion-training programs are behavioral rehearsal, modeling, coaching, and feedback.

In *behavioral rehearsal* clients are given the opportunity to practice and role-play appropriate assertive responses in problem situations. Brief scenes are enacted to closely approximate natural situations. As clients practice appropriate assertion, their ability to be assertive increases, as does the likelihood that the assertive-response tendency will be strengthened. Sometimes, especially for homework assignments, it is effective to have clients do covert behavioral rehearsal in which they simply imagine themselves responding to problem situations in an effective, assertive fashion.

Another important form of behavioral rehearsal is known as role reversal. Clients are required to play the recipient of the assertive response, and the counselor plays the role of the client in an assertive way. This type of rehearsal provides clients with a deeper understanding of their assertion deficit.

In *modeling,* clients observe the counselor acting in an appropriately assertive way. The model acts as a stimulus for similar behavior in the client. The counselor can adjust and improvise for the client's benefit. Additionally, the client is able to ask questions, and the counselor can demonstrate a broad array of responses. This live modeling in the office is a relatively efficient and inexpensive method to teach appropriate assertive behavior.

*Coaching* is similar to modeling, but in this procedure the counselor describes appropriate assertive behavior to the client.

Finally, *feedback* lets clients know how well their assertion training is progressing. Positive feedback ("You're doing a great job") is more effective than negative feedback ("No, that was a passive response"). It more rapidly changes the client's style of behavioral response and ultimately increases self-confidence, self-esteem, and assertive ability.

The major treatment components for assertion training are most effective when used in combination. Assertion is a complex behavior that substance abusers often lack, but acceptable assertion training can nevertheless usually be given in eight to ten one-hour sessions. Again, practice and positive reinforcement from the therapist are essential if one expects the behavior to be ingrained and well learned. Assertion training results in the expression of some anxiety. Therefore, it should always be preceded by a competent protocol of relaxation training.

## Modeling

As we have seen, modeling refers to learning through the observation and imitation of others. In general, this social-learning technique allows us to foster desired behaviors in our clients simply by demonstrating these behaviors. For example, we can model appropriate communication skills, eye gaze, posture, sympathy, and refusal of drugs (W. R. Miller, 1980; Upper & Cautela, 1979).

When a client observes the counselor or an actor performing appropriate behaviors, it is thought, the model acts as a stimulus for similar thoughts, attitudes, or behaviors on the part of the client (Wolpe, 1982). There are a number of ways to present modeled behavior. These include live modeling, in which the counselor performs the desired behavior in the presence of the client; modeling by video or audio recordings (relaxation tapes, assertion tapes); the use of multiple models (simulating real-life situations); and covert modeling with projected consequences (the counselor uses relaxation procedures and then has the client imagine situations in which he or she is engaging in the desired behavior). Live modeling tends to permit more flexible feedback, because there is always an opportunity for the model to adjust and improvise as the situation dictates. This type of modeling is frequently ad-libbed, however, and it does require a significant time commitment on the counselor's part. Recording of the desired model behavior allows editing of the work and a focus on specific problems. Another advantage of recording modeling is that tapes of modeled behavior can be used repeatedly, reducing the long-term costs while freeing the counselor to do other work.

Multiple models can demonstrate flexiblity and variability. The client sees a number of different behavioral styles in situations requiring the behavior in question. This variant requires a number of "helpers" to act as models, and it can be costly and difficult to arrange on a day-to-day basis. Another variant of the modeling technique is to have the client simply think of projected consequences of a model's behavior. This is easily done in the office, is cost effective, and is nonintrusive. Unfortunately, it is not as powerful as live or recorded models, and therefore its utility is limited.

Modeling is a powerful tool in therapy. Counselors tend to constantly model a number of behaviors, such as warmth, genuineness, and appropriate listening skills, but they must turn to well-designed modeling interventions for clients' specific deficits or problems.

## Contingency Contracting and Management

Another tool that can significantly improve substance abuse counseling is called contingency contracting and management. This technique might be used to limit the amount of alcohol consumed per occasion, encourage the ingestion of an Antabuse tablet each day, or facilitate open communication in a relationship dyad. It is readily applicable to a broad range of other situations and can be used in the treatment of all types of drug dependence to foster either abstinence or moderation.

Contingency contracting is an operant-conditioning procedure that links a reward (reinforcer) or a punisher to the occurrence or absence of a specified response. A reinforcer that follows a specific behavior (and only that behavior) is called a contingent reward. For instance, if one doesn't smoke for four days, one gets a gourmet dinner. If one does smoke during the four-day period, one does not get the dinner. As is evident, getting the reward is contingent on not smoking. Rimm and Masters (1983) have reviewed a large body of literature showing that there is little doubt that the contingent dispensation of reinforcement is an effective method for controlling behavior. In fact, it has been convincingly demonstrated that noncontingent reinforcement fails to control behavior, whereas the contingent application of the same reinforcer does exert effective control (Bandura, 1969; Caddy, 1982; Pomerleau, 1982; Rimm & Masters, 1983; Wolpe, 1982). As an example, consider a drug abuser who receives an achievement pin and a testimonial dinner every two months, regardless of his ability to maintain abstinence, as opposed to a drug abuser who receives a pin and testimonial dinner every two months *only* if she has successfully maintained abstinence. The first client is unlikely to strive for abstinence, since he is noncontingently reinforced, whereas the second client is likely to be highly invested in abstinence, since her reinforcement *is* contingent on such behavior. In a similar vein it is ineffective to use a contingent reinforcer that has no value to the client. In this respect, for instance, a night on the town will not be a potent reinforcer for the individual who dislikes crowds and spending money, nor will the opportunity to take an out-of-town vacation be an effective reinforcer for a homebody.

Contingency management then consists of the contingent presentation and withdrawal of rewards and punishments. Counselors can use these procedures themselves, and it is equally effective to train others (spouses, friends, children) to function as natural contingency managers. Additionally, clients must be trained in contingency management so that they can exercise increased self-control over their own problem behaviors.

Many more skills are involved in this procedure than the simple dispensation of reinforcements. For example, counselors must discover a number of reinforcers that can be manipulated and that are effective for the client whose behavior is being changed. Additionally, they must determine *what* behaviors will be changed, their frequency of occurrence (baseline), the situations in which they occur, and the reinforcers that appear to be responsible for the maintenance of these maladaptive behaviors. This knowledge will be gained through functional analysis. Failure to establish a baseline rate of behavior frequency, instituting procedures for measuring behavioral change, and assessing such things as the behaviors to be treated result in limited treatment effectiveness and a consequent waste of therapist and client time. Contingency-management techniques are flexible and can be applied in the community, individually, in a group, and in both inpatient and outpatient settings. They require creative treatment planning and individualizing and are both cost- and time-effective.

## Systematic Desensitization

Systematic desensitization (SD) is frequently talked about in terms of its relationship to relaxation training. In fact, all clients must be trained in relaxation before SD can be utilized. SD is used in combination with relaxation training to deal with specific environmental factors (such as highly feared situations) that typically provoke anxiety or resultant substance abuse. This procedure involves the gradual association between relaxation and images of anxiety-producing situations, presented in a hierarchical order. Initially, SD was used solely as a treatment for phobic clients, but it is now widely applied to a number of dysfunctions in which anxiety is thought to provoke an undesirable response. The rationale behind this procedure is that fears will diminish if they are repeatedly experienced and associated with a feeling of relaxation, both in imagination and, eventually, in real life. In terms of chemical-dependency counseling, this technique is particularly helpful with clients who are experiencing difficulty in using the standard relaxation training as a self-control technique in their day-to-day living because of intrusive and extreme anxiety. It is also very helpful for clients having difficulty implementing new social skills in interpersonal situations because of persistent anxiety and apprehension.

Before SD training begins, counselors must help clients develop a hierarchical list of situations within one general category that causes anxiety. The client who reports anxiety secondary to socializing in large groups, heterosexual interactions, and authority figures will need assistance in developing a separate list for each of these categories. Situations (or images) should be rank-ordered, from those producing the least anxiety near the bottom of the list to those producing the most anxiety near the top (P. M. Miller & Mastria, 1977). For example, a systematic-desensitization heirarchy could take the following form:

*Most anxiety-provoking:*
7. at a large social gathering where you know no one
6. at an office party where you are familiar with everyone but a few spouses
5. in a restaurant, with a friend, when you are introduced to someone you don't know
4. in a shopping center where you know no one, and no one knows you
3. at a small party with five or six of your closest friends
2. in your home with an old friend
*Least anxiety-provoking:*
1. alone in your bedroom

In constructing hierarchical lists, one must take special care to ensure that they are long enough so that they are gradual in terms of anxiety; large jumps in anxiety-producing situations could present difficulty in successful progression up the hierarchy.

Once the counselor and client have completed the hierarchy(ies), progressive muscle-relaxation training, as previously outlined in this chapter, must begin. Once the client is relaxed, he or she is instructed to imagine the least anxiety-provoking situation on the list. The client is further instructed to maintain the relaxation response while continuing to imagine the anxiety-provoking situation. If the client begins to feel any anxiety, he or she is asked to indicate this to the counselor simply by raising the right index finger. At this signal the counselor immediately advises the client to terminate the anxiety-provoking image and to engage in simple relaxation. This procedure is repeated until the client is able to imagine the scene for two minutes without experiencing any anxiety. Once the anxiety is reduced, the client should repeat the scene three to five times to consolidate gains and to create a learning history. Every item on the hierarchy list will be presented in just this fashion until the client is able to imagine all the scenes while maintaining a complete sense of relaxation (P. M. Miller & Mastria, 1977).

SD will typically be accomplished over a number of sessions but there are no set rules for time span. In general, progress is determined through the client's self-report. Following desensitization to the hierarchy list, the counselor should attempt to generalize these results to the client's real world. This is easily accomplished by establishing another hierarchical list that revolves around real-life situations that the client is likely to encounter in the days and weeks ahead.

Systematic desensitization is highly effective and easily utilized in all settings. It should be used as an adjunct to a comprehensive therapy program, and it will be particularly useful when anxiety or fear inhibits the client's ability to abstain or to moderate his or her substance use. This is a broadly used technique that enhances multi-faceted treatment programs, but as with other techniques, it is not useful for all substance abusers, and it should be used only when indicated.

## Covert Aversion Therapy

Covert aversion therapy, also known as covert sensitization or verbal aversion therapy, is frequently used as a component of broad-spectrum treatment for substance abuse. This technique attempts to interrupt drug-use behavior by creating an aversion to, or distaste for, alcohol or other drugs. In practice, this treatment technique is quite simple to use. Counselors simply train clients to use the relaxation response and then have them engage in directed imagination of aversion scenes that revolve around the use of alcohol or another drug. Typically, these scenes involve the imagination of nausea and vomiting, which are repeatedly paired with images related to the sight, smell, and taste of the drug and its use. Repetition of pairing the substance with an aversive imagined consequence results in a conditioned (uncontrollable and ingrained) aversion to the substance.

Covert aversion therapy permits the client and the counselor to adjust the topography of the aversive imagery to the unique specifics of the client's drug use behavior. It allows direct (imaginal) association between the aversion image, the behavior, and the environment associated with the drug use. It is sufficiently mobile and easily learned that it can be employed independently by the client when he or she feels tempted to drink or use other drugs (Caddy, 1982). This technique requires no administration of physically aversive stimuli (shock or chemically induced vomiting), and it is effective in maintaining treatment gains (W. R. Miller, 1985). Given these positives, in addition to its ease of administration and cost-effectiveness, covert aversion therapy is thought to be both a humane and an efficacious adjunct to a comprehensive treatment regime. Again, though, this technique is not to be randomly applied. It should be used only when indicated and when its application is likely to enhance treatment outcomes.

## ▌Alcoholics Anonymous and Narcotics Anonymous

Alcoholics Anonymous (AA) and Narcotics Anonymous (NA) are self-help groups that operate around the world. In general, these groups do not provide treatment. Rather, they exist to support recovering alcoholics or drug abusers in their rehabilitation process. Simply stated:

> Alcoholics Anonymous [Narcotics Anonymous] is a fellowship of men and women who share their experience, strength, and hope with each other that they may solve their common problem. The only requirement for membership is a desire to stop drinking. There are no dues or fees for AA membership; we are self-supporting through our own contributions. AA is not allied with any sect, denomination, political group, organization, or institution; does not wish to engage in any controversy, neither endorses nor opposes any causes. Our primary purpose is to stay sober and help other alcoholics to achieve sobriety.

This is the description that is read at the beginning of most AA and NA meetings throughout the world. These organizations have minimal formal structure, and they have no method of punishment or exclusion. They shun professionalism and report that their only authority is shared experience. The AA and NA programs are expressed in two sets of principles that have been developed since the inception of AA in 1935. The Twelve Steps came first as a program for personal recovery from drug or alcohol problems, and the Twelve Traditions, which are principles for relationships between groups, came second. NA, which was developed after AA, is a separate organization that uses most of the ideas and principles of AA.

The Twelve Steps of AA and NA are introduced with this sentence: "Here are the steps we took, which are suggested as a program for recovery":

> *Step 1:* Admitted we were powerless over alcohol [drugs]—that our lives had become unmanageable.
> *Step 2:* Came to believe that a Power greater than ourselves could restore us to sanity.

*Step 3:* Made a decision to turn our will and our lives over to the care of God as we understood Him.

*Step 4:* Made a searching and fearless moral inventory of ourselves.

*Step 5:* Admitted to God, to ourselves, and to another human being, the exact nature of our wrongs.

*Step 6:* Were entirely ready to have God remove all these defects of character.

*Step 7:* Humbly asked Him to remove our shortcomings.

*Step 8:* Made a list of all persons we had harmed and became willing to make amends to them all.

*Step 9:* Made direct amends to such people wherever possible, except when to do so would injure them or others.

*Step 10:* Continued to take personal inventory and when we were wrong, promptly admitted it.

*Step 11:* Sought through prayer and meditation to improve our conscious contact with God as we understood Him, praying only for knowledge of His will for us and the power to carry that out.

*Step 12:* Having had a spiritual awakening as the result of these Steps, we tried to carry this message to alcoholics [drug abusers], and to practice these principles in all our affairs.

As the Twelve Steps became more broadly known, AA grew. This growth necessitated guidelines for the interrelationships among groups, and hence the Twelve Traditions of AA were developed. These were consequently melded into the NA experience:

1. Our common welfare should come first; personal recovery depends upon AA [NA] unity. Each member of AA is but a small part of a great whole. AA must continue to live or most of us will surely die. Hence our common welfare comes first. But individual welfare follows close afterward.

2. For our group purpose there is but one ultimate authority—a loving God as He may express Himself in our group conscience. Our leaders are but trusted servants; they do not govern.

3. The only requirement for AA membership is a desire to stop drinking. Our membership ought to include all who suffer from alcoholism. Hence we may refuse none who wish to recover. Nor ought AA membership ever depend on money or conformity. Any two or three alcoholics gathered together for sobriety may call themselves an AA group.

4. Each group should become autonomous except in matters affecting other groups or AA as a whole.

5. Each group has but one primary purpose—to carry its message to the alcoholic who still suffers.

6. An AA group ought never endorse, finance, or lend the AA name to any related facility or outside enterprise, lest problems of money, property, and prestige divert us from our primary purpose.

7. Every AA group ought to be fully self-supporting, declining outside contributions. No contributions or legacies from nonmembers are accepted at the General Service Office in New York City, and

no more than $500 per year from any one member, and for only one year after death.

8. AA should remain forever nonprofessional, but our service centers may employ special workers.

9. AA, as such, ought never be organized; but we may create service boards or committees directly responsible to those they serve. The small group may elect its secretary, the large group its rotating committee, and the groups of a large metropolitan area their central committee, which often employs a full-time secretary. The AA General Service Board serves as the custodian of AA tradition and is the receiver of voluntary AA contributions. It is authorized by the groups to handle our overall public relations, and it guarantees the integrity of all our publications.

10. AA has no opinion on outside issues; hence the AA name ought never be drawn into public controversy.

11. Our public relations policy is based on attraction rather than promotion; we need always maintain personal anonymity at the level of press, radio, and films.

12. Anonymity is the spiritual foundation of all our traditions, ever reminding us to place principles before personalities.

AA and NA meetings are available almost everywhere. The recovering substance abuser can, if he or she looks hard enough, usually find at least one meeting each day. There are two types of meetings: open and closed. Anyone is welcome at the open meetings, where one or two members typically tell their own stories of "how they used to be" and "how they are now." Only members are allowed to attend closed meetings, since these tend to be much more personal and intimate. During these meetings personal problems or interpretations of the Twelve Steps or Twelve Traditions are usually discussed.

AA and NA, then, are widely available, cost-effective support programs for those alcoholics or drug-dependent individuals who choose to use them. We reiterate that AA is not a treatment regime and that it should be used only as a supportive adjunct to treatment and as a source of support throughout the recovery process. AA is not for everybody, as no approach is, and it is unwise to force this modality on clients. AA members clearly have a great belief in the Twelve Steps and Twelve Traditions, and if these are not compatible with a client's thinking or belief system, it is probably unwise to coerce him or her to conform to this mode of thought. Such coercion often results in resistance and treatment failure, and it is ultimately the counselor's responsibility to design individualized treatments for clients, as opposed to forcing them to adapt themselves to what is currently available. Judicious use of these systems will serve both counselors and clients well; using them injudiciously or as a matter of course will result in negative consequences.

# ▌Controlled Drinking

Whereas abstinence from alcohol or drugs is the preferred outcome of AA and NA, other approaches aim at controlling the drinking of clients. These treatments require a broad understanding of behavioral psychology and the principles of learning. Therefore, before controlled-drinking protocols are undertaken, counselors should receive highly specialized training from competent professionals who are very familiar with behavioral and social-learning perspectives and treatment techniques for the addictive behaviors.

Controlled drinking, or moderate drinking, is a relatively new concept for abusive drinkers. This notion naturally causes a great deal of controversy, since it is often thought that alcoholism is a chronic and progressive disease that only gets worse. Learning theorists, however, suggest that abusive drinking is not a disease process but rather a learned, maladaptive behavioral pattern. In this respect, then, it is thought that some problem drinkers can learn to drink in a nonproblematic way. Controlled drinking is not designed to lure successfully abstinent alcoholics back to drinking. Rather, it is intended for certain problem drinkers at the onset of treatment. No proponent of moderation-oriented therapies has ever advocated their use with all problem drinkers, nor has anyone ever suggested that abstainers can successfully resume drinking. Rather, it has been argued, quite successfully, that moderation is one of many viable treatment goals for problem drinkers.

There are several reasons for choosing moderation for some clients. Many alcohol abusers, especially those at early stages of problem development, are unwilling to label themselves as "alcoholic" or to even consider life-long abstinence as a goal. Controlled drinking is often a more acceptable goal to this type of problem drinker and in fact, several studies have shown that such users tend to do better when the treatment goal is moderation. Additionally, those clients who fail at abstinence programs may find that a moderation goal is more manageable and less aversive. Other possible advantages of a controlled-drinking goal are suggested by Heather and Robertson (1983):

1. In this society abstinence often implies deviance. This deviance label leads to problems of psychosocial adjustment.
2. Abstinent alcoholics often experience fatigue and depression, and enforced abstinence may have disastrous results for the personality organization of some individuals.
3. Abstinence is not highly correlated with an overall improvement in life functioning.
4. In some people, abstinence may introduce psychological or social problems that make a relapse more likely.

5. Abstinence during treatment hampers attempts to change alcoholics' drinking behavior.
6. The abstinence requirement of most treatment programs deters many alcoholics from entering treatment until their problem is seriously advanced.

Controlled drinking is used with about 15% of all alcohol abusers, according to W. R. Miller (1982) and others. Those who should not try controlled drinking fit the following criteria:

1. clients with liver dysfunction, stomach problems, an ulcer, or any other disease of the gastrointestinal tract
2. clients who have cardiac problems that would be adversely affected by alcohol
3. clients who have any physical illness or condition that would be negatively affected by alcohol
4. clients who have a diagnosis of alcohol idiosyncratic disorder intoxication (American Psychiatric Association, 1980, p. 132)
5. clients who are committed to abstinence
6. clients who have strong external demands for abstinence
7. female clients who are pregnant or considering pregnancy
8. clients who lose control of their behavior while drinking
9. clients who have been physically addicted to alcohol
10. clients using any medication or drug that is dangerous when combined with alcohol
11. clients who are abstaining from alcohol
12. those people with the following history: over 40, divorced and not in a supportive relationship, out of work, or with a family history of alcoholism
13. clients who have tried a *competently* administered moderation-oriented treatment and have failed

In general, the clients who do best with a controlled-drinking goal are those who show less resemblance to the classic diagnostic picture of advanced alcoholism. These people tend to have far fewer problems related to their drinking, a shorter history of alcohol problems, fewer symptoms of alcohol dependence or alcohol abuse, and no family history of alcoholism. These people are usually younger, more stable, supported, and less likely to consider themselves to be alcoholic.

Controlled drinkers are not normal social drinkers. In fact, they are quite different from social drinkers. One description of this difference has been advanced by Reinert and Bowen (1968). It says, in essence, that normal drinkers imbibe alcohol on occasion with the knowledge and confidence that well before they get into any trouble, they will lose their appetite for more. In contrast, controlled drinkers do not have these feelings of security, and they have

learned from experience about the bottomless pit that may sometimes be opened by the ingestion of even a small amount of alcohol.
Controlled drinkers are always on guard, and they must choose
carefully and compulsively the time, the place, and the circumstances of drinking and must rigidly and faithfully limit the amount
they drink.

W. R. Miller and Munoz (1982) define controlled drinkers as those
who:

1. have previously had life problems related to alcohol use
2. have decided that they need greater control over their drinking
3. choose to be neither abstinent nor an excessive drinker
4. have been trained by a competent clinician to use methods that
   will effectively increase their self-control over drinking
5. have effectively applied the methods for self-control that they
   have learned

Controlled drinking is an exceptionally complex protocol that is
implemented through a program known as behavioral self-control
training (BSCT) (W. R. Miller, 1980). BSCT is an educationally oriented approach to the treatment of alcohol problems. This approach
generally has the following hallmark characteristics: (1) it has an
educational format designed to facilitate moderate levels of drinking; (2) it is offered on an outpatient basis; and (3) it is amenable to
a number of presentation formats, including group and individual
(W. R. Miller, 1980). BSCT is inexpensive in that it requires no
special equipment and is not tied to an inpatient setting. It is less
intrusive than traditional treatments, and it has a demonstrated
effectiveness rate between 60% and 80% (W. R. Miller, 1980). A comprehensive BSCT consists of the following components (Hamburg,
Miller, & Rozynko, 1977; W. R. Miller, 1977, 1978a, 1978b, 1980; W.
R. Miller & Munoz, 1976):

1. A functional analysis of drinking behavior is made. The client
   and counselor determine specific and appropriate limits for alcohol consumption. These limits are based on scientific evidence
   concerning the effect of alcohol on the body and behavior.
2. The client monitors alcohol consumption.
3. The client is trained to control the rate of drinking.
4. The client is trained in self-reinforcement to encourage maintenance of gains.
5. The client undergoes stimulus-control training.
6. The client is taught coping skills to use in place of alcohol.

# Summary

In this chapter we addressed the issue of how to counsel individual substance abusers. We discussed the development of treatment plans, the necessity of pre-treatment preparation, general counseling techniques, specific behavioral techniques, the ongoing support offered by Alcoholics Anonymous and Narcotics Anonymous, and controlled drinking.

Clearly, a broad range of counseling techniques are available to the substance abuse practitioner. The ethical and professional responsibility to be competent and well trained requires a continuous investment of study and self-criticism and an openness to competent supervision. Clients are limited only by counselors' abilities, and counselors' abilities are limited only by their willingness to learn.

Individual counseling of substance abusers can be a most rewarding activity. It is never boring or unfulfilling so long as the counselor creatively applies a number of techniques. Counselors who choose to rely on one or a small number of techniques run the real risk of "burning out" and generally depriving their client population. If, on the other hand, counselors choose to remain open and inquisitive, they will enjoy long and exciting careers from which both they and their clients will benefit greatly.

# References

American Psychiatric Association. (1980). Diagnostic and statistical manual of mental disorders (3rd ed.). Washington, DC: Author.

Bandura, A. (1969). *Principles of behavior modification.* New York: Holt, Rinehart, and Winston.

Caddy, G. R. (1982). Evaluation of behavioral methods in the study of alcoholism. In E. M. Pattison & E. Kaufman (Eds.), *Encyclopedic handbook of alcoholism.* New York: Gardner Press.

Hamburg, S. R., Miller, W. R., & Rozynko, V. (1977). *Understanding alcoholism and problem drinking.* Half Moon Bay, CA: Social Change Associates.

Heather, N., & Robertson, I. (1983). *Controlled drinking.* New York: Methuen.

Jacobsen, E. (1968). *Progressive relaxation.* Chicago: University of Chicago Press.

Lawson, G. W., Ellis, D. C., & Rivers, P. C. (1984). *Essentials of chemical dependency counseling.* Rockville, MD: Aspen Systems Corp.

Miller, P. M., & Mastria, M. A. (1977). Alternatives to alcohol abuse: A social learning model. Champaign, IL: Research Press.

Miller, W. R. (1977). Behavioral self-control training in the treatment of problem drinkers. In R. B. Stuart (Ed.), *Behavioral self-management: Strategies, techniques, and outcomes.* New York: Brunner/Mazel.

Miller, W. R. (1978a). Behavioral treatment of problem drinkers: A comparative outcome study of three controlled drinking therapies. *Journal of Consulting and Clinical Psychology, 46,* 74–86.

Miller, W. R. (1978b, August). *Effectiveness of non-prescription theories for problem drinkers.* Paper presented at the annual meeting of the American Psychological Association, Toronto, Ontario.

Miller, W. R. (1980). Treating the problem drinker. In W. R. Miller (Ed.), *The addictive behaviors: Treatment of alcoholism, drug abuse, smoking, and obesity.* New York: Pergamon Press.

Miller, W. R. (1982). Treating problem drinkers: What works. *The Behavior Therapist, 5,* 15–19.

Miller, W. R. (1985, August). *Perspectives on treatment.* Paper presented at the 34th International Congress on Alcoholism and Drug Dependence, Calgary, Alberta.

Miller, W. R., & Munoz, R. F. (1976). *How to control your drinking.* Englewood Cliffs, NJ: Prentice-Hall.

Miller, W. R., & Munoz, R. F. (1982). *How to control your drinking.* Albuquerque: University of New Mexico Press.

Pomerleau, O. F. (1982). Current behavioral therapies in the treatment of alcoholism. In E. M. Pattison & E. Kaufman (Eds.), *Encyclopedic handbook of alcoholism.* New York: Gardner Press.

Reinert, R. E., & Bowen, W. T. (1968). Social drinking following treatment for alcoholism. *Bulletin of the Menninger Clinic, 32,* 280–290.

Rimm, D. C., & Masters, J. C. (1983). *Behavior therapy: Techniques and empirical findings.* New York: Academic Press.

Small, J. (1983). *Becoming naturally therapeutic.* Austin, TX: Eupsychian Press.

Upper, D., & Cautela, J. R. (1979). *Covert conditioning.* New York: Pergamon Press.

Wolpe, J. (1982). *The practice of behavior therapy.* New York: Pergamon Press.

# Family and Group Counseling

No substance abuser — in fact, no client — can be treated effectively unless his or her social interactions are taken into account. People influence their social environment and are influenced by it in return. Social support systems, which Caplan (1974) defines as enduring patterns of interaction that help the individual maintain a sense of self, provide the primary medium through which this process occurs.

> People have a variety of specific needs that demand satisfaction through enduring interpersonal relationships. . . . Most people develop and maintain a sense of well-being by involving themselves in a range of relationships in their lives that in toto satisfy these specific needs, such as marriage, parenthood, other forms of living and intimate ties, relationships with colleagues at work, membership in religious congregations and in social, cultural, political, and recreational associations, and acquaintanceships with neighbors, shopkeepers and providers of services [p. 5].

When an individual develops a substance abuse problem, *all* of these social support systems are likely to be affected. At the same time, the nature of the social environment will also have a reciprocal effect on the maintenance or resolution of the problem.

The system that tends to be most widely recognized as closely associated with addictive behaviors is the family. In discussing the nature of family dynamics associated with alcoholism, for instance, Wegscheider (1981) describes the adjustment of family members in the following terms:

> Trapped (or at least thinking they are trapped) in this highly disordered system, how do family members adjust? The only healthy response would be not to adjust to it but to open it up by voicing honestly their practical problems, their mental confusion, and their emotional pain and frustration. This course would protect their own psychological well-being and offer the best hope of bringing the [alcohol] Dependent [person] to treatment as well. But few family members choose it, for they risk losing the whole matrix of their lives. Instead, they opt for preserving the family system at whatever cost. Left with only unhealthy alternatives, they choose . . . the same defense as the Dependent: they hide their true feelings behind an artificial behavior pattern, a supporting role in the alcoholic drama, which seems to promise some kind of reward in a system that offers few [p. 84].

Yet if family members can have negative involvement in the maintenance of alcohol abusing behavior, they can also have highly positive effects on the maintenance of sobriety. As Finney, Moos, and Mewborn (1980, p. 27) have found, "The more cohesive and supportive the family . . . the better the prognosis for an individual who has been treated for alcoholism."

It becomes apparent, then, that substance abuse counselors need to pay close attention to the family dynamics affecting a client. Family systems obviously have the potential to influence the outcome of treatment. Just as important, however, is the fact that the family system itself can be seen as the most appropriate target for change. As family therapists have learned, one cannot legitimately separate the individual from the family, the "sick" from the "well," the cause of a dysfunction from the effect.

> Within a family therapy framework, problems are recast to take into consideration the fact that relationship difficulties and an individual's behavior cannot be understood without attention to the context in which that behavior occurs. Rather than seeing the source of problems or the appearance of symptoms as emanating from a single "sick" individual, the family therapy approach views that person simply as a symptom bearer—the identified patient—expressing a family's disequilibrium [Goldenberg & Goldenberg, 1985, p. 7].

Working with families from this perspective requires that counselors have an understanding of general systems theory and its applicability to counseling practice.

# Systems Theory

General systems theory is most often associated with the work of von Bertalanffy (1968), who developed it as an alternative New-tonian science. Traditional Newtonian physics was *reductionistic* in its attempt to break complex phenomena down into the smallest possible parts and was *linear* in its attempt to understand these parts as a series of less complex cause-and-effect relationships. Systems theory represents an entirely different mode of thought, viewing all living things as open systems best understood by an examination of their interrelationships and organizing principles. Attention is paid not to linear, causal relationships but to consistent, if circular, patterns of interaction.

> If a *system* is defined as a set of units or elements standing in some consistent relationship or interactional stance with each other, then the first concept is the notion that any system is composed of elements that are *organized* by the consistent nature of the relationship between these elements. Consistency is the key; consistent elements are related to each other in a consistently describable or predictable fashion [Steinglass, 1978, p. 305].

Living organisms are *open systems* in that they interact with their environment, taking in and discharging information or energy through boundaries that are sufficiently permeable to allow these transactions to take place. The system itself also encompasses *subsystems*, which interact in a predictable manner within the context of the larger system.

In order to apply the systems paradigm to family interactions, the counselor needs to understand several basic features of the approach, identified by Umbarger [1983, p. 17] in terms of the following list:

1. *Part and whole:* It is not the individual part or isolated content that deserves initial attention, but the larger system (itself greater and different than simply the sum of its parts) and the transactional process within this system. . . .

2. *Information, error, and feedback:* Living systems have communication-feedback loops that give information about the activities of the system. . . . Signals . . . tell any given subunit whether or not its behavior is dissimilar to the overall design for living of the total system.

3. *Feedback and homeostasis:* When information signals a difference from some baseline of the overall design, deviation-countering behaviors may occur. They induce constancy of homeostasis in the system, a steady state of being that is necessary for life.

4. *Feedback and growth:* When information signals a difference from some baseline of the overall design, deviation-amplifying behaviors may occur. They induce change and diversity in the system, a fluctuating state of being that is necessary for life.

5. *Life and tension:* The continual alteration of periods of growth with periods of stability . . . makes up the dynamic tension of life.

6. *Circularity:* Cause and effects are now viewed as circular, not as linear.

7. *Change:* Change in the total system as well as in any individual part occurs with intervention into the whole as well as into any part. Both part and whole must change in some conjunction with each other, though not always simultaneously.

Although family therapists may differ in their personal approaches and theories, they tend to share a general perception that the family is a system, clearly conforming to the principles described above.

> The human family is a social system that operates through transactional patterns. These are repeated interactions which establish patterns of how, when, and to whom to relate. . . . Repeated operations build patterns, and these patterns underpin the family system. The patterns which evolve become familiar and preferred. The system maintains itself within a preferred range, and deviations which pass the system's threshold of tolerance usually elicit counterdeviation mechanisms which reestablish the accustomed range [Minuchin, 1979, p. 7].

Thus, each family has its own homeostasis, or preferred steady state, that may or may not be "healthy" but that is monitored through feedback and control mechanisms and protected by the system as a whole. Each family has a set of rules that governs its interactions and makes them predictable. Each includes subsystems (for example, spousal, parental, or sibling) that carry out specialized functions and attempt to preserve the integrity of the overall system. Each is an organized whole, making it impossible to consider intervening in one part without taking the others into account.

## ▌Approaches to Family Therapy

The development of systems theory laid the groundwork for the growth of family therapy in the second half of the 20th century. Intervention approaches have also been affected, however, by alternate models of human behavior and competing theories of counseling and therapy. Family therapy, like all other approaches to counseling, reflects highly varied viewpoints. One of the most helpful categorizations is provided by Goldenberg and Goldenberg

(1985), as shown in Table 5.1. Each of the six viewpoints described in the table has unique characteristics. Yet each is built—albeit, to varying degrees—on the notion that individual clients affect and are affected by their family unit. Each examines the development of the individual in a social context. Each recognizes the potential inherent in interventions that go beyond individual, intrapsychic phenomena.

## Psychodynamic Family Therapy

In 1970 the Group for the Advancement of Psychiatry (GAP) attempted to put varying theories of family therapy into perspective by placing them on a continuum, with the two extreme positions indicating the degree to which a theoretical orientation tended to emphasize the individual or the family system.

> At one extreme, position A, were those therapists who saw the family as a means of gathering information about specific family members. These therapists retained a primary focus on the individual and were contrasted with their hypothetical opposite, the position-Z therapists, who focused entirely on the family as the unit of both change and pathology. Consequently, position-Z therapists were more likely to view traditional psychiatric problems as social and interpersonal symptoms of maladaptive family functioning [Kolevzon & Green, 1985, pp. 26–27].

Of all the theoretical frameworks reviewed in Table 5.1, the psychodynamic approach comes closest to the position-A pole of the GAP's hypothetical continuum. This approach, which is based to a large degree on psychoanalytic thought, emphasizes the effects of individual pathologies on the family system, tends to view the family as a group of interlocking personalities, and stresses the importance of insight for personal change.

The psychoanalytic bases of this model are apparent in its emphases on bringing unresolved conflicts to the surface, on dealing with past experiences, and on addressing both intrapsychic and interpersonal change. Yet the psychodynamic viewpoint as it is applied to family practice has been strongly affected by systems thought and is therefore very different from analytic therapy as it is applied to individuals. Nathan Ackerman, one of the earliest pioneers in family therapy, has probably done more than any other single theorist to bridge the gap between these two epistemologies. He summarizes the family therapist's role and functions in the following terms:

1. The therapist establishes a useful rapport, empathy, and communication among the family members and between them and himself.

**Table 5.1** A comparison of six theoretical viewpoints in family therapy

| Dimension | Psychodynamic | Experiential/humanistic | Bowenian | Structural | Communication | Behavioral |
|---|---|---|---|---|---|---|
| 1. Major time frame | Past; history of early experiences needs to be uncovered. | Present; here-and-now data from immediate experience observed. | Primarily the present, although attention also paid to one's family of origin. | Present and past; family's current structure carried over from earlier transactional patterns. | Present; current problems or symptoms maintained by ongoing, repetitive sequences between persons. | Present; focus on interpersonal environments that maintain and perpetuate current behavior patterns. |
| 2. Role of unconscious processes | Unresolved conflicts from the past, largely out of the person's awareness, continue to attach themselves to current objects and situations. | Free choice and conscious self-determination more important than unconscious motivation. | Earlier concepts suggested unconscious conflicts, although now recast in interactive terms. | Unconscious motivation less important than repetition of learned habits and role assignments by which the family carries out its tasks. | Family rules, homeostatic balance, and feedback loops determine behavior, not unconscious processes. | Problematic behavior is learned and maintained by its consequences; unconscious processes rejected as too inferential and unquantifiable. |
| 3. Insight versus action | Insight leads to understanding, conflict reduction, and ultimately intrapsychic and interpersonal change. | Self-awareness of one's immediate existence leads to choice, responsibility and change. | Rational processes are used to gain self-awareness into current relationships as well as intergenerational experiences. | Action precedes understanding; change in transactional patterns more important than insight in producing new behaviors. | Action-oriented; behavior change and symptom reduction brought about through directives rather than interpretations. | Actions prescribed to modify specific behavior patterns. |
| 4. Role of therapist | Neutral; makes interpretations of individual and family behavior patterns. | Active facilitator of potential for growth; provides family with new experiences. | Direct but non-confrontational; detriangulated from family fusion. | Stage director; manipulates family structure in order to change dysfunctional sets. | Active; manipulative; problem-focused; prescriptive, paradoxical. | Directive; teacher, trainer, or model of desired behavior; contract negotiator. |

|  | | | | | |
|---|---|---|---|---|---|
| **5. Unit of study** | Focus on individual; emphasis on how family members feel about one another and deal with one another. | Dyad; problems arise from interaction between two members (for example, husband and wife). | Entire family over several generations; may work with one dyad (or one partner) for a period of time. | Triads; coalitions, subsystems, boundaries, power. | Dyads and triads; problems and symptoms viewed as interpersonal communications between two or more family members. | Dyads; effect of one person's behavior on another; linear view of causality. |
| **6. Major theoretical underpinnings** | Psychoanalysis. | Existentialism; humanistic psychology; phenomenology. | Family systems theory. | Structural family theory; systems. | Communication theory; systems; behaviorism. | Behaviorism; social-learning theory. |
| **7. Major theorists and practitioners** | Ackerman, Framo, Boszormenyi-Nagy, Stierlin, Skinner, Bell | Whitaker, Kempler, Satir | Bowen | Minuchin | Jackson, Erickson, Haley, Madanes, Selvini-Palazzoli | Patterson, Stuart, Liberman, Jacobson, Margolin |
| **8. Goals of treatment** | Insight, psychosexual maturity, strengthening of ego functioning; reduction in interlocking pathologies; more satisfying object relations. | Growth, more fulfilling interaction patterns; clearer communication; expanded awareness; authenticity. | Maximization of self-differentiation for each family member. | Change in relationship context in order to restructure family organization and change dysfunctional transactional patterns. | Change dysfunctional, redundant behavioral sequences ("games") between family members in order to eliminate presenting problem or symptom. | Change in behavioral consequences between persons leads to elimination of maladaptive or problematic behavior. |

*Note:* From *Family therapy: An overview* (2nd ed.) (pp. 126–127) by I. Goldenberg and H. Goldenberg. Pacific Grove, CA: Brooks/Cole, 1985. Copyright 1985 by Wadsworth, Inc. Reprinted by permission of Brooks/Cole Publishing Company.

2. He uses this rapport to catalyze the expression of major conflicts and ways of coping. He clarifies conflict by dissolving barriers, defensive disguises, confusions and misunderstandings. By stages, he attempts to bring to the members a clearer and more accurate understanding as to what is really wrong.
3. He counteracts inappropriate denials, displacements and rationalizations of conflict.
4. He transforms dormant, concealed interpersonal conflicts into open, interactional expression.
5. He lifts intrapersonal conflict to the level of interpersonal exchange.
6. He neutralizes processes of prejudicial scapegoating that fortify one part of the family while victimizing another part.
7. He fulfills, in part, the role of a great parent figure. . . .
8. He penetrates and undermines resistance, and reduces the intensity of shared conflict, guilt, and fear. . . .
9. He serves as a personal instrument of reality testing. . . .
10. He serves as the educator and personifier of useful models of family health [Ackerman, 1981, pp. 171–172].

Thus, Ackerman succeeds in focusing concurrently on individual pathology and family patterns, on "intrapersonal conflict" and "interpersonal exchange." Although he and other psychodynamic family therapists stop short of labeling all individual symptoms as indications of system dysfunctions, they do recognize the high degree of reciprocity between individual and family problems and conflicts.

## Experiential/Humanistic Therapy

The work of Virgina Satir (1967, 1972) has been closely associated with that of the communications theorists, but it is placed by Goldenberg and Goldenberg in the experiential/humanistic category because of her increasing concern for feelings and because of the strongly humanistic underpinnings of her approach.

> To Satir . . . the rules that govern a family system are related to how the parents go about achieving and maintaining their own self-esteem; these rules, in turn, shape the context within which the children grow and develop their own sense of self-esteem. Building self-esteem, promoting self-worth, exposing and correcting discrepancies in how the family communicates — these are the issues Satir tackles as she attempts to help each member of the family develop "wellness" and become as "whole" as possible. The humanistic influence of the human-potential movement on these goals is unmistakable [Goldenberg & Goldenberg, 1985, p. 160].

The process of family counseling, as practiced by Satir, focuses on the communication patterns that typify the functioning of the specific family. Among the dysfunctional communication styles that Satir has identified are:

- *the placater:* the individual who always agrees with others at the expense of the self, possibly in the hope of gaining approval
- *the blamer:* the family member who dominates and accuses others, who places the responsibility for problems on other people
- *the super-reasonable person:* the individual who avoids emotional involvement and tends to intellectualize and consider all issues in a detached, computerlike way
- *the irrelevant person:* the family member who distracts others and communicates material that is out of context

In contrast to these dysfunctional communicators, the *congruent communicator* is able to express his or her messages clearly and genuinely; there is true congruence between what is meant and what is said, what is felt and what is expressed. One of the primary goals of the family therapy of Satir and other humanistic theorists is to make congruent communication the norm for the family as a whole.

Closely associated with the family's communication patterns are the self-esteem of the members and the rules that govern family interactions. Functional families reflect and enhance the self-esteem of individual members and are free to develop reasonably flexible rules that encourage open communication. Dysfunctional families, in contrast, fail to maintain the members' self-esteem and tend toward rules that limit authentic communications. Therapy attempts to move family systems away from dysfunctional patterns and toward congruent, flexible, open transactions.

## Bowenian Family Therapy

The approach developed by Murray Bowen places a unique emphasis on the differentiation of the self.

> This concept is a cornerstone of the theory. . . . [It] defines people according to the degree of *fusion* or *differentiation* between emotional and intellectual functioning. This characteristic is so universal that it can be used as a way of categorizing all people on a single continuum. At the low extreme are those whose emotions and intellect are so fused that their lives are dominated by the automatic emotional system. . . . These are the people who are less flexible, less adaptable, and more emotionally dependent on those about them. . . . At the other extreme are those who are more differen-

> tiated. . . . Those whose intellectual functioning can retain relative autonomy in periods of stress are more flexible, more adaptable, and more independent of the emotionality about them. They cope better with life stresses, their life courses are more orderly and successful, and they are remarkably free of human problems [Bowen, 1982, p. 362].

Bowen's formulation sees those who are less differentiated as being most likely to develop any type of problem. Moreover, those who show low degrees of differentiation between emotion and intellect — the ones at the end of the continuum characterized by fusion — also show intense fusion in their marriages. People tend to choose partners with equal degrees of differentiation. Thus, two poorly differentiated individuals, each with a weak sense of self, will join together into a "common self" with a high potential for dysfunction.

According to Bowen, the poorly differentiated family will tend to be subject to one of several common symptoms: marital conflict, dysfunction in one spouse, or the projection of problems onto children. Whether these symptoms become serious — whether, for instance, the projection of problems onto children brings about impairment in one or more — depends on the degree of stress with which the family must contend. If anxiety remains low, the family may remain reasonably functional. High anxiety levels bring more intense symptoms. Whether or not the family actually becomes dysfunctional, the potential for problems is transmitted through multiple generations both because undifferentiated individuals have difficulty in detaching from their parents and because impaired children tend to marry other poorly differentiated individuals and to pass their problems on to the next generation.

Just as anxiety affects the degree of fusion within the family, it also affects the working of triangles, which Bowen sees as the smallest stable relationship systems and therefore as the building blocks on which all human systems are based. The intensity of these triangles within the family is affected both by the degree of differentiation of self among the members and by the level of anxiety that is present.

Bowenian therapy, then, is based on the concepts of differentiation, of triangulation, and of multigenerational transmission processes.

> The therapy focuses on the most important triangle in the family. It is designed to help one or more family members to become aware of the part that the self plays, and to avoid participation in the triangle moves. . . . When it is possible to modify the central triangle in a family, the other family triangles are automatically modified without involving other family members in therapy. The therapy also involves a slow process of differentiation between emotional

and intellectual functioning and slowly increasing intellectual control over automatic emotional processes [Bowen, 1982, p. 307].

Gradually, the therapeutic process leads to the increased differentiation of each family member and therefore to the increased health of the family system as a whole.

## Structural Family Therapy

Salvador Minuchin (1974, 1979) has had a major impact on family practice through his development of structural family therapy, a strongly systems-oriented approach. In Minuchin's terms, a family system can be understood only to the degree that its *structure* is observed and recognized. This structure involves "enduring interactional patterns that serve to arrange or organize a family's component subunits into somewhat constant relationships" (Umbarger, 1983, p. 13). These patterned relationships regulate the family's transactions, allowing the system to remain consistent over time.

Family subsystems form an important aspect of this structure and are rule-bound in terms of participation and boundaries. An *enmeshed* family system is characterized by an absence of clear boundaries differentiating one subsystem from another and by a complete lack of distance among family members. In contrast, some family systems can be characterized as *disengaged;* the boundaries between subsystems are rigid, and personal distance among family members is great. The pathologically enmeshed family has overly rigid boundaries separating the family system from its environment, whereas the disengaged family complements rigid internal boundaries with a lack of clear boundaries separating it from the outside world.

Family systems may be enmeshed or disengaged to varying degrees. What makes a structure dysfunctional is the family's inability to change any of its behaviors in response to the necessity for a new adaptation.

> The family therapist's definition of a pathogenic family, then, is a family whose adaptive and coping mechanisms have been exhausted. Family members are chronically trapped in stereotyped patterns of interaction which are severely limiting their range of choices, but no alternatives seem possible. In this time of heightened rigidity of transactional patterns, conflict overshadows large areas of normal functioning. Often one family member is the identified patient, and the other family members see themselves as accommodating his illness. . . . A family with an identified patient has gone through a reification process which overfocuses on one member. The therapist reverses this process [Minuchin, 1979, pp. 10–11].

Minuchin's therapeutic method begins with the counselor joining the family system, sharing and imitating its communication style through *mimesis,* and taking a position of leadership. Once the counselor has elicited enough information to understand the family's structure, the process of change begins. Gradually, the counselor confronts the family's view of the problem, moving attention from the individual symptom-bearer to the family system, manipulating the subsystem boundaries, presenting alternate concepts of reality, and encouraging the family's attempts to grow. Ultimately, the aim of the therapy is to change the structure of the family system, making it more functional in its own environmental context.

## The Communications Model

If psychodynamic therapy falls at the A position of the theoretical continuum developed by the Group for the Advancement of Psychiatry, the communication model holds position Z. Rather than adapting existing therapeutic models to family practice, the communications model was developed from a systems framework.

Much of the pioneering work in applying systems theory to the study of family relationships was begun in the 1950s by a group organized in Palo Alto, California, by Gregory Bateson.

> Bateson's work was instrumental in shifting the focus of family therapy from the single individual to the exchange of information and the process of evolving relationships between and among family members. It was also Bateson who stressed the limitations of linear thinking in regard to living systems. . . . He called instead for an epistemological shift — to new units of analysis, to a focus on the ongoing process, and to the use of a new descriptive language that emphasizes relationships, feedback information, and circularity [Goldenberg & Goldenberg, 1985, p. 6].

Bateson was joined in Palo Alto, in what was to become the Mental Research Institute, by Jay Haley, John Weakland, and Donald Jackson. This interdisciplinary team developed the double-bind theory of schizophrenic family relationships, hypothesizing that families with schizophrenic members tended to communicate through contradictory messages (Bateson, Jackson, Haley, & Weakland, 1956). As family therapy has evolved, the double-bind theory of schizophrenia has been less important than the attention it focused on communications models for understanding families and other human systems. It is now readily understood that communications have both content and "command" aspects and that the command aspects, or metacommunications, define relationships.

The communication approach is probably best exemplified by the strategic therapy of Haley (1976) and Madanes (1981), with its focus on active methods for changing repetitive communication patterns between family members. Haley (1976, p. 9) suggests that "if therapy is to end properly, it must begin properly — by negotiating a solvable problem and discovering the social situation that makes the problem necessary." If problems or symptoms serve some purpose in the social context, they can be resolved only through a strategy that focuses on interpersonal relationships.

Once the problem has been redefined in terms that make it solvable, the therapist develops a strategy unique to the needs of the specific family system. He or she then uses a variety of mechanisms, emphasizing the use of directives for families to follow between therapeutic sessions. One type of directive, the "paradoxical directive," actually prescribes that a family member continue in a behavior that would be expected to be targeted for change. The therapist redefines the symptom in terms of the function it serves and suggests that the behavior be continued or emphasized. If used very carefully, prescribing of the paradoxical tasks can help the therapist bring about change while avoiding family resistance.

> [The therapist] wants the members to resist him so that they will change. These tasks may seem paradoxical to family members because the therapist has told them he wants to help them change but at the same time he is asking them not to change. . . . Usually a family has stabilized around one family member being the problem. When the therapist moves to make a change in the situation of the problem person, he is moving to unstabilize the family and he will meet resistance in varying degrees. The paradoxical tasks are designed to deal with this problem [Haley, 1976, pp. 67–68].

To Haley, Madanes, and other communications theorists, the best way to eradicate the problem or symptom being addressed is to make it unnecessary for the stability of the family system.

## Behavioral Family Therapy

Liberman (1981, p. 152) sees the family as a "system of interlocking, reciprocal behaviors" and points out that problem behaviors are learned in a social context and maintained as long as the social system is organized to reinforce them.

> Changing the contingencies by which the patient gets acknowledgment and concern from other members of his family is the basic principle of learning that underlies the potency of family or couple therapy. Social reinforcement is made contingent on desired, adaptive behavior instead of maladaptive and symptomatic behavior. It is the task of the therapist in collaboration with the family or couple to (1) specify the maladaptive behavior, (2) choose reasonable goals which are alternative, adaptive behaviors, [and] (3) direct

and guide the family to change the contingencies of their social reinforcement patterns from maladaptive to adaptive target behaviors
[pp. 153–154].

Also important to Liberman's approach to behavioral family therapy
is the concept of *modeling*.

The model, sometimes the therapist but also other members of the
family, exhibits desired adaptive behavior which then is imitated
by the patient. . . . The amount of observational learning will be
governed by the degree to which a family member pays attention
to the modeling cues, has the capacity to process and rehearse the
cues, and possesses the necessary components in his behavioral
experience which can be combined to reproduce the more complex,
currently modeled behavior [1981, p. 154].

Thus Liberman, like other family counselors using behavioral or
social-learning approaches, focuses attention on specific, measurable behaviors and on the environmental contingencies that tend
to develop and maintain these behaviors. When behavioral therapists work with families, they set concrete goals to increase positive behaviors, at least in part by altering the patterns of reinforcement and the models offered by the social unit. Just as important is
the counselor's effort to provide skills training for family members,
focusing on ways to communicate effectively, techniques for managing stress, and self-controlled methods to change behavior.

Stuart (1980), in his approach to marital therapy, begins by asking clients to complete a Marriage Pre-Counseling Inventory, which
highlights the major areas of concern to be addressed by the couple.
Once the clients have identified their goals in therapy, he describes
the methods he will use and clarifies the connections between these
immediate interventions and the longer-range goals that the couple
may find more meaningful. His step-by-step therapeutic process
involves initiating "caring days," when clients carry out positive
behaviors that have been identified as desirable by their partner;
teaching communication skills; working on specific behavior changes;
and planning for the long-term maintenance of positive changes.

In the final analysis, all of these approaches to family therapy
seek verifiable changes both in the behaviors of family members and
in family relationships. Although the alternate perspectives vary
widely in their emphases, they all recognize the importance of the
family as a social system that influences and is influenced by individual behaviors.

# Substance Abuse and the Family System

As we have seen, family therapy calls for a reframing of the presenting problem from a focus on individual symptoms to a focus on family structure and interactions. Even when the identified client is alcohol- or drug-dependent, the family counselor sees the goal of intervention not just as abstinence for the affected family member but also as improved functioning for the family unit as a whole.

Substance abuse or dependence, like any other presenting problem, can be seen as a "systems-maintaining and a systems-maintained device" (Kaufman, 1985, p. 37). It is often central to a family's functioning, becoming a primary organizing factor in the system's structure. A family with an alcoholic member, for instance, learns to maintain its homeostasis around that person's drinking. Alcohol may even be a stabilizing factor, producing "patterned, predictable and rigid sets of interactions which reduce uncertainties" (Steinglass, 1979, p. 163). In fact, a number of families studied by Steinglass and his associates seemed to use the alcoholic's intoxicated state as a way of dealing with conflict and restabilizing their interactions.

> The transition from sober to intoxicated behavior appeared to serve a specific functional role for these marital couples, a role that was felt to be primarily problem-solving in nature. Although it was felt that three different types of problem-solving activities were associated with alcoholism (problem-solving associated with individual psychopathology, intrafamilial conflict, or conflict between the family and the external environment), in each case the emergence of the intoxicated interactional state appeared to temporarily restabilize the marital system [Steinglass, 1978, pp. 357–358].

These findings do not mean that unstable family dynamics "cause" alcohol problems or that the homeostasis found by alcohol-affected families should be considered a healthy or positive state. What they do imply is that families develop consistent, predictable methods for adapting to alcoholism, just as they create rules and interactional styles for dealing with other problems. At the same time, alcohol or drug abuse may also be one method—if a spectacularly ineffective one—for coping with the stresses of a family system.

> Drinking behavior interrupts normal family tasks, causes conflict, shifts roles, and demands adjustive and adaptive responses from family members who do not know how to appropriately respond. A converse dynamic also occurs: marital and family styles, rules, and conflict may evoke, support, and maintain alcoholism as a symptom of family system dysfunction or as a coping mechanism to deal with family anxiety [Kaufman, 1985, pp. 30–31].

If a counselor recognizes this conceptualization as being based in reality and wants to work from a family perspective, he or she is forced to reconsider most of the commonly held assumptions related to substance abuse, its etiology, and its treatment. A family-systems counselor views the alcoholic or addict simply as the identified symptom-bearer in the family, rather than as the primary focus of attention, and wants to know what function the drinking behaviors perform in the family unit. With this perception comes a major alteration in desired outcome goals.

> If alcohol consumption is part of an ongoing interactional pattern within the family system, then the traditional therapeutic intervention aimed toward abstinence is totally inadequate to the task. . . . A logical extension of this theoretical model is to view family therapy not so much from the point of view of involving family members as a mechanism for improving treatment with the identified alcoholic, but rather to view the entire family, or the marriage itself, as the patient. Therapeutic intervention becomes interactionally rather than intrapsychically oriented, and goals for treatment center around an improvement in the functioning, flexibility, and growth potential of the family system as a whole rather than the more limited focus on reduction in drinking on the part of the identified alcoholic [Steinglass, 1979, pp. 165–166].

As in individual counseling, the counselor's goals and methods depend on an assessment of the specific family situation. Bepko and Krestan (1985, p. 89) suggest, however, that generalizations can be made about the needs of alcoholic family systems at varying stages of the recovery process, and there is no reason to believe that the same principles would not hold true for families affected by drugs other than alcohol. The three stages of treatment, and their accompanying goals, are the following:

1. attainment of sobriety: unbalancing the system
2. adjustment to sobriety: stabilizing the system
3. long-term maintenance of sobriety for the whole family: rebalancing the system

The first stage of treatment, then, involves the counselor's attempt to unbalance the system by interrupting patterns that have been characteristic of the family system in the past. "In general, the therapist is attempting to help the family achieve a more functional structure which eliminates the need for alcohol as an interactional fulcrum" (p. 96).

Part of the counselor's role at this point involves helping the family confront problem drinking behaviors and, if possible and appropriate, press the alcohol-dependent member into accepting treatment. Attention should continue to be placed on the family system, however, with the counselor helping other members achieve a degree of detachment from the alcohol-related problems.

> In brief, the therapist may need to initiate family action to achieve a dry system. If that fails, then the next option is to disengage the family from the drinking member so that a clear family definition of responsibility can be developed. In doing so, the family becomes disengaged from perpetuating a wet system [Kaufman & Pattison, 1981, pp. 956–957].

This process of disengagement can help the family draw clearer boundaries among subsystems, interrupt rigid patterns of interaction, and recognize the impossibility of accepting responsibility for the behavior of others. For many families, a referral to Al-Anon or another self-help organization at this point provides much-needed support as sober family members attempt to withdraw from the performance of roles that have enabled the alcohol abuser to avoid the negative consequences of drinking.

When the alcohol-abusing family member does achieve sobriety, the counselor is in a position to help the family cope with what is, in fact, a crisis. Families that have built their lives on transactional patterns involving alcoholism often find it difficult to adapt to the sudden need for change. Sometimes they have difficulty finding a new homeostatic state. Often they face disappointment when they realize that every aspect of their lives does not suddenly improve. Usher, Jay, and Glass (1982) identify four responses to the crisis of abstinence:

1. The family "can resolve the crisis most easily by reintroducing alcohol into the system, i.e., by returning to their old patterns and reestablishing an alcoholismic homeostasis" (pp. 932–933).
2. The family may separate (a not uncommon response to an alcoholic member's new sobriety).
3. The family may develop a new structure based on support from outside the family (for example, involvement in Alcoholics Anonymous accompanied by an avoidance of family interactions).
4. The family may make genuine changes in the family structure, "allowing for more effective interaction, closeness, and increased success at meeting each other's affective needs" (p. 933).

The model developed by Bepko and Krestan (1985) suggests that the problems of the newly sober system be addressed in two phases. First, the family system needs to be stabilized as members try to adjust to change. Stabilizing treatment goals (pp. 124–125) include:

1. Keep system as calm as possible: focus predominantly on stepping down conflict, stress.

2. Address individual issues of family members more than interactional ones.
3. Stress self-focus for all family members.
4. Anticipate and predict extreme reactions to sobriety on the part of the co-alcoholic (the sober family member who has been most involved in and affected by the alcohol problem).
5. Address fear of relapse.
6. Begin to teach new behavioral skills for coping with stress and conflict.
7. Make minor structural changes that will ensure at least minimally adequate parenting.

Once stability has been achieved, the family can begin to work toward "rebalancing the system" and developing the roles and relationships that characterize healthy, effectively-functioning social units.

## Children of Alcoholics

The problems inherent in the alcoholic family system have important implications for the development of children who must spend their preadolescent and adolescent years attempting to cope with a unique set of difficulties. Although families affected by substance abuse obviously vary, they do tend toward some common patterns, at least as far as child rearing is concerned.

In a family affected by parental alcoholism, at least one parent is likely to be somewhat impaired in the ability to provide consistent child-rearing practices. The interactions of the alcoholic parent may show extreme variations, with the parent being effective or ineffective, warm or cold, distant or affectionate depending on current alcohol consumption. The nonalcoholic parent may also show variations as a result of focusing on the partner's drinking. Thus, in some alcoholic families neither parent is truly available to the child on a consistent basis.

The structure and boundaries of the alcoholic family system may also be problematic. Within the family unit, boundaries between subsystems may be weak, with the unity of the parental subsystem broken and children taking on what should be adult responsibilities. At the same time, boundaries between the family and its environment may be overly rigid, as the family tries to maintain secrecy about the alcohol problem. Thus, children who are unable to count on consistent support from their parents may also be prevented from reaching out beyond the family for fear of breaking the family's rule of silence. The delicate homeostasis of the alcoholic family system is maintained, but at high cost to the development of self-esteem of individual family members.

Children raised in these circumstances may need to work to provide consistency and order that are otherwise lacking in their home life.

> Children need consistency and structure. As an alcoholic progresses into alcoholism, and the co-alcoholic becomes more and more pre-occupied with the alcoholic, children experience decreasing consistency and structure in the family unit, and their lives become less and less predictable. Some days, when dad is drinking, no disruption or tension occurs, but on *other* days when he is drinking, he becomes loud, opinionated and demanding in his expectations of the children. Mom, at times, reacts to this disrupting behavior by being passive and ignoring it; other times, she makes arrangements for the children to go to the neighbors until dad goes to bed, or tells them to go outside and play until she calls for them. The children don't know what to expect from dad when he drinks, nor do they know what to expect from mom when dad drinks. When structure and consistency are not provided by the parents, children will find ways to provide it for themselves [Black, 1981, pp. 17–18].

Individual children differ in the mechanisms they use to adjust to their family situation. Some writers and counselors believe that children of alcoholics play a limited number of identifiable roles that give their family system a semblance of order.

Wegscheider (1981), for instance, identifies four basic roles that children may adopt in alcoholic families: (1) the family hero, (2) the scapegoat, (3) the lost child, and (4) the family mascot. The "family hero" takes over many functions that would normally be carried out by adults, assuming the responsibility for solving family problems and making sure that stability is provided for himself or herself and for younger children. This leadership is carried over into other childhood situations, including school, and into adulthood, making the family hero a success at most tasks attempted. The "scapegoat" is identified as the troublemaker in the family and tends to receive attention for his or her misbehavior. The "lost child," in contrast, remains in the background and seems to need little in the way of attention from the family. The "mascot" becomes the focus of attention as a way of lessening anxiety; he or she uses clowning as a way of distracting other family members from tension-provoking problems. Each of these roles is used by the individual as a coping mechanism and by the family system as a set of transactions to maintain homeostasis.

Black (1981) also provides a typology of family coping roles taken on by children raised in alcoholic families, including the responsible one, the adjuster, and the placater. The "responsible one," like

Wegscheider's family hero, provides consistency and structure in the home environment, taking over parental roles on a routine basis.

> The responsible child makes life easier for the parents by providing more time for the alcoholic to be preoccupied with drinking, and for the co-alcoholic to be preoccupied with the alcoholic. Whether or not responsible children are blatantly directed into this role, or more subtly fall into it, it is typically a role which brings them comfort. Playing the responsible role provides stability in the life of this oldest, or only, child and in the lives of other family members. These responsible children feel and are very organized. . . . [They] have learned to rely completely on themselves [Black, 1981, pp. 19–20].

The "adjuster" copes with a disorganized family system by detaching, by going along with events as they occur and thinking about them as little as possible. Black's "placater," like Satir's, focuses on the needs of others. In the alcoholic system this process tends to involve an attempt to salve the family's wounds.

> The placater finds the best way to cope, in this inconsistent and tension-filled home, is by acting in a way which will lessen his own tension and pain, as well as that of the other family members. This child will spend his early and adolescent years trying to "fix" the sadness, fears, angers and problems of brothers, sisters, and certainly, of mom and dad [Black, 1981, p. 24].

It may be an oversimplification to identify and label a limited number of roles played by children of alcoholics and to assume that these roles differ substantially from those played by the children of non-substance-abusing parents. It is important, however, to understand that the alcoholic family is at risk of being dysfunctional and to recognize that children of alcoholics might be required to develop extraordinary mechanisms for coping.

Black (1986) points out that children of alcoholics need to cope with a great deal of stress but may have fewer physical, social, emotional, and mental resources available to them than children living in more functional family systems. Their physical resources may be sapped because they are tired due to a lack of sleep at night, because they have internalized stress, or because they have been abused. (Of course, they may also be the victims of fetal alcohol syndrome, which causes developmental problems in the infants of alcoholic mothers.) Social resources may also be limited; hesitance to bring other children into the home or to share information about the family may interfere with the development of intimate relationships. Emotional resources are affected by the pain, fear, and embarrassment that come with unstable living arrangements, financial difficulties, broken promises, accidents, and public intoxication. Even mental resources may be affected by a lack of parental help and by difficulties in maintaining regular school attendance. Children in this situation can benefit by receiving the help and support provided by counseling.

## Counseling Children of Alcoholics

Counseling for children still living in the alcoholic home environment should concentrate on providing empathy and support and on helping clients develop coping skills that can serve them effectively both in the current situation and in the future. Ideally, this process should help children deal with their uncertainties and prevent the development of chronic emotional problems.

One way to look at appropriate directions for counseling is to consider Ackerman's (1983) conceptualization of the family's potential for progressing from a "reactive" to an "active" phase of development.

> The reactive phase is consistently dominated by the behavior of nonalcoholic family members reacting to the alcoholic's behavior. During this time most family members [are] extremely cautious in their behavior in order to avoid or to further complicate the existing problems of alcoholism. However, by being reactive they are constantly adapting their behavior in order to minimize or survive an unhealthy situation [p. 11].

The reactive phase is characterized by the attempts of family members to deny the alcohol problem, even to themselves. Parents try to protect children by covering up problems and by avoiding discussion of unpleasant realities. The reactive phase is characterized by social disengagement, with the family becoming isolated from others. Emotional disengagement also occurs, with children learning to deny their negative feelings. The coping roles described by Wegscheider and by Black may become rigidified.

Ackerman's notion, however, is that a family can move to an active phase.

> The main difference between the active and reactive phases is the responses of the nonalcoholic family member even though the alcoholic is still drinking. Rather than being passive to the effects on themselves from alcoholism they begin to take an active interest in themselves. . . . In this manner, the family begins to "de-center" itself from alcoholism. . . . They are willing to abandon their anonymity in exchange for help and a viable alternative to how they have been existing [p. 28].

The most useful approach to take with children of alcoholics may be to help them move from a reactive to an active state. If children are isolated in their home environment, counseling should help them reach out to others. If children are afraid of their feelings, counseling should help them recognize and express their previously forbidden emotions. If children feel they are alone in their situation, counseling should convince them that others share their problems. Children of alcoholics need to know that they are not to blame for family difficulties and that their attempts to meet their own needs are in no way deterimental to other family members. These counseling goals can probably be accomplished most successfully in group, rather than individual, settings.

> One of the primary tasks in the treatment of the latency-age child from an alcoholic home is to help the child bear the burden of the shameful and frightening family secret by bringing it out in the open. This process is immediately relieving to the child and causes her or him to feel less isolated. For this reason and because children from alcoholic homes often have deficits in the areas of social development and peer interaction, group is the treatment of choice [Brown & Sunshine, 1982, p. 70].

Group counseling for children of alcoholics should follow a structured process that helps group members understand more about substance dependence but that goes beyond the cognitive dimension to deal with affect and with acquiring skills. A good example of a structured approach is provided by Hastings and Typpo (1984) in a book designed for use by a counselor with a child or a group of children. Their design includes materials dealing with topics that are likely to meet the needs of the target population, including:

1. *drinking and drug problems:* a knowledge-building module discussing the effects of alcohol and other drugs
2. *feelings:* exercises designed to elicit awareness of negative and positive emotions and to explore the use of defenses
3. *families:* discussions of family rules, feelings, and relationships
4. *coping with problems:* exercises eliciting fresh ideas about coping methods, along with suggestions for dealing with some of the more prevalent alcohol-related family problems
5. *changes:* material encouraging children to make changes in the areas over which they do have some control, including taking care of themselves and handling their uncomfortable feelings
6. *choices:* decision-making exercises with an emphasis on the nature of choices

This structured approach, like many others becoming available to counselors, can help children develop the skills and resources they need for coping with family stress. Underlying most of these approaches is an emphasis on bringing hidden family dynamics to the surface. The introduction by Hastings and Typpo (1984) to their workbook says it best:

Imagine an ordinary living room . . . chairs, couch, coffee table, a TV set and, in the middle, a

LARGE, GRAY ELEPHANT.

The ELEPHANT stands there, shifting from one foot to another and slowly swaying from side to side.

Imagine also the people that live in this house; you, along with your mother and father and maybe some sisters and brothers. People have to go through the living room many times a day, and you watch as they walk through it very . . . carefully . . . around . . . the . . . ELEPHANT. No one ever says anything about the ELEPHANT. They avoid the swinging trunk and just walk around it. Since no one ever talks about the ELEPHANT, you know that you're not supposed to talk about it either. And you don't.

But sometimes you wonder why nobody is saying anything or why no one is doing anything to move the ELEPHANT. After all, it's a very big elephant and it's very hard to keep walking around it all the time and people are getting very tired. You wonder if maybe there is something wrong with *you*. But you just keep wondering, keep walking around it, keep worrying and wishing that there was somebody to talk to about the ELEPHANT.

Living in a family where drinking is a problem is a lot like living with an ELEPHANT in the living room.

## Counseling Adult Sons and Daughters of Alcoholics

People who grow up with an "elephant in the living room" may develop coping mechanisms that serve them poorly in adulthood. Only a minority of children of alcoholics respond by acting out; these individuals tend to receive some kind of attention or help during their adolescence. But most children in these situations respond instead by exerting control, burying feelings, and doing the best they can to adapt and survive. Until recently, these children have received little notice. If anything, their behavior has been seen as mature, and well adjusted. They pay a price for this adjustment, one that many clinicians and writers believe leads to a common set of concerns in adulthood. Seixas and Youcha (1985, pp. 47–48) ask adult children of alcoholics whether they identify with the following list of very prevalent feelings and attitudes:

Lack of trust?
Feel isolated and lonely?
Deny or suppress deep feelings?
Feel guilty?
Feel unnecessarily embarrassed and ashamed?
Wish for closeness, yet fear it?
Have a low opinion of yourself?
Feel sad?

Need to control yourself?
Need to control others?
Split the world into all good or all bad?
Have an exaggerated sense of responsibility?
Want desperately to please?
Have trouble standing up for your own needs?
Overreact to personal criticism?

Adult children of alcoholics are certainly not the only people who exhibit the attitudes and behaviors listed above. It does seem, however, that a significant number of adults from alcoholic homes are troubled by difficulty in trusting others, relinquishing control, identifying and expressing feelings, or abandoning behavioral rigidity. Coping mechanisms that are necessary in a difficult childhood situation may be less appropriate for a mature life-style.

The counselor attempting to work with adult children of alcoholics needs to address these issues in a two-stage process. Black (1986) suggests that clients must be encouraged to face their fears of loss of control and express their guilt, sadness, and anger, but that this catharsis must then be replaced with an attempt to learn new behavioral skills. If counselors accept this idea, they can approach these clients as they would any others, completing a careful assessment of each one's strengths and deficits and developing a plan for behavioral change based on these unique needs. If clients' needs are addressed through a group process, emphasis should be placed on developing such skills as assertion, relaxation, stress management, and interpersonal communication, depending on the areas that group members need to have addressed. Although the group can also serve as a mechanism for providing information about substance abuse and its effects on family dynamics, it is probably less useful to focus on children of alcoholics as an alcoholism risk group than to stress the individual's potential for successful adaptation and self-control. Attempts to eliminate the individual's sense of isolation and guilt may work best in concert with a referral to one of the many self-help groups for adult children of alcoholics now available in many areas of the world.

# ▌ Group Counseling

The fact that substance abuse problems are so closely tied to social relationships has focused attention on the possibility of using group counseling as an appropriate mechanism, both for prevention and for treatment. Group counseling has a number of positive attributes that can make it an approach of choice for dealing with a variety of issues (Dagley, Gazda, & Pistole, 1986, pp. 137–138):

1. A group offers each individual the opportunity to test self-perceptions against reality.
2. Distorted perceptions and false assumptions of both self and others may become more apparent and lose their value.
3. Groups may provide a sense of psychological safety to support the elimination of self-defeating behaviors.
4. Groups approximate real-life interaction situations, thus providing members with chances to try out new behaviors in a safe environment.
5. The responses of others can help an individual appreciate the universality of some personal concerns.
6. Members can increase their ability to give and solicit appropriate self-disclosures and feedback.
7. Interaction with others in a group can enhance one's empathy and social interest.
8. Groups of some duration offer individuals reinforcement for personal changes.
9. Groups have unique ways of helping members develop a deeper understanding and acceptance of individual differences.
10. Consistent feedback from others in a group can enhance a person's accuracy of perception and communication.

Many of the characteristics described by Dagley, Gazda, and Pistole seem highly relevant to the issues faced by substance-abusing clients. Yet despite years of experimentation with group approaches, especially for alcoholics, the literature shows little in the way of consistent, measurable benefits attributable to this modality (Miller & Hester, 1985). Although group counseling holds a great deal of promise, that promise has not yet come to fruition.

If group approaches have not demonstrated measurable benefits, it may be because of their overly restricted focus. In general, group work with substance-abusing clients has tended to take one of two avenues: an emphasis on verbal confrontation or an emphasis on a didactic presentation of information. Neither of these approaches is consistent with what is known about human behavior change.

Frequently, group sessions for substance abusers focus on confrontation, with leaders and members putting a great deal of effort into "breaking through denial," or convincing clients to accept the reality of their addiction. In these sessions the group process is considered successful only when the client verbalizes his or her acceptance of the label "alcoholic" or "addict."

This approach has become prevalent, especially in inpatient settings, perhaps because group leaders fail to recognize how tenuous the connections are between "correct" verbalizations and actual behavior change. It is possible that many clients bow to coercion and accept, at a superficial level, labels that they have not internalized.

Using the group interaction to encourage such compliance ignores realities of group interaction and influence that have long been understood. There are clear and widely understood differences between compliance and internalization.

> *Compliance* can be said to occur when an individual accepts influence because he hopes to achieve a favorable reaction from another person or group. He adopts the induced behavior not because he believes in its content but because he expects to gain specific rewards or approval and avoid specific punishments or disapproval by conforming. . . . *Internalization* can be said to occur when an individual accepts influence because the content of the induced behavior — the ideas and actions of which it is composed — is intrinsically rewarding. . . . He may consider it useful or the solution of a problem or find it congenial to his needs. Behavior adopted in this fashion tends to be integrated with the individual's existing values. Thus the satisfaction derived from internalization is due to the *content* of the new behavior [Kelman, 1971, p. 203].

Compliance, then, takes place because the individual accepts the influence of the group and wishes, consciously or unconsciously, to gain acceptance. Internalization takes place when the individual actually believes in the efficacy of the newly acquired behavior. The implications of this framework become clear when we consider the differing effects of compliance and of internalization on behavior outside of the group setting. "When an individual adopts an induced response through compliance, he tends to perform it only under conditions of surveillance by the influencing agent" (Kelman, 1971, p. 204). In sharp contrast, "when an individual adopts an induced response through internalization, he tends to perform it under conditions of relevance of the issue, regardless of the surveillance or salience" (p. 204). Thus, if substance abusers accept their new labels only at the compliance level, the effects on their behaviors may be limited to the context of the group or treatment setting, where "surveillance by the influencing agent" is a reality. What has been seen as the success of "breaking through denial" may not, in fact, have any influence on the real-life behaviors we seek to influence.

Similarly, group modalities that focus on providing cognitive information may also lack relevance to behavior change. "Educational" approaches in the form of lectures about the dangers of drugs and alcohol are used very widely, both as preventive tools and as treatment methods. In inpatient alcoholism treatment programs, for instance, a great deal of time is likely to be spent on lectures concerning the disease concept and the negative effects of alcohol. Although this approach may affect cognitive knowledge, it does not appear to have any measurable effect on behavior. As is the case with confrontation groups, clients appear to have changed, but these changes fail to make the transition to another environment.

> Because the persuasive power of groups is so great . . . an illusion
> that individuals have changed is often created when in fact their
> alterations of behavior within the group context are perhaps only
> accommodations to a new referent group, to a different set of
> norms. The "change," therefore, is often ephemeral because it is
> more a response to specific group conditions and depends on the
> treatment group for maintenance. . . . Too often, after participation
> in the group, the individual faces the external world little prepared
> to use what he has learned [Lieberman, 1977, pp. 49–50].

If the substance abuse field is to make use of group counseling,
it will have to concentrate on using methods that encourage the
transfer of newly learned attitudes and behaviors to nontreatment
settings. Most promising are those activities that focus on the development of concrete, usable skills and that provide the opportunity
to rehearse new behaviors in the group environment. Many of the
approaches used in the group setting parallel the methods used in individual counseling. The group context, however, provides increased
opportunities for modeling, for rehearsing interpersonal behaviors,
for sharing feelings and ideas, and for gaining reinforcement as
attempts at behavior change begin to succeed. Among the activities
that lend themselves well to the group modality are analysis of
drinking or drug-taking behaviors, development of alternative methods of coping, and training in problem solving and assertiveness.

## Behavior Analysis

Substance-abusing clients need to begin by assessing their behaviors. This can be accomplished either through homework assignments completed individually and then shared with other group
members or through group activities designed to elicit ideas concerning the antecedents and reinforcements associated with target behaviors.

If clients are outpatients, an initial homework assignment can
involve use of an alcohol consumption record. An example of such
a record-keeping device is shown as Exhibit 5.1. This form has
been used for members of a group of clients being seen because of
multiple arrests for driving under the influence of alcohol. Careful
record keeping helps them become more conscious of the amount
they have been drinking; the people, places, and feelings associated
with their drinking; and the risks and potential problems their
drinking behaviors might bring.

Clients are asked to complete the consumption record during the
week between group meetings. When they return to the group setting, they are asked to share the results of this record with a partner
and then to discuss their general impressions with the group as a
whole. This set of activities helps individuals increase their knowl-

# ▌Exhibit 5.1

## Alcohol Consumption Record

Name _____

Date record begun _____ Date record ended _____

| Date | | | | | | | | | | |
|---|---|---|---|---|---|---|---|---|---|---|
| Place where drinking occurred | | | | | | | | | | |
| Whom were you drinking with (relationship and number of people)? | | | | | | | | | | |
| Feelings before drinking (see #3) | | | | | | | | | | |
| Time drinking began | | | | | | | | | | |
| Why did you begin drinking at this time? | | | | | | | | | | |
| Number of standard drinks consumed (see #1) | | | | | | | | | | |
| Feelings during drinking (see #3) | | | | | | | | | | |
| Time drinking stopped | | | | | | | | | | |
| Feelings after drinking (see #3) | | | | | | | | | | |
| Amount of money spent on alcohol | | | | | | | | | | |
| Did you drive after drinking? | | | | | | | | | | |
| How risky do you think this drinking was for you on a scale of 1–4 (see #2) | | | | | | | | | | |

#1  *Standard drink*
   10 oz. beer
   4 oz. wine
   1 oz. hard liquor

#2  *Risk scale*
   4 — very risky          1 — no risk
   3 — moderately risky
   2 — slightly risky

#3  *Feelings codes*
   1. Happy              4. Relaxed          7. Calm, at ease
   2. Bored              5. Angry            8. Sick
   3. Tense, nervous     6. Tired, sleepy    9. Depressed

edge of their own drinking behaviors, recognize similarities and differences among other group members, and perceive their own difficulties more clearly through identification with the behaviors of others. The fact that the forms are discussed in a group reinforces careful and accurate reporting.

In an inpatient setting or in a group whose participants have already achieved abstinence, similar results can be achieved through exercises carried out in the group. For example, McCrady, Dean, Dubreuil, and Swanson (1985) describe a group situation in which alcoholic clients are asked to brainstorm as many responses as they can think of to the question "Why do you think some people develop drinking problems?"

> Usually, the brainstormed answers fit into the following categories: (1) life stresses (e.g., retirement, death of loved one); (2) emotional-physiological (e.g., chronic anxiety, depression, chronic pain); (3) other people's behavior (e.g., unfaithful spouse, recalcitrant business partner, alcoholic parent); (4) drinking environments (e.g., "All my friends drink"); (5) heredity and early socialization (e.g., "My father is an alcoholic"); and (6) positive consequences (e.g., "I could socialize better") [p. 432].

Once the brainstormed items have been placed in these categories, responses can be labeled as antecedents or as reinforcements, thus laying the groundwork for a discussion of behavioral models of problem drinking while helping clients recognize similarities in their responses.

In another exercise used by McCrady and her colleagues, clients focus on antecedents to drinking. Group brainstorming allows clients to become aware of the many possible antecedents to drinking by asking them to list as many triggers as they can. Group sessions can also focus on individuals, asking one client at a time to list the factors that seem to trigger drinking behaviors. Other group members provide support and help individuals identify connections or problems that might not otherwise be readily apparent. Although similar activities can be carried out on an individual basis, the group context for this effort helps to generate fresh ideas and to encourage the recognition that people can learn to take active responsibility for meeting their own special needs.

## Coping Mechanisms

Group exercises also lend themselves well to the process of helping substance abusers develop other methods for coping with stressors or high-risk situations. A workshop strategy can be used both to help group members recognize stressful situations that trigger substance use and to help them develop more effective mechanisms for dealing with these pressures. In terms of the stress intervention model developed by Barrow and Prosen (1981), clients can learn to deal with environmental demands and their responses to them by: (1) altering their environment through problem solving, life-style changes, and the development of assertiveness and other interpersonal skills; (2) altering their own mental processes; or (3) altering nervous system activation through relaxation training, meditation, or biofeedback. A number of group exercises can be used to bring about this kind of learning.

**Identifying stressors and high-risk situations**    Group members can work together to brainstorm a list of environmental factors that they tend to find stressful or that trigger their own drinking or drug-taking behavior. Clients can use the list to identify both the scope and the commonality of their concerns. Even more important is the fact that this list building brings stressors to the conscious level so that they can be addressed in a realistic fashion.

**Cognitive restructuring**    The group context can also be helpful for working on clients' reactions to demanding situations. Restructuring (Goldfried & Goldfried, 1980) involves helping clients recognize the role of their own cognitions in mediating arousal. This recognition allows them to change unrealistic cognitions to more rational interpretations that will, in turn, lead to more appropriate responses.

> Clients must consciously and deliberately engage in doing something differently when feeling upset. This emotional reaction must now serve as a "cue" for them to stop and think: "What am I telling myself that may be unrealistic?" They must learn to "break up" what was before an automatic reaction and replace it with a more realistic appraisal of the situation. . . . Clients eventually can totally eliminate the initial upset phase by having made the more realistic appraisal an automatic reaction [p. 107].

Group members can assist one another in their attempts to recognize examples of their own irrational responses and to identify and rehearse alternate self-messages that can, in time, become automatic.

**Relaxation training**    Not all stressors can be prevented or reinterpreted. Clients also need to be able to intervene at the point of the physiological stress response. Probably most appropriate for use in a group situation is the muscle-relaxation procedure we discussed in Chapter 4, with clients being trained to tense and relax muscles and to note the difference between tension and relaxation. Clients can also practice relaxation exercises on their own between sessions and learn to monitor their tension levels on a daily basis.

**Identifying successful approaches**    As group members become more familiar with models of stress reduction and coping, they can also begin to identify methods they have used in the past to cope with situations that might otherwise have been connected with drinking or drug use. As they discuss these coping mechanisms, they may notice that their strategies include a combination of environmental problem solving, cognitive changes, and relaxation methods. This recognition can lead, in turn, to the development of individual plans for dealing with troublesome issues. Group members can help one another identify alternatives to substance-abusing behaviors, that can come close to being as reinforcing as drinking or drug use have been in the past.

## Problem Solving

Exercises can be designed both to help group members understand problem-solving concepts and methods and to provide practice in applying these methods to their problems. The concept of problem solving should be introduced with a discussion of its relevance for substance abuse. Discussion can focus on the fact that some people tend to ignore their problems and expect drinking or drug use to solve them. Approaching problems in an orderly fashion is a better choice for all types of issues. Beyond this, problem-solving skills can be useful for dealing with specific substance use problems—for example, avoiding driving under the influence of alcohol or planning alternatives to celebrations that would have involved alcohol or drug use.

A series of sessions that has been used with groups of multiple DUI offenders begins with an overview of the following problem-solving steps:

1. recognizing and defining problems
2. devising alternatives
3. judging the alternatives
4. implementing and evaluating the chosen solution

The four steps are explained one by one, with the group leader then applying the model to several general examples. As members become more familiar with problem-solving steps and substeps, they contribute additional situations and assist one another by refining problem definitions, brainstorming alternatives, listing positive and negative aspects of the proposed solutions, and preparing implementation plans.

Learning is enhanced by written homework assignments that give participants a chance to apply their problem-solving skills to hypothetical problem situations such as the following:

1. There is a big party next Saturday that you want to attend, but you usually get very drunk at this person's parties.
2. Your bowling team always meets afterward at a bar. You plan to go but want to keep your drinking under control.
3. Your friends like to stop for a drink after work and you think they'll be upset if you don't join them.
4. Your car has broken down and you need to find some way to get to work.
5. You never seem to have enough money.

This exercise allows clients to choose between applying the problem-solving exercise to a drinking-related issue or to a more general problem. Once participants have completed the activity on their own, they bring their solutions to the next group meeting to compare notes. Such practice allows group members to become adept at using the model when real-life problems present themselves.

## Assertiveness Training

Assertive behaviors, like problem-solving skills, depend for their development on both understanding and practice. In the group setting, assertiveness needs first to be defined, with participants learning to differentiate among assertiveness, aggressiveness, and passivity and to recognize the suitability of assertion in human interaction. Group discussion can also point up the relationships between assertiveness deficits and drinking problems; people may drink to overcome dissatisfaction with their nonassertive behavior or to attempt assertions that they find difficult in a sober state. Most important for alcohol-abusing clients attempting sobriety is the fact that assertiveness skills will be needed when refusing a drink.

Understanding of assertiveness needs to be followed by modeling of assertive behavior and by rehearsing of assertive behaviors in the group. In a group exercise for clients with alcohol-related problems, the focus can be placed on assertive drink refusal, with the leader explaining that the same skills can be applicable to a variety of interpersonal situations. After the group leader models assertive refusal of a drink offered by a role-playing group member, participants can role-play similar situations, alternating between the roles of drink "pusher" and assertive refuser. The group leader's coaching and feedback can help to improve each client's skills. Repetitions of the behavior rehearsal can focus on issues being faced by the clients. As with all group interventions, the ultimate purpose must be to develop healthy, adaptive behaviors that can be transferred from the group setting to the client's real-life situation.

# ▌ Summary

Effective treatment for individual clients depends on the counselor's recognition that substance abuse has a major impact on the individual's social network and that the social environment, in turn, affects the maintenance or resolution of each presenting problem. General systems theory has helped practitioners understand that human behaviors cannot be well understood through reductionistic, linear analyses. Human beings, like all other living organisms, need to be thought of as open systems in constant, organized interaction with their environment. Systems thinking has helped counselors focus on predictable transactions, on communication and feedback loops, on circular rather than cause-and-effect relationships, and on each system's quest for equilibrium.

Practitioners involved with family therapy have been most influenced by systems theory. Although family counselors vary widely in their approaches, they tend to share a recognition that effective interventions must focus on the family system, rather than on the individual, and that problems must be understood within the context of the environments in which they occur. Among the currently important theories of family counseling are the following:

1. psychodynamic therapy, which continues to place some emphasis on unresolved intrapersonal conflicts and on past experiences, albeit within the context of family practice
2. experimental/humanistic therapy, which focuses on communication patterns that help to build self-esteem and self-worth among family members
3. Bowenian family therapy, which emphasizes the differentiation of the self
4. structural family therapy, which understands families through the enduring interactional patterns that make their structure functional or dysfunctional
5. communication models, which consistently focus on family interactions and relationships rather than on individuals and their presenting problems
6. behavioral family therapy, with its emphasis on behaviors that are learned and reinforced in the social context

Systems thinking has been especially useful in enhancing our understanding of the family context of alcoholism. Family counseling focuses broadly on family structure and interactions, rather than narrowly on the problems presented by one individual. This focus has helped substance abuse counselors see the family system as a whole as the appropriate target for change. The abuse of alcohol or another substance may become central to a family's organizational structure, with the members learning to maintain homeostasis around the continued drinking or drug use of the affected individual. Counselors therefore need to help the family as a whole interrupt rigid patterns of interaction and find a new equilibrium after sobriety has been achieved.

Attention to family systems has also brought an emphasis on the problems faced by children of alcoholics. Children utilize a variety of roles to attain stability in what may be a chaotic situation. Counseling for children still in the alcoholic home generally focuses on reducing anxiety, eliminating feelings of isolation, and building coping skills. Counseling for adult sons and daughters of alcoholics emphasizes such issues as control, guilt, sadness, and lingering anger.

Because substance abuse and social interactions are interwoven, counselors have also become increasingly interested in using group methods. Groups that focus narrowly on verbal confrontation or didactic providing of information have not had demonstrable effects on behavior. More promising are group interventions that focus on developing skills that can be transferred to real life. Among the activities that lend themselves well to group counseling are behavioral analyses of substance use behaviors, development of alternative coping mechanisms, problem-solving exercises, and assertiveness training.

# ▌ References

Ackerman, N. W. (1981). Family psychotherapy—theory and practice. In G. D. Erickson & T. P. Hogan (Eds.), *Family therapy: An introduction to theory and technique* (2nd ed.) (pp. 165–172). Pacific Grove, CA: Brooks/Cole.

Ackerman, R. J. (1983). *Children of alcoholics: A guidebook for educators, therapists, and parents* (2nd ed.). Holmes Beach, FL: Learning Publications.

Barrow, J. C., & Prosen, S. S. (1981). A model of stress and counseling interventions. *Personnel and Guidance Journal, 60,* 5–10.

Bateson, G., Jackson, D. D., Haley, J., & Weakland, J. H. (1956). Towards a theory of schizophrenia. *Behavioral Science, 1,* 251–264.

Bepko, C., & Krestan, J. A. (1985). *The responsibility trap: A blueprint for treating the alcoholic family.* New York: Free Press.

Black, C. (1981). *It will never happen to me.* Denver: M.A.C.

Black, C. (1986, March). *Children of alcoholics.* Paper presented at the Conference on Children of Alcoholics, Gestalt Institute for Training, Chicago.

Bowen, M. (1982). *Family therapy in clinical practice.* New York: Aronson.

Brown, K. A., & Sunshine, J. (1982). Group treatment of children from alcoholic families. *Social Work with Groups, 5*(1), 65–72.

Caplan, G. (1974). *Support systems and community mental health.* New York: Basic Books.

Dagley, J. C., Gazda, G. M., & Pistole, M. C. (1986). Groups. In M. D. Lewis, R. L. Hayes, & J. A. Lewis (Eds.), *An introduction to the counseling profession*. Itasca, IL: F. E. Peacock.

Finney, J. W., Moos, R. H., & Mewborn, C. R. (1980). Posttreatment experiences and treatment outcome of alcoholic patients six months and two years after hospitalization. *Journal of Consulting and Clinical Psychology, 48*(1), 17–29.

Goldenberg, I., & Goldenberg, H. (1985). *Family therapy: An overview* (2nd ed.). Pacific Grove, CA: Brooks/Cole.

Goldfried, M. R., & Goldfried, A. P. (1980). Cognitive change methods. In F. H. Kanfer & A. P. Goldstein (Eds.), *Helping people change* (2nd ed.) (pp. 97–130). New York: Pergamon Press.

Haley, J. (1976). *Problem-solving therapy*. New York: Harper & Row.

Hastings, J. M., & Typpo, M. H. (1984). *An elephant in the living room*. Minneapolis: CompCare Publications.

Kaufman, E. (1985). *Substance abuse and family therapy*. Orlando, FL: Grune & Stratton.

Kaufman, E., & Pattison, E. M. (1981). Differential methods of family therapy in the treatment of alcoholism. *Journal of Studies on Alcohol, 42*, 951–971.

Kelman, H. C. (1971). Compliance, identification, and internalization: Three processes of attitude change. In B. L. Hinton & H. J. Reitz (Eds.), *Groups and organizations: Integrated readings in the analysis of social behavior* (pp. 201–209). Belmont, CA: Wadsworth.

Kolevzon, M. S., & Green, R. G. (1985). *Family therapy models: Convergence and divergence*. New York: Springer.

Liberman, R. (1981). Behavioral approaches to family and couple therapy. In G. D Erickson & T. P. Hogan (Eds.), *Family therapy: An introduction to theory and technique* (2nd ed.) (pp. 152–164). Pacific Grove, CA: Brooks/Cole.

Lieberman, M. A. (1977). Up the right mountain, down the wrong path— theory development for people-changing groups. In R. T. Golembiewski & A. Blumberg (Eds.), *Sensitivity training and the laboratory approach* (3rd ed.). Itasca, IL: F. E. Peacock.

Madanes, C. (1981). *Strategic family therapy*. San Francisco: Jossey-Bass.

McCrady, B. S., Dean, L., Dubreuil, E., & Swanson, S. (1985). The problem drinkers' project: A programmatic application of social-learning-based treatment. In G. A. Marlatt & J. R. Gordon (Eds.), *Relapse prevention: Maintenance strategies in the treatment of addictive behaviors* (pp. 417–471). New York: Guilford Press.

Miller, W. R., & Hester, R. K. (1985). The effectiveness of treatment techniques: What works and what doesn't. In W. R. Miller (Ed.), *Alcoholism: Theory, research, and treatment* (pp. 526–574). Lexington, MA: Ginn Press.

Minuchin, S. (1974). *Families and family therapy*. Cambridge, MA: Harvard University Press.

Minuchin, S. (1979). Constructing a therapeutic reality. In E. Kaufman & P. Kaufmann (Eds.), *Family therapy of drug and alcohol abuse* (pp. 5–18). New York: Gardner Press.

Satir, V. M. (1967). *Conjoint family therapy* (2nd ed.). Palo Alto, CA: Science and Behavior Books.

Satir, V. M. (1972). *Peoplemaking.* Palo Alto, CA: Science and Behavior Books.

Seixas, J. S., & Youcha, G. (1985). *Children of alcoholism: A survivor's manual.* New York: Harper & Row.

Steinglass, P. (1978). The conceptualization of marriage from a systems theory perspective. In T. J. Paolino & B. S. McCrady (Eds.), *Marriage and marital therapy: Psychoanalytic, behavioral, and systems theory perspectives* (pp. 298–365). New York: Brunner/Mazel.

Steinglass, P. (1979). Family therapy with alcoholics: A review. In E. Kaufman & P. Kaufmann (Eds.), *Family therapy of drug and alcohol abuse* (pp. 147–186). New York: Gardner Press.

Stuart, R. B. (1980). *Helping couples change: Clinical demonstrations and client guides for material therapy* [cassette recording]. New York: BMA Audio Cassettes, a division of Guilford Publications.

Umbarger, C. C. (1983). *Structural family therapy.* New York: Grune & Stratton.

Usher, M. L., Jay, J., & Glass, D. R. (1982). Family therapy as a treatment modality for alcoholism. *Journal of Studies on Alcohol, 43,* 927–938.

von Bertalanffy, L. (1968). *General systems theory.* New York: Braziller.

Wegscheider, S. (1981). *Another chance: Hope and health for the alcoholic family.* Palo Alto, CA: Science and Behavior Books.

# Relapse and Relapse Prevention

A relapse, or an uncontrolled return to drug or alcohol use following competent treatment, is one of the greatest problems substance abusers and their counselors face. In fact, Polich, Armor, and Braiker (1981) have reported that close to 90% of all clients treated for substance abuse relapse within one year after their discharge from treatment. This figure is astounding and overwhelming, yet relapse and relapse prevention tend to receive very short shrift in most substance abuse treatment agencies. This critical inattention must stop if we expect to consolidate treatment gains, decrease the frequency of the "revolving door" syndrome, and increase the willingness of drug and alcohol users to enter treatment programs. It seems important, then, that we spend some time learning about relapse prevention, obviously one of the ultimate goals of substance abuse counseling.

A relapse has usually been defined as a return to substance use. This could be a minor event, such as a slip in which the substance is used only once. Traditionally, these slips are called relapses, and their occurrence is thought to obviate all prior success; thus, the substance abuser must, if he or she is willing, reinitiate the process of recovery and begin at the beginning. In traditional circles, the significance of a slip is great. It is thought and taught that one drink, one joint of marijuana, one pill, or one shot of a narcotic will lead, inevitably, to intoxication and pretreatment levels of abuse. This belief stems from the disease conceptions of drug and alcohol dependence, which hold that these conditions are progressive. In this view the substance abuser, whether using drugs or not, is always involved with a progression of his or her disease, and any reinitiation of substance use will reactivate the disease process. Within this framework clients are taught that their only chance of recovery is abstinence; it is commonly thought that abstinence means health, and substance use means illness. In addition, traditionalists tell their clients that alcoholism and drug dependence are chronically relapsing diseases. It seems that these two injunctions (you must be abstinent to be well, and you have a chronically relapsing disease) create a double bind for substance-abusing clients. This double bind, combined with the belief that a relapse leads inevitably to complete deterioration, must be, at best, confusing and anxiety-provoking for clients.

It seems wise, therefore, to differentiate a slip (a temporary lapse) from a relapse (a return to uncontrolled substance use) and also from a return to nonproblem drinking. In this regard, a slip should be considered a temporary lapse that is neither catastrophic nor regressive. It should provide an impetus for learning, and the client and counselor should spend time examining what precipitated the slip and how the client can learn by analyzing it. A slip is not devastating in and of itself. It can be devastating if defined as a disaster and as a failure. The counselor should help the client understand slips—for example, as testing behavior or as a response to environmental cues—and redefine them as learning experiences. This redefinition should effectively reduce guilt, anxiety, and embarrassment and enable the client to quickly get back on track without turning the slip into a full-blown relapse. On the other hand, 19% of all substance abusers spontaneously discontinue their pattern of abusive substance use (W. R. Miller, 1982). These people tend to return to moderate use following a period of abstinence. This new way of using alcohol or drugs should not be considered a relapse, since use, in this group, is not problematic. These clients tell us a lot about drug abuse problems not being progressive. In fact, they show that problem use waxes and wanes and that there is a great variability in substance use and abuse patterns (Vaillant, 1983).

A true relapse, in contrast, is a serious situation. It occurs when the client resumes an abusive pattern of use after a period of treatment-induced abstinence or controlled use. Thus a relapse occurs, in our conception, following a slip. It is thought that the slip, if not managed correctly and redefined as a learning experience, will result in what Marlatt (1985) has called the *abstinence violation effect* (AVE). This effect is frequently overwhelming, in that it includes great conflict ("I shouldn't be drinking, but I drank"), intense anxiety, great confusion, profound guilt, decreased self-esteem, extreme embarrassment, and a pervasive sense of shame. These powerful negative emotions lead to a belief pattern of noncontrol and a resumption of substance abuse to manage the resultant negative emotional states. Our conceptualization, then, is to train clients to redefine relapses as learning experiences, which when analyzed will tell them and their counselors a great deal about environmental stressors and gaps in treatment. This view reduces shame, doubt, and guilt, allows clients to maintain their integrity, and encourages them not to elope from treatment but rather to embrace it. There is no going back to square one, and all treatment gains are consolidated. If a client relapses for three weeks after four months of sobriety, he or she simply has 120 days of sobriety and 21 days of substance use. There are no moral injunctions against the client and no hints of failure. The experience of relapse is seen as therapeutic, understandable, and acceptable.

# Models of Addiction

Prevailing models of addiction heavily influence which treatment we choose for our clients and, consequently, how, or even whether we address the issues of relapse and relapse prevention. It is impossible to use certain treatment techniques while operating from certain models, and within some models it is impossible to effectively address the critical issues of relapse. Typically, the addiction field is influenced by three models: (1) the moral model, (2) the medical model, and (3) the social-learning model.

## Moral Model

The moral model utilizes religious concepts and philosophical ideals to differentiate between behaviors that society considers "normal" and those it considers "abnormal." Under this model those who use drugs or alcohol are thought to be immoral deviants. Such people, then, are thought to have to suffer the legal, physical, and psychological consequences of their actions. Proponents of this model assume that substance abusers are "willful sinners" who freely choose to use drugs or alcohol. They maintain that drinkers or drug abusers are responsible for their "vice" and that drinking and drug use are signs of moral weakness and not the products of physical, psychological, or social factors (Guydish, 1982; Tarter & Schneider, 1976).

Since abusive substance use cannot be objectively defined within the context of the moral model (because any drinking or drug use is bad), there remain both ambivalence and vagueness over what constitutes abuse. In cultures where drinking and drug use are prohibited, one is likely to be identified as an alcoholic or drug addict more readily than in cultures where substance use is tolerated and sanctioned on both religious and secular occasions (Tarter & Schneider, 1976). Devotees of the moral model tend to support an "all or none" attitude toward substance use, viewing the substance itself as evil.

The moral model is not at all scientific, but it is still utilized by some people to define and understand substance-abusing behavior. It is not a formidable factor in shaping scientific thought about substance abusers, but it is an easy model to adopt when treatment fails and one wants to conveniently blame clients for their relapse or failure to grow. The moral model is relatively ineffective in helping us adopt or devise relapse-prevention treatments. Its use in chemical dependency work is not suggested, and counselors who find themselves tempted to rely on a conceptual framework like this should make a decision to seek further training and supervision.

## Medical Model

The moral model has declined as a dominant mode of thought in the United States. Its decline coincides with the emergence of the medical model of substance abuse (Cole & Ryback, 1976). The concepts of evil and wickedness have given way to the concepts of sickness and disease, and alcoholism and drug dependence are frequently regarded as disease entities unto themselves. In this respect substance abuse is thought to be either a primary illness or a symptom of an underlying physiological or structural disturbance. This model applies disease terminology and places responsibility for the care of substance abusers in the hands of physicians. In a broad conception, the medical model should include theories related to genetics (Murray & Stabenau, 1982), endocrinology (Stokes, 1982), brain dysfunctions (Blum, 1982; McEvoy, 1982), and biochemistry (Tewari & Carson, 1982). But because of reductionism and a non-scientific stance, the medical model's disease conception has been reduced to the simplistic notion that alcoholism and drug dependence are primary, progressive, chronic, and relapsing diseases. This description does not describe or enlighten and is more philosophical than scientific. It makes relapse prevention or treatment planning very difficult.

Further, the medical model's disease concept, which has been fastidiously described in Jellinek's *The Disease Concept of Alcoholism* (1960), is a large, implicit component of the Alcoholics Anonymous and Narcotics Anonymous treatment approaches. These approaches tend to relieve substance abusers of personal responsibility and instead acknowledge that alcoholism and drug dependence are "bigger" than the alcoholic or drug abuser. AA and NA also posit that substance abusers are not weak-willed but that they are affected by a disease and therefore unable to drink or use drugs. Although the disease concept and related AA and NA approaches have enjoyed wide acceptance, predominant support for their acceptance is based on anecdotal reports (W. R. Miller, 1982; Tarter & Schneider, 1976).

In fact, the medical model is based primarily on unproven assumptions that are not synthesized from strict scientific study. Pattison, Sobell, and Sobell (1977) have outlined the prevailing assumptions of this model, which are adapted as follows:

1. There are unitary and well-defined phenomena that can be identified as alcoholism and drug dependence.
2. Alcoholics and drug-dependent individuals are essentially different from nonalcoholics and non-drug-dependent individuals.
3. Alcoholic and drug-dependent individuals may sometimes experience an irresistible physical craving for alcohol or drugs or a strong psychological compulsion to drink or use drugs.
4. Alcoholics and drug-dependent individuals develop "loss of control" over drinking and drug use and a related inability to stop drinking or using drugs.
5. Alcoholism and drug dependence are irreversible conditions.
6. Alcoholism and drug dependence are progressive diseases with distinct phases.

The medical model, then, has been used to describe the behaviors of chemically dependent individuals, speculate about the etiology and pathogenesis of chemical dependency, and initiate treatment and prevention programs for substance users and abusers. Much debate, however, has centered on the utility of the model and its applicability to substance abuse. Substance abusers who are labeled "sick," it has been argued, are being robbed of their freedom and their responsibility for themselves and are being deluded with the hope of a "cure" (Szasz, 1972). This model is also questioned on the ground that assuming a physiological causation places emphasis specifically on the individual while ignoring the social millieu, which may have been instrumental in establishing a response of excessive substance use in the first place and in maintaining that response in the long run (Pomerleau, 1982). Not only may it be a false premise to call a substance abuser "sick," but it may also hinder more than aid the helping agents, who are reluctant to apply pressure on a sick person (Finlay, 1974). Furthermore, this conception makes it easier for the counselor to disown treatment failures ("He has a disease—what more could I do?"), and it forces a dichotomous view of relapse (the client either is abstinent or has relapsed) as an expected component of the disease. It is expected that counselors operating in this model can only grit their teeth and tell their clients to struggle for abstinence by exerting their will. Exertion of will against the powerful and uncontrollable forces of the disease is, of course, difficult, and in this conception the ugly head of relapse is likely to be reared again and again. The reduced and simplified medical model is seen as lacking by many mental-health professionals, and it has spurred initiative toward a broader and more integrated view, which is being taken by social-learning theorists.

## Social-Learning Theory

The ascendance of scientific psychology in this century has had a profound effect on theory, research, and treatment in the substance abuse field. The social-learning theory defines substance abuse as an individual phenomenon, yet it does not exclude or minimize social factors, environmental factors, and the importance of significant individuals in the development of the abuse pattern (Tarter & Schneider, 1976).

Learning theories of substance abuse have emerged from a larger body of knowledge relating to reinforcement theory. They have also been influenced by attempts to explain substance abuse without the overtones of either the disease model or the moral model. Rather, social-learning theorists think that substance use and abuse are a result of a certain history of learning in which the behavior of drinking alcohol or using drugs has been increased in frequency, duration, and intensity for the psychological benefits it affords (P. M. Miller, 1976). There are many divergent learning theories.

One learning theory variant is a drive-reduction theory, which defines the stimulus as internal tension that, regardless of its cause, creates a drive state. Drinking or drug use becomes a prepotent response (habit) in an effort at reducing the drive. The psychological effects of alcohol or drugs are thought to be initially tension reducing and, therefore, reinforcing. The reinforcement, in turn, strengthens the drinking response, which will therefore occur more frequently in response to tension. This cycle, then, eventually leads to habitual drinking or drug use (Conger, 1956; Dollard & Miller, 1950).

Learning theory also deals with the seeming incongruity that excessive alcohol or drug use brings on social punishment in the forms of job loss, social ostracism, emotional upset, and psychological and physical deterioration. This incongruity is explained by the principle of delayed reinforcement. Thus the morning-after hangover or social punishment will not be effective in stopping a drinking or drug use response because of the delayed negative reinforcing effects (Tarter & Schneider, 1976). Furthermore, if the drive is intense, the immediate drive-reduction effects afforded by substance use will be more heeded than competing social punishment, which may actually cause new stress and lead to more substance use (Tarter & Schneider, 1976).

A second social-learning perspective (Bandura, 1969) suggests that excessive substance use is initiated by environmental stressors and is maintained by the hypothesized depressant and anesthetic effects of alcohol and drugs on the central nervous system. In this view the potential alcoholic or drug addict has acquired substance use, through differential reinforcement and modeling, as a widely generalized dominant response to stress because of the substance's reinforcing qualities. This powerful reinforcement cements the substance-taking response, and continued drug or alcohol use leads, eventually, to a physiological state of dependence that manifests itself by producing withdrawal symptoms when the substance is removed (Tarter & Schneider, 1976).

Consequently, the drug use or drinking response is continued in order to forestall withdrawal. Aversion reduction is itself a reinforcement of drug and alcohol use and thus becomes a secondary maintaining mechanism for excessive consumption (Smith, 1982). One major advantage of learning theory is that it can be integrated with the many other theories that posit a drive that can be reduced by substance ingestion.

Since Bandura, social scientists have given careful consideration to the conceptualization of substance abuse. In a more pointed opposition to the medical and moral models, an emergent model based on empirical research has been developed. After an extensive review of research into addictions, Pattison and his colleagues (1977) proposed 11 emergent concepts that offer a broad perspective from which to approach the treatment of alcohol and drug problems (see Chapter 3). This model respects psychosocial factors and implies the need for change in the individual and his or her relations with the environment. The model goes beyond an exclusively medical approach and encompasses a broad range of human experiences.

The emergent social-learning model has stimulated new investigations and interpretations in the addictive behaviors. This reality is seen most clearly in the *Diagnostic and Statistical Manual of Mental Disorders* (American Psychiatric Association, 1980), which classifies substance abuse problems only in terms of consumption patterns,

symptoms of intoxication, withdrawal symptoms, and related adverse personal and social consequences. In this same vein W. R.
Miller (1985) and Marlatt (1985) have concluded that excessive substance use is the result of a combination of factors, including cognitive, emotional, situational, social, and physiological variables. This
outlook typifies the emergent model, and it is representative of
broad thinking in the addiction field. This approach is proactive,
since it allows us to pinpoint the cues and high-risk situations that
may lead to a slip or relapse in our clients. In this regard relapse
prevention is possible, and relapse is not inevitable. Substance-
abusing clients are given skills training and other interventions (to
be discussed later in this chapter) that allow them to function normally and without risk in an environment that is ordinarily very
hostile to the recovering substance abuser. Treatments based on
social-learning theory are manageable and flexible. They respond to
the needs of clients and allow for a life-style of moderation, which,
in all respects, improves the client's quality of life.

The three models of addiction relate to relapse in the following
ways: The moral model does not and cannot consider relapse in an
objective way. In this framework a "relapse" would simply be seen
as a willful return to a hedonic life-style. The medical model's disease conception considers relapse to be an all-or-nothing endeavor
in which any use of a substance following abstinence is thought
to be a relapse. Additionally, relapse is viewed as a major symptom
of the "disease of chemical dependency," and clients are typically
urged to exert their will to prevent a relapse. The social-learning
perspective, however, looks at a return to substance use as a learning experience that can be successfully used to bolster gains previously made in treatment. Furthermore, social-learning theorists
think that relapse is a response to environmental cues that constantly impinge on clients. In this regard relapse determinants and
high-risk situations can be picked up early on, and clients can be
treated and given relapse-prevention strategies that can effectively
decrease the probability of an initial use of a substance (slip) and a
consequent full-blown relapse.

# Determinants of Relapse

Now that we have a guide to frame our thinking about relapse, we
can look specifically at the factors that initiate it. Understanding the
determinants of relapse—those telltale signs—will enable the
counselor to prevent the disastrous return to substance abuse that
many clients experience.

## High-Risk Situations

It is important to consider first the precipitants to a slip; that is, what are the conditions or situations that initially lead an abstinent or controlled substance user back to substance abuse and all the associated problems? We must start by considering the notion of perceived self-control, or self-efficacy, that clients possess while they are successfully adhering to a prescribed treatment regime. During these times clients feel strongly that they can control themselves and their environment, and they develop a strong sense of self-efficacy. This powerful feeling of mastery tends to maintain itself nicely while the client is in the hospital and for some period after discharge. Unfortunately, these feelings of mastery and self-control quickly give way to feelings of insecurity, anxiety, and doubt when the client is confronted by a high-risk situation (Marlatt & Gordon, 1985).

High-risk situations are, very generally, incidents, occurrences, or situations that threaten clients' sense of self-control (for example, walking into a room where all their old drinking buddies are drinking) and increase the probability of their return to substance use. Cummings, Gordon, and Marlatt (1980) have analyzed the precipitants to relapse in a large number of substance abusers and have found that in this group negative emotional states accounted for 35% of all relapses, interpersonal conflicts accounted for 16%, and social pressure accounted for 20%. Negative emotional states are feelings like anger, anxiety, frustration, depression, and boredom. Interpersonal conflicts are those arguments or confrontations that occur between clients and their family, friends, lover, or coworkers. Social pressure involves situations in which clients respond to environmental or peer pressure to drink or use drugs. These categories, then, represent high-risk situations that can result in a return to uncontrolled substance use.

Consider the client who comes to the counselor's office saying that he has been feeling depressed and hopeless recently. His wife accuses him of self-pity, and they wind up having a fight. After the fight the client goes for a walk in his old neighborhood, and he happens to run into some of his old friends, who are drinking. Given his depression, his fight with his spouse, and the fact that he has met some drinking friends, he abandons abstinence in favor of consumption, since he has no coping skills to effectively diffuse his negative feelings or to resist the advances of his friends. In Marlatt and Gordon's cognitive-behavioral model this client would, when he realized that he had no coping response, begin to feel less self-control and more anxiety. These feelings would yield positive thoughts about what drinking would do for him, and he would take his first drink. Following this ingestion the client would experience the abstinence

violation effect, and the guilt, shame, embarrassment, and dissonance that he felt would lead to further drinking (to relieve the psychological discomfort he felt) and, inevitably, to a full-blown relapse.

Had this client been given coping-skills training in treatment, he
could have used these skills in the high-risk situation and effectively
short-circuited his initial use of the substance. Utilization of a coping response would have resulted in increased self-efficacy, positive
reinforcement, and a strong sense of self-control. These positive feelings, of course, greatly reduce the likelihood of an initial use of the
substance and a consequent relapse. This scenario is clearly illustrated in Figure 6.1.

## Covert Antecedents of a Relapse

Before we look more closely at what leads up to successful resolution of high-risk situations, let us examine the critical antecedents of
a high-risk situation. These covert antecedents of a relapse are conceptualized by Marlatt and Gordon (1985) as shown in Figure 6.2.

Covert antecedents are basically life-style imbalances that yield
a chain of events inevitably leading to cognitive distortions and
eventual arrival at a high-risk situation. In this veiw the life-style
imbalances occur when people's balance between external demands
(their "shoulds") and pleasure and self-fulfillment (their "wants") is

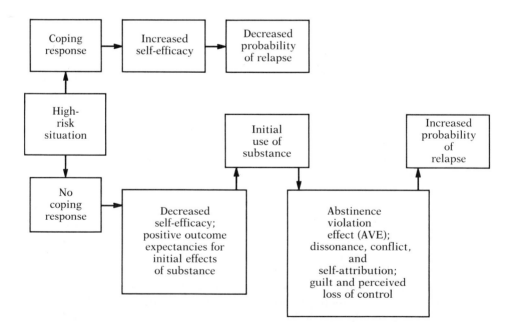

**Figure 6.1**  A cognitive-behavioral model of the relapse process

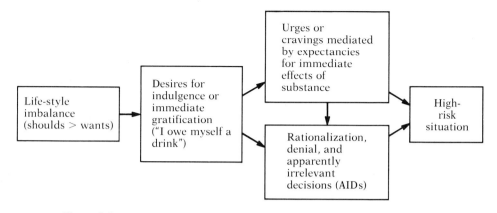

**Figure 6.2**  Covert antecedents of a relapse situation

inordinately weighted to the side of the shoulds. When this happens, clients begin to feel imposed on and deprived and are very likely to begin believing that they deserve indulgence and gratification. People who feel "put upon" all day may very well believe that they deserve to fully indulge themselves at night by getting intoxicated. According to the Marlatt and Gordon model these people would, following the desire for indulgence and gratification, begin to have increasingly strong urges and cravings for their preferred substance. As these cravings and urges develop, they will grow stronger because the client will begin to think very positively about the immediate effects of the substance ("I'll feel so relaxed; it'll taste so good"). As the urges and cravings grow and the desire for indulgence increases, clients will begin to rationalize ("I owe myself . . .") and begin to deny any possible negative outcomes that could be associated with reinitiation of substance use.

As their cognitive processes change, clients move ever closer to the high-risk situation, and as this movement occurs, they begin to make apparently irrelevant decisions (AIDs). These AIDs are thought to be a product of rationalization ("What I'm doing is OK") and denial ("This behavior is acceptable and has no relationship to relapse") that manifest themselves as certain choices that lead inevitably to a relapse. In this respect the AIDs are best conceptualized as "minidecisions" that are made over time and that, when combined, lead the client closer and closer to the brink of the triggering high-risk situation (Marlatt & Gordon, 1985). Examples of these AIDs include the refusal by a recovering alcohol abuser to empty her liquor cabinet because her problem should not adversely affect other people's ability to drink in her house. Another example might be the smoker who refuses to tell his office mates that he has quit smoking because "it's nobody's business but my own." This person may neglect advertising the situation so that he can more easily approach a co-worker for a cigarette ("Oh, I've run out"). As the AIDs are developed, the substance abuser moves closer and closer to a possible high-risk situation. This situation, of course, if not averted by a coping response, can, and quite often does, lead to a slip, an abstinence violation effect, and then a full-blown relapse.

Given this situation, then, the relapse process to this point could be depicted as shown in Figure 6.3.

# ▋ Relapse Prevention

Marlatt and Gordon's conceptualization of the relapse process enables us to prescribe certain treatments at all stages of this model to prevent relapses. This activity is most critical in maintaining our clients' successful treatment outcomes. Relapse prevention is not a matter of will or teeth-gritting determinism. Rather, it is a broad-spectrum treatment approach that provides a method of assessment, specific intervention procedures to limit or avoid slips and relapses, and global intervention procedures for self-control strategies to avoid the life-style imbalance that ultimately leads to a high-risk situation and possible return to uncontrolled substance use.

Frequently counselors ask, Why bother with relapse prevention? Traditional wisdom suggests that merely mentioning a relapse might trigger this unfortunate situation to occur. Surely, however, it makes better sense to learn precise prevention skills and related cognitive strategies to cope with the omnipresent danger of relapse than to simply sit idly by waiting for it to happen (Marlatt & Gordon, 1985).

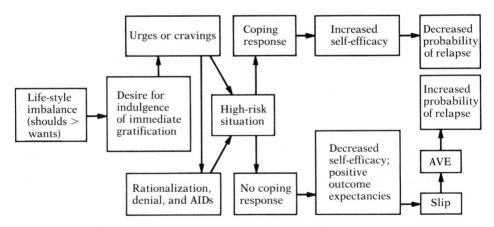

**Figure 6.3**  The relapse process from life-style imbalance to abstinence violation effect

In this view relapse-prevention strategies should become part and parcel of the complete treatment regime.

Although overall treatments will vary, all clients should receive comprehensive relapse-prevention treatment. This type of training will typically weave through the entire treatment period, but the specific concept of relapse and the training central to this issue should be introduced just beyond the midpoint of treatment and continue until termination. Further, relapse-prevention strategies should be bolstered after termination at brief (half-hour) booster sessions 1, 3, 6, 9, 12, 15, 18, and 24 months after formal treatment ends. In addition to the booster sessions, clients should be advised that they can come in or call at any time. This open-door policy plus booster sessions will consolidate treatment gains, provide a sense of continuity, and greatly decrease the probablity of a relapse. Typically, clients are discharged and not seen again! This posture results in an extinction of learning that occurred in treatment and often leads to a return to uncontrolled substance use.

Relapse-prevention strategies do not work if clients are told that they have no control over their lives. They are not, in this perspective, seen as "victims of disease" but, rather, as objective participants in a process designed to understand why they do what they do. This participant-observer model is critical if we are to restore a sense of control and ability to our clients, and it is this self-efficacy that will enable substance abusers to operate on their environment as opposed to having the environment operate on them. As you develop this sense of self-mastery in your clients, move slowly. Do not overwhelm the clients, but allow them to pick and choose acceptable techniques and strategies in a fashion that enhances their self-efficacy and allows them to feel good about the process.

## Specific Intervention Strategies

Marlatt and Gordon (1985) have provided, in their relapse-prevention model, a scheme of specific intervention strategies to be used after a client is exposed to a high-risk situation (see Figure 6.4). This typology gives the counselor highly specific treatment interventions that can be used to effectively stop the relapse process before it advances to actual substance abuse. Even if clients progress all the way to the abstinence violation effect, it is thought, they can still prevent the relapse from occurring. Each of these techniques should become part of the treatment protocol for all clients, and the training should occur in the order that they are presented in Figure 6.4. Booster sessions and treatment for relapse prevention will focus on mastery of these techniques as well as mastery of the global intervention techniques to be discussed in the next section.

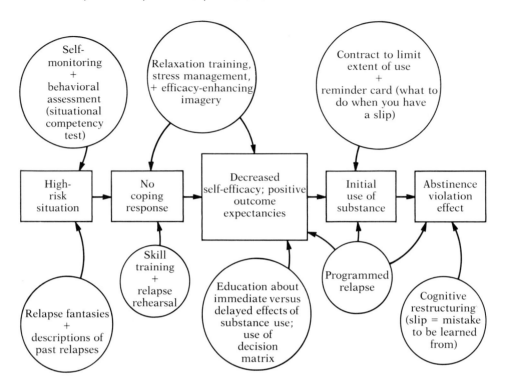

**Figure 6.4**   Relapse prevention: specific intervention strategies

Of primary importance in this model is the high-risk situation. Once clients are in a high-risk situation where they have no adaptive coping response, they are almost destined to engage in substance use. Thus it is extremely important that clients be able to identify high-risk situations, since this awareness will enable them to quickly and effectively realize what is going on and what they can do about it.

**Self-monitoring**   The first tool in training clients to recognize high-risk situations is called self-monitoring. It can be used with either currently using or abstinent clients. Current users will self-monitor when, where, and why they use drugs or alcohol, and abstinent clients will self-monitor when, where, and why they wanted to use drugs or alcohol. Self-monitoring is a simple tool that requires clients to keep a complete record of their substance use or their urges to use substances. As can be seen in Exhibits 6.1 and 6.2, the self-monitoring sheets will also show what feelings the clients were having and what coping skills they used to avoid substance use or limit the amount consumed.

Self-monitoring in this fashion serves as both an assessment procedure and an intervention strategy. The counselor gathers a great

# ▮ Exhibit 6.1

## Self-Monitoring Sheet for Substance Use

| Time of drug or alcohol ingestion | Feeling when you began to drink or use drugs* | Coping skill used to avoid continued use | Location |
|---|---|---|---|
| | | | |
| | | | |
| | | | |
| | | | |

*Feeling code:
1. Happy
2. Relaxed
3. Angry
4. Bored
5. Sick
6. Tense/nervous
7. Confused
8. Depressed
9. Tired/sleepy
10. Sad
11. Other

# ▮ Exhibit 6.2

## Self-Monitoring Sheet for Urges to Use Substances

| Time of thought about drinking or drug use | Feeling when you noticed thought* | Coping skill used to avoid drug use | Location |
|---|---|---|---|
| | | | |
| | | | |
| | | | |
| | | | |

*Feeling code:
1. Happy
2. Relaxed
3. Angry
4. Bored
5. Sick
6. Tense/nervous
7. Confused
8. Depressed
9. Tired/sleepy
10. Sad
11. Other

deal of information about cues to substance use and existent coping skills, and clients develop a much more acute awareness of their urge and use pattern as they continue to self-monitor. Awareness of critical points where a choice is made whether to use and utilization of alternative responses are thought to be two powerful and significant components of the substance abuse clients' coping repertoire (Marlatt & Gordon, 1985). Addictive behaviors such as drug and alcohol abuse tend to take on a life of their own after many years and to look like automatic responses. Self-monitoring forces clients to be consciously aware of their actions, and this awareness is very effective in dehabitualizing the substance use response (Marlatt & Gordon, 1985). As clients become more aware, they tend to use less and to report fewer pleasurable feelings from the drugs or alcohol.

**Direct observation methods**   Another set of techniques that helps identify high-risk situations is known as direct observation methods. Clients are presented with a comprehensive list of situations and asked to rate them for degree of temptation and the level of confidence they would have in their capacity to avoid a relapse (Marlatt & Gordon, 1985). Similarly, the Situational Confidence Questionnaire (Annis, 1982) can be used to elucidate exactly what clients would do in a high-risk situation. In this test clients imagine themselves in each of 100 situations and report on a scale how confident they are that they would be able to resist drinking ("What would you do if you found yourself at a wedding reception where everyone was drinking?"). This technique allows counselors to determine their clients' coping-skill level and to increase their awareness of high-risk situations. Other exercises involve the client's recounting of past relapse episodes and analysis of relapse fantasies. Past episodes provide a way for both client and counselor to see more clearly what led up to these relapses, what high-risk situations were involved, and how these unfortunate experiences could have been avoided. Relapse fantasies, too, will tell a great deal about the expectancies involved in a relapse and will give clear indications of what situations are seen as high-risk.

Once the counselor and client (remember, it's a collaborative effort) have determined the high-risk situations, the client can be taught to respond to these situations in an adaptive and forthright manner. Some situations will be simply avoided, some will require escape, and others will require the use of coping skills to successfully negotiate the difficult situation without relapsing.

**Coping skills**   Coping skills are thought by Marlatt and Gordon to be the single most important tool that substance abuse clients must have to avoid a relapse. Remember, the relapse-prevention model is not a strategy of will. It is, rather, a strategy of preparedness that is based on the client's ability to cope with high-risk situations. Relaxation training, assertion, and proper communication are coping skills. The therapist needs to fully assess clients to determine which skills they possess, which skills need to be bolstered, and which skills they need to learn.

Stress-management techniques, too, are coping skills. These include cognitive and behavioral components that can be taught, such as the following: (1) taking one thing at a time; (2) working tension off physically; (3) learning not to be a perfectionist; (4) humor; (5) seeking outside help when needed; (6) allowing time alone; (7) hobbies and activities not involving substance use; (8) moderation, as opposed to rigidity, in thought and action; (9) sleeping and eating correctly; and (10) balancing the costs and benefits of life.

Another tool is an efficacy-enhancing imagery technique. Here, counselors have clients fully relax and then present them with images of possible relapse situations. Instead of relapsing, clients imagine that they have a great degree of control and can manage the difficult situation effectively. This tool is very similar to relapse rehearsal, in which clients imagine a relapse situation in which they successfully use a coping skill and therefore avoid using drugs or alcohol.

**Decision matrix**    Coping skills tend to be quite effective, when learned correctly, in avoiding further progression of the relapse process. If, however, clients do not at first succeed with coping skills and proceed to the next step in the relapse process, experiencing decreased self-efficacy and positive outcome expectancies, they can use their coping skills or a decision matrix. This matrix is a form on which clients list immediate and delayed positive and negative consequences for both continuation and discontinuation of abstinence. Clients should be trained in the use of this matrix before treatment ends and should be advised to create (on paper) a new matrix every time they are considering a resumption of substance use. An example of a completed matrix for an alcohol abuser is given in Exhibit 6.3.

**Behavioral contracting**    The matrix in combination with factual education about immediate and delayed effects of substances should provide clients with a great deal of staying power to avoid initial use of the substance. If, however, clients are simply swept away by the idea of using and do indeed try the substance, some training should have been done in treatment on avoiding continued use. First of all, the client and counselor should have developed a behavioral contract (signed, sealed, and delivered) that will limit the extent of substance use following a slip. The contract should be simple, nonjudgmental, and nonpunitive. It is, of course, not a legal document, but contracts like this can have a powerful effect on client behavior.

# ■ Exhibit 6.3

## Decision Matrix for Resumption of Alcohol Use

|  | Immediate consequences | | Delayed consequences | |
|  | Positive | Negative | Positive | Negative |
|---|---|---|---|---|
| Alcohol abstinence | Improved self-efficacy, confidence, and esteem; family approval; better health; financial gains; continued success | Frustration; denial of pleasure; anger at myself for not doing what I want | Enhanced ability to control my life; more money; more respect; greater popularity | Denial of immediate and seemingly easy gratification |
| Alcohol use | Immediate reduction of anxiety; revenge against my wife; better feeling about work; immediate gratification | Feeling that I've lost control; anger at family and boss; financial loss; weakness | Being in a fog, so I won't have to deal with reality | Continued deterioration; loss of my family; loss of my job; poor health; loss of my friends; greater self-hatred |

Clients tend to take them seriously and become invested in their ability to keep the contract. An example is given in Exhibit 6.4.

**Reminder cards**    Additionally, all clients should be given a small wallet card that has tips and suggestions on what to do should a slip occur. This card should outline coping skills, thoughts to be engaged in, and numbers to call. It should be simple and straightforward. An example of a reminder card is given in Exhibit 6.5.

**Programmed relapse**    Another technique for limiting the negative consequences of a slip is known as programmed relapse. This is a complex procedure known as paradoxical intention, in which the client is required to consume the first drink, smoke the first cigarette, or use some other substance under the direct supervision of the counselor. The goal of this technique is to enable an objective experience of returning to substance use under the guidance of the therapist. Try scheduling the "relapse" at a time and place you designate (programmed). This precludes the otherwise dangerous possibility that the client will relapse under highly stressful conditions (Marlatt & Gordon, 1985). This is an exceptionally advanced technique, and counselors should not consider using it until they have received comprehensive training in this area and have received permission from their supervisor and agency director. It is a method of last-ditch proportions, and counselors should rely on other techniques before using this one.

# ▌ Exhibit 6.4

## Client's Contract to Limit Substance Use after a Slip

---

**Behavioral Contract**

I, John Smith, agree that I do not want to engage in substance use. If, for whatever reason, I slip and return to using (*preferred substance*), I am aware that I have not failed my treatment, myself, or my counselor. I am also aware that this slip is only temporary and that I have the skills to control it. I agree to use no more than <u>(fill this in after consulting with client)</u>, and I will not use for more than ___ day(s).

I recognize that a slip is only that. It is not a disaster, and I can use it to learn more about myself. To facilitate this process I agree to call my counselor at 555-5555 as soon as I discontinue the slip.

| | |
|---|---|
| _____ | _____ |
| Signature | Counselor |

---

# ▌ Exhibit 6.5

## Reminder Card for Client in Case of a Slip

---

**What to Do If You Slip**

1. Remember that you are in control.
2. You have not failed but are responding to a series of environmental cues.
3. Relax and do efficacy-enhancing imagery.
4. Consider the long-term consequences of continued use.
5. Call _____ at 555-5555.
6. Contact (*friend/spouse*).

---

**Cognitive restructuring**    Finally, if clients advance through the relapse process and are experiencing the abstinence violation effect, they will have one final technique left to them. The cognitive restructuring that will have been done while clients were still in treatment enables them to "rethink" what is happening to them. They are trained to use different thought processes, so that a slip becomes a mistake that they can learn from. Additionally, they are imbued with the notion that the slip is a product of the situation and not a reflection on the self ("I am not a bad person!"). This procedure requires some effort and is often referred to as positive mental attitude training. Clients are taught to be objective, rational, and fair. They are taught to reframe the situation while recognizing that not all is lost. If this technique does not halt the process, clients may go on to relapse. If counselors have done their job, they are not to blame; if, however, they have incompletely treated their clients, then they have failed.

A relapse in this situation is not hopeless. Clients will still be able to utilize all that they have learned and may, at some point in the future, end the relapse.

## Global Intervention Strategies

Global self-control strategies can be used to bolster the relapse-prevention effort. These skills and techniques will, in some cases, allow clients to completely avoid high-risk situations precipitated by imbalanced life-styles. These global procedures, too, should be used throughout counseling and will also be specifically targeted for the relapse-prevention phase of treatment. Marlatt and Gordon (1985) have succinctly and effectively demonstrated this part of the model (see Figure 6.5).

**Life-style imbalance**   The relapse process begins with a life-style imbalance. This imbalance manifests itself as too much stress or as negatives in a client's life. Global self-control strategies are intended to increase the client's overall capacity to deal with stress and to cope with high-risk situations with an increased sense of self-efficacy; to train the client to identify and respond to situational and covert early warning signals; and to help the client exercise self-control strategies to reduce the risk level of any situation that might otherwise trigger a slip (Marlatt & Gordon, 1985).

The initial goal is to avoid the onset of an imbalanced life-style. In this regard it is critical that clients effectively balance their shoulds and wants. This effort involves balancing work and recreation, good times and bad, happiness and sadness, and pain and pleasure. Such a balance can best be effected by alerting clients to the fact that they may become obsessive and overwhelmed, now that they are sober, with a million details that can present themselves in day-to-day life. These details can be managed, but not to the exclusion of "the good things" in life. Clients should be encouraged to have leisure activities, nonstressful hobbies, and plenty of time for themselves. Additionally, positive addictions such as jogging, meditation, and knitting are therapeutic and effective stress-reduction

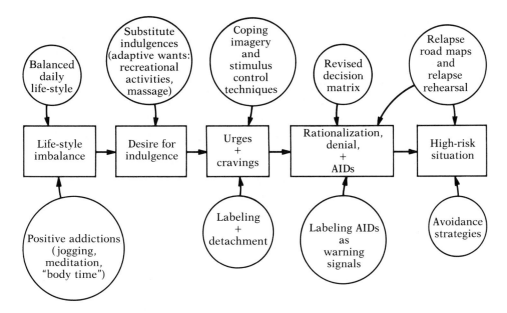

**Figure 6.5**   Relapse prevention: global self-control strategies

techniques. These activities, when combined with a healthy style of living (sleeping and eating correctly), greatly enhance a balanced life-style. They are easy to do, inexpensive, and always available. Booster sessions and follow-up should always assess these activities, and, if necessary, corrective action should be taken to maintain a balanced life-style.

**Desire for indulgence**   The next step in the relapse process centers on a desire for indulgence that stems from the frustrating experience of a life-style imbalance. If a desire to indulge manifests itself, clients must have substitute indulgences that they can engage in. These should be adaptive (good for the person) as opposed to maladaptive (bad for the person—for example, a return to substance use), and they should be developed creatively and broadly with the client's best interests in mind. In this respect adaptive substitute indulgences could include buying a long-wanted item, going shopping, or even helping someone else (L. P. Dana, personal communication, April 1986). Additionally, substitute indulgences could include such things as buying or cooking a gourmet meal, going boating, vacationing, seeing a movie, or taking a bath. Other simple ideas would include getting a massage, reading, going to bed early, making love, or walking on a beach. The list is endless, and substitute indulgences can be developed easily for each individual client. These activities should be determined individually, and they should be very reinforcing. Remember, substance use is, in and of itself, exceptionally rewarding, so the substitute indulgence ideally has a reinforcement potential equal to or greater than use of the preferred substance.

**Urges and cravings**   Further along in this model we see the introduction of urges and cravings, which are a direct result of the desire for indulgence. These urges and cravings are compensatory conditioned responses that develop from an anticipation of the effects of substance use. They result from external cues (seeing a syringe, passing a favorite bar, smelling cigarette smoke) and are therefore very common experiences following discontinuance of drug or alcohol use. Given this reality, it is critical that clients be taught about cuing responses and that they learn that exposure to cues can and does lead to a sense of deprivation and a desire to use. To cope with this situation, the client should be taught to use coping imagery ("Imagine yourself in X situation; now, when you feel the desire to use, make the decision to flee, relax . . ."). Basically, the counselor must give clients a number of scenes in which they successfully cope with an intense desire to use drugs and alcohol. Additionally, stimulus-control techniques (removal of as many tempting stimuli as possible from clients' everyday living environment) will effectively limit the amount of cuing that goes on, and the frequency of urges and cravings will be greatly diminished. Stimulus-control techniques are particularly useful during the early stages of recovery, since nonexposure simply results in less temptation.

**Labeling and detachment**   One of the most effective tools clients can use to survive urges and cravings is labeling and detachment. In this method clients are taught to be critical observers of their bodily responses, and they become exceptionally sensitive to environmental influences on their behavior. Use of this technique would allow a client to say: "I'm experiencing a conditioned response that manifests itself as craving. This response stems directly from my walking by Fifth Street, where I used to do all my drinking. This feeling is temporary, and it will pass. If I respond to it, I will strengthen it and consequently be forced to experience this feeling more and more frequently. If I experience the feeling and do not give in to it, it will pass, and eventually the frequency of these feelings will decrease greatly." In this example the client assumes a sense of control and objectivity. She has a heightened awareness of what is happening and is consequently less anxious and less likely to succumb to the urge.

**Rationalization, denial, and AIDs**   If the techniques used to this point fail and clients begin to engage in rationalization, denial, and apparently irrelevant decisions, they will be able to call on the training previously received that shows rationalization and denial to be precursors of a high-risk situation. In this regard a decision matrix could be formulated that would show the positive aspects of a behavior change away from returning to substance use. Additionally, AIDs should be considered in treatment, and clients can be sensitized to these most ominous actions. Given this sensitization, they can relabel AIDs as warning signs and effectively abort the relapse process.

If the process continues on to introduction of a high-risk situation, the client should be able to fall back on relapse rehearsals (see the previous section) or engage in an avoidance strategy such as calling the counselor, fleeing from the situation, calling a friend, and the like (see Figure 6.5).

The relapse-prevention model in its entirety is shown in Figure 6.6.

# ▎Summary

Relapse prevention is an important part of a comprehensive treatment program. The relapse-prevention model covered in this chapter requires coping skills that enable all recovering clients to handle the high-risk situations they encounter. If they can cope, they do. If they cannot cope, the likelihood of relapse is great. It is the therapist's responsibility to educate clients about relapse and to give them a wide-ranging treatment that is focused on relapse prevention. Every skill that enables the client to resist relapse is a coping skill. It is no small task to help clients develop the skills they need, but it is easily accomplished. Take a head-on perspective to this problem and it begins to be resolved—neglect it and it grows larger.

The new cognitive-behavioral model we have examined in this chapter hinges on the development and maintenance of coping skills in the substance-abusing client. These skills, learned in counseling, are applicable to the broad range of unique experiences that each client encounters. We discussed models of addiction (moral, medical, and social), determinants of relapse, covert antecedents of relapse, relapse prevention, specific intervention strategies for relapse prevention, and global intervention strategies for relapse prevention. Relapse prevention should be ongoing throughout the counseling process. It is important that the counselor be sensitive to individual differences and create relapse-prevention strategies that closely match the needs and experiences of individual clients.

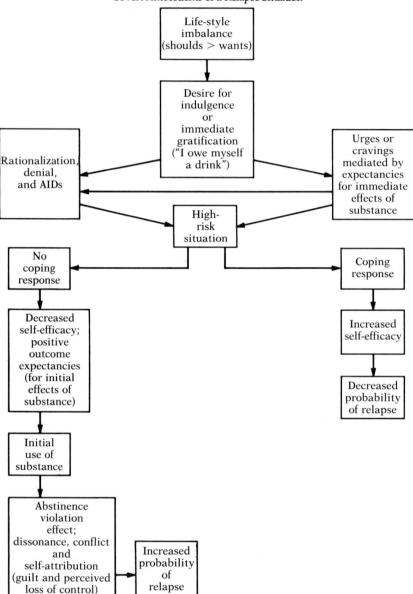

Covert Antecedents of a Relapse Situation

A Cognitive-Behavioral Model of the Relapse Process

**Figure 6.6**    The relapse-prevention model: a comprehensive view

Relapse Prevention: Global Self-Control Strategies

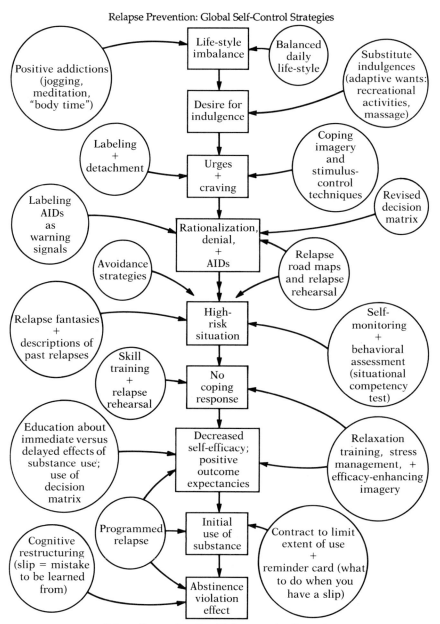

Relapse Prevention: Specific Intervention Strategies

# ■ References

Alcoholics Anonymous World Services. (1953). *Twelve steps and twelve traditions.* New York: Author.

American Psychiatric Association. (1980). *Diagnostic and statistical manual of mental disorders* (3rd ed.). Washington, DC: Author.

Annis, H. M. (1982). *Situational Confidence Questionnaire.* Toronto: Addiction Foundation of Ontario.

Bandura, A. (1969). *Principles of behavior modification.* New York: Holt, Rinehart & Winston.

Blum, K. (1982). Neurophysiological effects of alcohol. In E. M. Pattison & E. Kaufman (Eds.), *Encyclopedic handbook of alcoholism.* New York: Gardner Press.

Cole, J. A., & Ryback, R. S. (1976). Pharmacological therapy. In R. Tarter & A. A. Sugerman (Eds.), *Alcoholism: Interdisciplinary approaches to an enduring problem.* Reading, MA: Addison-Wesley.

Conger, J. (1956). Reinforcement theory and the dynamics of alcoholism. *Quarterly Journal of Studies on Alcohol, 17,* 296–305.

Cummings, C., Gordon, J. R., & Marlatt, G. A. (1980). Relapse: Prevention and prediction. In W. R. Miller (Ed.), *The addictive behaviors.* New York: Pergamon Press.

Dollard, J., & Miller, N. (1950). *Personality and psychotherapy.* New York: McGraw-Hill.

Finlay, D. (1974). *Constructive coercion and the problem drinking employee: Prospects and problems.* Vancouver: Alcoholism Foundation of British Columbia.

Guydish, J. (1982). Substance abuse and alphabet soup. *Personnel and Guidance Journal, 7,* 392–401.

Jellinek, E. M. (1960). *The disease concept of alcoholism.* New Brunswick, NJ: Millhouse Press.

Marlatt, G. A. (1985). Relapse prevention: Theoretical rationale and overview of the model. In G. A. Marlatt & J. R. Gordon (Eds.), *Relapse prevention.* New York: Guilford Press.

Marlatt, G. A., & Gordon, J. R. (Eds.). (1985). *Relapse prevention.* New York: Guilford Press.

McEvoy, J. P. (1982). The chronic neuropsychiatric disorders associated with alcoholism. In E. M. Pattison & E. Kaufman (Eds.), *Encyclopedic handbook of alcoholism.* New York: Gardner Press.

Miller, P. M. (1976). A comprehensive behavioral approach to the treatment of alcoholism. In R. Tarter & A. A. Sugerman (Eds.), *Alcoholism: Interdisciplinary approaches to an enduring problem.* Reading, MA: Addison-Wesley.

Miller, W. R. (1982). Treating problem drinkers: What works. *The Behavior Therapist, 5,* 15–19.

Miller, W. R. (1985). Controlled drinking: A history and critical review. In W. R. Miller (Ed.), *Alcoholism: Theory, research, and treatment.* Lexington, MA: Ginn Press.

Murray, R. M., & Stabenau, J. R. (1982). Genetic factors in alcoholism pre-disposition. In E. M. Pattison & E. Kaufman (Eds.), *Encyclopedic handbook of alcoholism*. New York: Gardner Press.

Pattison, E. M., Sobell, M. B., & Sobell, L. C. (1977). *Emerging concepts of alcohol dependence*. New York: Springer.

Polich, J. M., Armor, D. M., & Braiker, H. B. (1981). *The course of alcoholism: Four years after treatment*. New York: Wiley.

Pomerleau, O. F. (1982). Current behavioral therapies in the treatment of alcoholism. In E. M. Pattison & E. Kaufman (Eds.), *Encyclopedic handbook of alcoholism*. New York: Gardner Press.

Smith, J. W. (1982). Treatment of alcoholism in aversion conditioning hospitals. In E. M. Pattison & E. Kaufman (Eds.), *Encyclopedic handbook of alcoholism*. New York: Gardner Press.

Stokes, P. E. (1982). Endocrine disturbances associated with alcohol and alcoholism. In E. M. Pattison & E. Kaufman (Eds.), *Encyclopedic handbook of alcoholism*. New York: Gardner Press.

Szasz, T. (1972). Bad habits are not diseases. *Lancet, 7766*, 83–84.

Tarter, R. E., & Schneider, D. U. (1976). Models and theories of alcoholism. In R. E. Tarter & A. A. Sugerman (Eds.), *Alcoholism: Interdisciplinary approaches to an enduring problem*. Reading, MA: Addison-Wesley.

Tewari, S., & Carson, V. G. (1982). Biochemistry of alcohol and alcohol metabolism. In E. M. Pattison & E. Kaufman (Eds.), *Encyclopedic handbook of alcoholism*. New York: Gardner Press.

Vaillant, G. E. (1983). *The natural history of alcoholism: Causes, patterns, and paths to recovery*. Cambridge, MA: Harvard University Press.

# Preventing Substance Abuse

A man out walking in the woods one day came upon a tragic scene in a beautiful but turbulent river. Several people were struggling against the raging waters, and others had already drowned. Our friend immediately jumped into the river to help as many as he could to reach shore safely.

A second person came upon the scene. He saw that despite the first man's best efforts, many people were not being helped. He thought to himself that there must be a better way, and he proceeded upriver. At a clearing where the river was calmer, the second man noticed that although many people were in the water, few were in grave trouble. Our second man waded into the river and began to pull some of the people to shore and warn others of the impending dangers downriver.

A third person came upon the river and noted the actions of the first two men. While many people were being helped, many others were still being caught by the current and drowned. The third man went still farther upstream, to an area where people were entering the river — some by accident and others by choice. The third man erected fences and other barriers to keep people from accidentally falling into the waters, posted warnings of the dangers downstream, and taught people to swim so that they would not drown.

This rescue tale represents the field of substance abuse counseling today. Our first man might be called treatment, the second, intervention, and the third, prevention. Although alcoholism education was first mandated by Vermont in 1882, substance abuse prevention is, in many ways, "the new kid on the block."

Traditionally, community responses to perceived substance abuse problems have focused on treatment or on legal approaches. Neither of these alternatives has been demonstrated to be particularly effective in reducing what is perceived by many to be an epidemic growth in substance abuse problems. Thus, since the mid-1970s there has been a growing interest in the development of prevention strategies (DuPont, 1979). This chapter reviews some of the issues in substance abuse prevention in the expectation that identifying those problems will help us develop more effective prevention programs.

# ▌ The Concept of Prevention

Prevention refers to activities that reduce or stabilize the incidence (occurrence of new cases) of substance abuse and thereby reduce or stabilize its prevalence (the total number of cases). As we will see, the development, implementation, and evaluation of substance abuse prevention programs has not been an easy process (Blane & Chafetz, 1979; Miller & Nirenberg, 1984).

## Practical Difficulties

Preventing substance abuse involves two key difficulties. The first problem is that we have little valid and reliable data on the prevalence and incidence of substance abuse in society, for many reasons, including disagreements over how we should define and measure the existence of the problem. Furthermore, we have even less information on the endemic level (the attainable minimum) or the susceptibility level (the possible maximum) of users. Thus, we are uncertain how widespread substance abuse is and the extent to which we could reduce or prevent it.

The second difficulty with prevention lies in identifying and carrying out programs and activities that will work. We must (1) understand the causal factors in the development of substance abuse; (2) design programs and activities that will modify these risk factors; (3) obtain the resources necessary to implement our programs; and (4) demonstrate the effectiveness of programs. At present, etiological research and theory have articulated an impressive array of possible risk factors for substance abuse (Jones & Battjes, 1985), and program designers have been equally energetic in developing activities to modify those risk factors (Glynn, Leukefeld, & Ludford,

1983). However, obtaining the resources (including financial and social support) for substance abuse prevention has been difficult, and frequently those programs that are implemented seem unable to demonstrate the desired effects.

## Community Responses to Substance Abuse

Bourne (1974) has argued that community responses to substance abuse can be viewed as evolving through the four stages depicted in Figure 7.1. The first stage is one of denial. That is, community leaders and members typically find it difficult to accept the idea that substance abuse is a problem in their community. Thus, the community may actively or passively resist the development of prevention and treatment programs on the basis that there is no need for them.

The second stage is typified by panic. This stage is generally initiated in response to a crisis of some sort (the drug-related death of a local athlete) but may be stimulated through a needs assessment survey or similar demonstration of the extent of substance abuse. The panic stage is transitory and involves rather vociferous demands that "something must be done immediately."

The third, or fragmentation, stage, according to Bourne (1974), involves the development of diverse proposals and counterproposals for how to respond to this crisis. Typically, one or more actions will be accepted and endorsed as "the solution." Such solutions often take the form of developing treatment alternatives for "those people" or increasing law enforcement to reduce the availability of drugs as well as the motivation to use drugs. The key characteristic of the fragmentation stage is that the community response is based on considerations of cost, political clout, ease of implementation, and similar factors. What is missing is a comprehensive, integrated approach to the prevention of substance use, misuse, and abuse.

Deviating somewhat from Bourne's model, it should be noted that if the actions taken during the fragmentation stage are even partially "successful" (that is, the panic subsides, and there is a general community consensus that the problem is being corrected), the community may regress to the denial stage or stagnate in the fragmentation stage. Successive "crises" or other information that substance

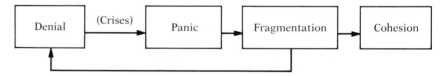

**Figure 7.1**   Community reactions to substance abuse

abuse is continuing or increasing can result in increased commitment to the already existing programs and activities. After all, those existing programs and activities worked before, and therefore if we renew our commitment and increase our resources, they will work again.

Bourne (1974) indicates that relatively few communities have progressed beyond the fragmentation stage. This assessment is probably as valid today as it was in 1974. That is, when existing programs no longer seem to be working, the typical community response is to divert increased resources into the existing substance abuse service providers and, maybe, to add an additional program or two to satisfy perceived needs.

Eventually, several factors can combine to move a community from a fragmentary to a cohesive response to substance abuse. These factors include the ever-increasing costs of supporting the existing and often competing programs, the persistence of substance abuse, and increasing community awareness of the inadequacies inherent in the ad hoc system that has been developed. The cohesive stage of a community's response to substance abuse is typified by a comprehensive planning process based on a thorough needs assessment to determine what services are needed and what are already available. The community can then begin to develop new or expanded programs to meet unmet needs as well as coordinate existing programs.

The importance of this discussion of community responses to substance abuse is that prevention programs have generally been one of the last components considered. Thus, substance abuse prevention can be said to be in its infancy. It has not had the opportunity to develop the social support necessary for its growth and so has not been able to demonstrate its effectiveness.

# General Models of Prevention

The National Institute on Drug Abuse (NIDA) and the National Institute on Alcohol Abuse and Alcoholism (NIAAA) have adopted somewhat different conceptual schemes to organize prevention activities and programs. The NIDA uses a drug abuse program continuum, as depicted in Figure 7.2. It should be noted that the NIDA model seems based on the assumption that substance abuse is primarily an individual problem resulting from inadequate information, education, alternatives, and intervention programs. Information programs imply that accurate, honest, and timely information will allow people to make responsible decisions, to adopt socially approved behavior; that is, not to use drugs. Education pro-

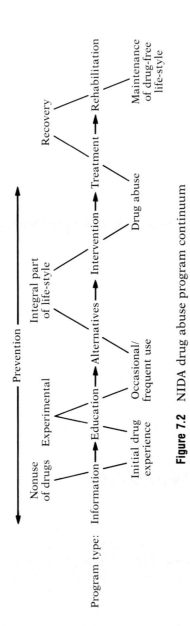

**Figure 7.2** NIDA drug abuse program continuum

grams assist people in developing or enhancing crucial life skills (such as decision making, stress reduction, and communication) that help satisfy basic personal and social needs so that drugs aren't desirable. An alternatives program tries to counter substance abuse by providing alternatives that are enjoyable, rewarding, and acceptable to the target population. Intervention programs preclude substance abuse by "giving assistance and support to people during critical periods in their lives" (French & Kaufman, 1981, p. 5). Treatment is designed to prevent drug abuse morbidity and mortality, by helping abusers change their behavior. Finally, rehabilitation is aimed at relapse prevention, through long-term activities that support the maintenance of a drug-free life-style.

In contrast the NIAAA has adopted a public health approach to prevention planning. This utilizes two dimensions, level of activities and target of activities, as depicted in Table 7.1. The levels of prevention activities are defined as follows (Davis, 1976): primary prevention refers to activities designed to minimize the development of new cases; secondary activities are those that focus on early identification and intervention; and tertiary activities focus on treatment and rehabilitation of substance abusers. The target of prevention activities, when applied to substance abuse, would include the drug or drugs being used (the *agent*), the user (*host*), and those aspects of the physical and social *environment* that facilitate or impede substance abuse.

Two features of these general models of prevention deserve some discussion. First, note that the NIDA continuum model and the NIAAA public health model are compatible with each other. The NIDA's model can be seen as a partial explication of row 2 (*host*) of the NIAAA's model. Thus, following Swisher (1979), information, education, and alternatives would constitute primary prevention activities targeted at the user (*host*); intervention programs would fall within the secondary prevention area; and treatment, rehabilitation, and relapse prevention programs would be within the purview of tertiary prevention.

**Table 7.1**   NIAAA public health model of prevention activities

| Target of Activities | Level of Activities | | |
|---|---|---|---|
| | Primary | Secondary | Tertiary |
| Agent | | | |
| Host | | | |
| Environment | | | |

The second feature of particular note is that treatment programs constitute only a partial response to substance abuse problems (NIAAA, 1982a). The NIDA's continuum model clearly indicates that treatment and rehabilitation programs are focused on late stage or chronic abusers of drugs. Similarly, in the NIAAA public health approach, treatment programs would at best satisfy only the third column (tertiary prevention) of the model. Thus, both models indicate that treatment is an incomplete response to substance abuse problems and, as such, imply that treatment per se is unlikely to greatly reduce the prevalence of substance abuse in a community. Likewise, both models imply the need to develop and implement comprehensive prevention systems. These systems would utilize multiple programs designed to meet the needs of diverse populations of potential and actual substance users and abusers.

The public health model utilized by the NIAAA is conceptually the broader of the two, in the sense that it can incorporate both modalities and programs identified in the NIDA's continuum model and activities not so easily visualized through it. For example, legal or law enforcement approaches to preventing substance abuse are compatible with the public health model insofar as they affect the availability of the agent or alter the environment within which abuse takes place. Thus, the NIAAA approach provides a broad, general model for conceptualizing the development of substance abuse prevention activities.

As might be expected, the NIAAA public health approach has been both lauded and criticized. Beauchamp (1980), for example, advocates this perspective to drug abuse as preferable to a disease conception. Blane (1976), on the other hand, has criticized the public health model on the basis of (1) dissimilarities between substance abuse and the infectious diseases that were the basis for the model, and (2) conventional usage that tends to ignore important distinctions in primary–secondary–tertiary activities as well as agent–host–environment relationships.

A third general framework for organizing prevention efforts is found in the work of Koch and Grupp (1971). These authors utilize an economic model of supply and demand. Any activity or program that reduces the supply, or availability, of substances in society or reduces the demand for drugs is preventive. The primary means of reducing the supply of drugs are inhibition of the importation, production, and distribution processes. Reduction in supply is a principal focus of law enforcement and taxation regulations. Reducing the demand for drugs might include some combination of the following strategies: (1) treatment of existing abusers; (2) early identification and intervention with users; (3) coercion or the threat of punishment for use; (4) information on the personal and social risks of drug use; (5) restrictions on advertising of drugs and the presumed benefits of use; (6) provision of acceptable alternatives to substance use; (7) training in the appropriate use of drugs; and (8) social changes designed to enhance the quality of life for at-risk populations. This supply and demand model also indicates the need to approach substance abuse problems from a broader perspective than treatment or law enforcement.

# Determining the Purpose of Prevention

One of the continuing problems in the area of substance abuse prevention is disagreement over what we wish to prevent. There are three separate but related foci for prevention. First, the purpose of prevention can be defined as achieving abstinence. However, abstinence as used in the substance abuse prevention literature has several meanings. Abstinence can be used to refer to a general prohibition against the use of any drug by any individual. A review of the history of substance use across time and cultures suggests that general prohibition may be unattainable and that we should seek other prevention goals. A second meaning of abstinence focuses on either prohibition of selected drugs or on prohibition for particular groups within society (for example, minors). Such specific forms of abstinence should rest on pharmacological and etiological research that demonstrates that either controlled use of a drug cannot and does not occur or that certain identifiable groups cannot safely use drugs. Such research on the inevitable addiction to any particular drug does not exist. In fact, epidemiological research suggests that non-problematic use of most drugs can and does occur. However, there may be justifiable grounds for encouraging abstinence as a form of prevention among some groups (for example, pregnant women).

Instead of abstinence, a program may have as its goal preventing the abuse of a substance (Brotman & Suffet, 1975). Abuse of a substance generally refers to the pattern of use in terms of quantity, frequency, or duration. Although such an approach is conceptually consistent with the general models used by the NIDA and the NIAAA (as is abstinence) and is probably a more realistic goal than abstinence in a drug-using society, the controlled-use approach to prevention is inconsistent with legal codes and popular conceptions regarding the dangers of drug use. Furthermore, in order to differentiate substance use from substance abuse, we need either a pharmacological or a statistical definition of what is a permissible pattern of use (Hartford, Parker, & Light, 1980). Lacking such standards, the controlled-use approach to prevention is forced to rely on before-and-after data that would demonstrate an improvement by reducing the quantity, frequency, or duration of use. Generally speaking, only with regard to the "social drugs"—that is, alcohol, caffeine, and nicotine—and prescription drugs has there been much support for controlled-use prevention programs.

The third and final goal of prevention efforts can be on reducing the undesirable consequences of substance use or abuse (Mills & McCarty, 1979). Such programs shift our focus from the drug per se to a consideration of the interaction between a substance, the user, and the environment. They tend to focus on critical circumstances and inappropriate situations. Thus, a number of proscriptions and prescriptions have developed regarding the use of substances when operating an airplane, a public transportation conveyance, or one's personal automobile. These prevention programs or activities do not focus so much on abstinence or on controlled use as they do on the consequences of substance use in critical or inappropriate situations.

Given that prevention programs can focus on any of these three goals, we may ask why so many programs seem to seek abstinence in preference to either controlled use or reducing the consequences of using substances. There are several reasons. First, there is a historical tradition that emphasizes nonuse of drugs. Second, there is a simplified logic that specifies that if people do not use drugs, they cannot abuse them. Third, a mystique and mythology regarding the evils of drugs have developed. Finally, the emphasis on abstinence is easier to carry out than trying to define acceptable levels of controlled use.

There are, however, some very serious drawbacks to emphasizing abstinence as a prevention goal: First, many abused drugs also have legitimate and widely accepted therapeutic uses in medicine. Thus, there is a potential conflict and difficult distinction to be made between the use of a substance under the direction of a physician and the use of the same substance without the approval of an authority. Second, abstinence denies the historical fact that virtually every known culture permits, if not actually encourages, the use of one or more psychoactive drugs for social and recreational purposes. By what criteria are we to distinguish between caffeine and other stimulants, tobacco and marijuana, or alcohol and other depressants? Third, and related to the second, the bulk of pharmacological, etiological, and epidemiological research provides little support for the so-called "logic of abstinence" or for much of the mystique and mythology that have been created around substance use and abuse. Fourth, abstinence as a prevention goal may be inconsistent with developmental processes emphasizing decision making, clarification of values, independence, and responsible behavior. Finally, the emphasis on abstinence is one reason so many prevention programs have been seemingly ineffective, since any use of a substance following completion of the program or activity would be construed as a negative outcome (Bacon, 1978). Thus, a new generation of prevention programs focusing on controlled use or reducing the adverse consequences of substance abuse may show greater promise of being successful than the abstinence-oriented programs (Segal, Palsgrove, Sevy, & Collins, 1983).

# Developing a Causal Model

Having determined what the purpose, or goal, of a substance abuse prevention program is, we need to determine how to achieve that goal. Achieving a change in the prevalence of substance abuse, or the consequences of abusing drugs, depends on the development of a causal model. Such a model specifies the presumed antecedents of substance abuse, so that we can identify those factors that are subject to change and thereby reduce the occurrence of abuse.

Robinson (1982), in discussing the prevention of alcoholism, notes that most prevention proposals proceed from one of three causal assumptions: the problem is alcohol, the problem is alcoholics, or the problem is society. Such parochialism is unsupported by research and deters the development of effective prevention strategies. Progress in developing effective prevention programs depends on recognizing the diversity of etiological factors involved and utilizing a coordinated approach to prevention. An adequate causal model of substance abuse, as Lettieri, Sayers, and Pearson (1980) suggest, is one that includes, at a minimum, an explanation for each of the following phenomena:

- initiation of drug-using behavior
- maintenance of drug use
- transition from use to abuse
- termination of use and abuse of drugs
- relapse

In addition, the causal model should also account for biological, psychological, and sociocultural influences on each of the foregoing processes or stages. Failure to fully articulate the presumed causal model can result in both overestimating the importance of the factors selected for inclusion and underestimating compensatory processes among correlated factors not included in the model. Both of these errors imply that even when we are successful in modifying our selected antecedents of substance abuse, the impact of the prevention program or activity can be insignificant or nonexistent.

For example, concern over drinking and driving generally focuses on either restricting drinking or identifying and punishing drivers who have been drinking. Restrictions on drinking are generally attempted by way of public education campaigns regarding the risks of drinking and driving or, more recently, by way of dramshop laws, training of those who serve alcohol, and encouraging hosts to be responsible. Identifying and punishing drunken drivers is a law enforcement concern. Although these approaches are needed, they are incomplete. Both approaches ignore the acute and chronic effects of alcohol on subjective perceptions and the lack of intent by many individuals to overuse alcohol and then drive. We need to develop activities that will deter driving by intoxicated individuals, such as devices to keep the people from entering or starting their automobile and the provision of alternative transportation. Only by focusing on both the factors that result in drinking and the factors that contribute to driving after drinking can we begin to develop successful programs to prevent driving while intoxicated.

Likewise, analyses of adolescent substance abuse suggest that a broad array of factors contributes to the initiation of illegal drug use. A partial listing of these factors, as suggested in Kandel (1978), would include:

- legal drug use (beer, wine, liquor, and tobacco)
- personal adjustment problems, including rebelliousness, stress on independence, low sense of psychological well-being, and low self-esteem
- poor school performance and lower academic aspirations and motivation
- delinquency and deviant activities
- attitudes favorable to the use of drugs
- peer drug-related attitudes and drug-use behavior
- parental distance, attitudes, and behaviors
- social settings favoring drug use

The preceding list clearly indicates that preventing the initiation of adolescent substance abuse is a complex problem requiring a comprehensive approach. Such an approach would involve multiple strategies (information, life skills, alternatives, and social policy) targeted at multiple systems (youth, families, schools, and community). Moreover, the earlier the age of initiation of substance use, the greater likelihood of subsequent substance abuse problems (Kandel, 1978). Therefore, prevention-oriented programming should be initiated before adolescence.

As the preceding examples illustrate, developing substance abuse prevention programs requires a careful analysis of the factors that contribute to the use and abuse of drugs. Only through etiological research that identifies and explicates the relationships among causal factors can we hope to successfully reduce the incidence of substance abuse.

# Producing Change

Having identified a number of presumed causal factors that contribute to the occurrence of substance abuse problems, we will encounter several issues in actually changing the prevalence of those problems. These issues include (1) obtaining sufficient resources to initiate and maintain the change process; (2) anticipating counterprevention programs and activities; (3) allowing enough time for the prevention activities to work; (4) providing programs of sufficient intensity; (5) ensuring that the proposed changes do not create new problems; (6) targeting populations; and (7) demonstrating the effectiveness of prevention programs.

## Obtaining Resources

Obtaining sufficient resources to begin and maintain prevention programs continues to be a major obstacle. Although it is difficult, if not impossible, to determine the total amount of private and public funds committed to prevention, the National Association of State Alcohol and Drug Abuse Directors reported that prevention program funding would account for approximately 11.5% of the total state funds for alcohol and drug abuse programs in 1984–1985 (Butynski, Record, & Yates, 1984). This may represent an increase over previous funding levels, but it remains clear that federal and state commitment to substance abuse prevention is lacking (Nathan, 1983).

The absence of federal and state resources can be largely attributed to both the lack of any social policy calling for prevention and the entrenched treatment orientation to substance abuse. Swisher (1979), among others, has indicated that substance abuse prevention overlaps in several respects with an array of other social and personal problems, such as mental health, education, law enforcement, and health care. Thus there is competition among community agencies for funds, clients, and other resources. Although coordination and integration of these diverse agencies are desirable, as Sanford (1972) notes, it is unclear to what extent these agencies can fulfill diverse objectives (for example, reducing both teenage drinking and pregnancies) without extensive training and education in the substantive issues related to each type of problem. In the absence of a social policy committed to the prevention of substance abuse problems, it is unlikely that significant resources will be committed to prevention programs and activities.

A second obstacle to obtaining resources for prevention is the institutionalization and elaboration of a treatment system for substance abusers. Blane (1976) has noted that helping professionals are understandably more oriented toward services for afflicted individuals than toward preventive programs. It should be obvious that vested interests have developed around the concept of treatment. In recent years the treatment network has been elaborated in a number of directions, including earlier identification of, intervention with, and referral of suspected substance abusers; identification of special populations with special treatment needs (women, youth, the elderly); and increases in the number of agencies for indirectly afflicted individuals (spouses and children of substance abusers). The appropriateness of such elaboration is not at issue here. What is important is that prevention is a latecomer and is often opposed, overtly or covertly, because it is perceived as diverting funds from needed treatment resources.

## Resisting Counterprevention

Given the diversity of prevention models, purposes, and etiological factors, the absence of a clear social policy, and the vested interests of the treatment network, it should not be surprising that there is no consensus on how to prevent substance abuse. When prevention proposals, programs, and activities also infringe, or are perceived as infringing, on other established institutions such as the alcoholic beverage industry, pharmaceutical manufacturers, advertising, law enforcement, medicine, or education, there is little doubt that there will be controversy, debate, and resistance to the proposals (Grant & Ritson, 1983). The resulting disagreement over the means and ends of prevention can result in counterprevention (Low, 1979). For example, prevention and educational programs in the schools may encounter resistance from various community groups (including parents), who may oppose the program on a wide variety of grounds, such as that they are an inappropriate or nonessential part of the curriculum or that the focus should be on abstinence, not responsible use. Similarly, national, state, and local efforts may be disjointed in such a way as to create countervailing forces. Thus, one of the problems a prevention initiative should anticipate is the development of counteractivities by those agencies or organizations that do not concur with the program's purpose or techniques.

## Allowing Enough Time

A third issue to be considered in trying to prevent substance abuse is the amount of time required for the expected changes to accrue. Prevention programs or activities need to give careful attention to the period required to demonstrate expected changes. Unrealistic expectations by prevention planners in combination with demands from the community or funding sources can result in unrealistic promises of change within short periods. For example, a 5th-

through 8th-grade information program designed to reduce the prevalence of substance abuse among 9th- through 12th-graders may not show significant effects for at least four years (when the first group of 8th-graders become seniors) and may reasonably require seven years (when the first group of 5th-graders finally become seniors). Such a delay in demonstrated effectiveness is generally (1) not recognized by program planners; (2) not acceptable to community groups who want something done now; or (3) inconsistent with funding agencies, which make periodic (usually annual) assessments of effectiveness a prerequisite for continued funding. Thus, the proposed program may not be implemented or, if implemented, is likely to be terminated or substantially modified before a true assessment of its impact can be obtained.

Low (1979) suggests that it may take considerably longer than ten years to demonstrate the effectiveness of a well-planned, systematic prevention program. This is particularly true if we add time for planning, designing, pilot testing, and implementation to the amount of time required for the program to demonstrate its impact. Within the general area of health promotion and risk reduction, there are numerous examples of this kind of delay. Antismoking programs (initiated about 1964) and seat-belt-usage campaigns (initiated around 1972) are two examples in considering the length of time necessary to substantially alter social behavior. It is rare to find an agency with this kind of long-range perspective on substance abuse prevention.

## Ensuring Intensity

In addition to allowing enough time for prevention to work, we must recognize the importance of providing programs of sufficient intensity to make changes occur. The intensity of a program is particularly important when we examine school programs, but it should also be considered when designing other prevention activities.

Most educational facilities appear to assume that knowledge and skill in a particular area accrue slowly, sequentially, and with practice. Thus, we teach spelling, writing, reading, mathematics, history, athletics, music, and the like, beginning in grammar school and extending into college. Even such activities as learning to drive an automobile or how to handle a gun involve intensive learning processes. Substance abuse education, on the other hand, often seems to assume that a single film or guest speaker, or maybe a four-week series of activities, is sufficient to prevent the use, misuse, or abuse of drugs.

Substance abuse in contemporary society is a multifaceted issue crosscut by multiple perspectives drawn from moral, legal, medical, psychological, and sociological considerations. For prevention activities to have an impact, they must be of sufficient intensity and duration to provide appropriate opportunities for acquisition, retention, and practice or recall.

## Maintaining Positive Balance

A program has a positive balance when the positive effects outweigh the negative effects (Low, 1979). In designing, implementing, and evaluating substance abuse prevention programs and activities, we must give careful attention to both their intended and their unintended effects at both the personal and social levels of analysis.

The importance of positive balance can be observed in several areas. First, as Low notes, the benefits of substance use are primarily personal and subjective, whereas the problems associated with such behavior are more likely to be interpersonal and objective. Thus, there is a distinct tendency to underestimate the benefits of substance use and to emphasize the problems associated with using drugs. Second, there is a clear tendency to overgeneralize research based on clinical populations and to assume that other users of drugs have (or will have) the same kinds of problems (health, occupational, legal, familial, or other) found among those already in treatment. Third, it seems that many, if not most, substance abuse professionals persistently view substance use as the cause of other problems when it is entirely possible that the substance use is the result of some other problem. Finally, it should be noted that agency definitions of behaviors as either desirable or undesirable are often constructed on the basis of implicit normative standards. These standards, in turn, are based on judgments of what should be, what is conventional, and what is politically acceptable rather than empirical assessments of the etiology and epidemiology of substance abuse.

An example of the importance of positive balance is found in the law-enforcement approach to the control of substance abuse (Pekkanen, 1980). The underlying logic of this approach seems to be that (1) by reducing the availability or supply of drugs (through legal restrictions on the importation, manufacture, distribution, and sale of drugs) and (2) by reducing the demand for drugs (through imprisoning or deterring users and dealers) we can reduce the prevalence of substance use and abuse. Furthermore, it is often argued that reductions in prevalence of substance use will result in a reduction in drug-related crime. Finally, a corollary of this approach contends that if legal restrictions are initially ineffective, we need to strengthen the penalties for noncompliance.

Advocates of the law-enforcement approach use arrest, prosecution, and prison statistics and data from programs designed to divert substance abusers into treatment to support assertions that this approach can be effective in containing drug abuse. These possible benefits of drug laws and enforcement must be balanced against the costs of this approach, such as the following:

> *financial costs*, such as the $2.55 billion spent by the U.S. government on law enforcement in fiscal 1985 (Drug Abuse Policy Office, 1984)
>
> *criminal justice problems*, including the number of personnel diverted from other law enforcement areas; difficulty in enforcing a "victimless" crime; possible corruption of officers, prosecutors, and judges; and hostility and alientation of community members who oppose this approach
>
> *stigmatization* of individuals arrested under these laws
>
> *increased health risks* for users from the poor quality control of "street" drugs and from the spread of disease and septic problems in the use of drugs (for example, acquired immune deficiency syndrome)
>
> *increased criminal activity* in the form of both a black market to supply the drugs and the need to acquire the money to purchase drugs
>
> *perpetuation of myths* about drugs and drug use because of the difficulties in studying an illegal activity

Clearly, the concept of positive balance calls into question the efficacy of drug laws and their enforcement in preventing substance abuse.

## Targeting Populations

A sixth issue in prevention is the selection of target populations. Three sets of variables are relevant in deciding which groups will be the target of a prevention program or activity: general versus specific, direct versus indirect, and delayed versus immediate.

A general prevention program is one that is applicable to a wide array of individuals regardless of their degree of involvement in substance use and abuse. Specific prevention programs, on the other hand, focus on certain groups, with the specificity defined in terms of a presumed or empirically validated common characteristic. For example, drug information programs are usually general, since they try to enhance knowledge of how drugs affect behavior. However, specific information programs have been developed that target the drug use and abuse problems among, for example, Black Americans, Native Americans, older Americans, and Hispanic Americans (NIAAA, 1982b).

The second variable in selecting a target population focuses on whether the prevention activities will be direct or indirect. Direct prevention activities are specific to substance abuse, whereas indirect activities focus on more general issues that are correlated in some way with substance abuse. Health promotion activities can be viewed as indirect substance abuse prevention, since they may not only affect the use and abuse of drugs but also have an impact on a variety of other behaviors (nutrition, exercise, and stress control). Substance abuse education, in contrast, would presumably focus on changing some combination of affective, behavioral, and cognitive factors related to the use and abuse of drugs and would involve nutrition, exercise, and stress control only to the extent that they are correlates in the use and abuse of drugs.

Finally, in targeting a prevention program, it is well to keep in mind the distinction between delayed and immediate variables. For example, since both parent and peer behaviors have been found to correlate with adolescent substance abuse (Kandel, 1978), prevention programs or activities must focus on both variables. However, the development of functional families, appropriate parenting skills, and satisfactory parent–child relationships precedes and contributes to peer relationships. Thus, prevention programs targeting parents would have delayed effects, and peer-oriented programs would have more immediate effects on the use and abuse of substances.

A consideration of the preceding three categories (general versus specific, direct versus indirect, and delayed versus immediate) indicates that there are at least eight types of prevention programs, as represented in Table 7.2. Selection of a particular type or combination of types requires a determination of the characteristics of the population or group to be targeted by the prevention program. Thus, once a target population for substance abuse prevention has been provisionally selected, a needs assessment should be conducted.

## Evaluating Programs

Well-designed studies to assess the effectiveness of substance abuse prevention programs are essential (Schaps, DiBartolo, Palley, & Churgin, 1978). There are extensive reviews of both general issues

**Table 7.2**   Types of prevention programs

|  | Direct | | Indirect | |
|  | Delayed | Immediate | Delayed | Immediate |
|---|---|---|---|---|
| General |  |  |  |  |
| Specific |  |  |  |  |

related to evaluation (Rossi & Freeman, 1985) and specific concerns related to the evaluation of substance abuse prevention programs and activities (French, Fisher, & Costa, 1983; French & Kaufman, 1981). We will not examine them here, but there are several issues that do deserve special mention: (1) evaluation as a social judgment process; (2) the relationship between what is desired, what is intended, and what is accomplished; (3) the contrast between immediate and delayed effects; (4) the strength of the effects; and (5) the concept of declining marginal utility.

Evaluation research ultimately involves a social judgment regarding the utility or acceptability of a program or activity. Although the data used to support an evaluation are essentially neutral, decisions regarding what data to collect, how to collect them, and what their results mean involve a variety of implicit and explicit judgments. Thus, there may be considerable disagreement among the evaluation research team, the program developers and managers, and the community over the relative success or failure of a prevention program or activity.

For example, a drug education program may be designed to enhance students' knowledge of the benefits and risks of various substances in the expectation that such information will reduce the use and abuse of drugs. Evaluation research may show that although there appears to have been an increase in knowledge about drugs, the research design was inadequate to show that this change in knowledge was a direct result of the program. It may further indicate little or no impact on drug-using behavior. Thus, the results are inconclusive. The community, observing little change in adolescent behavior, may conclude that the program does not work.

One major source of disagreement regarding the effectiveness of substance abuse prevention programs derives from the distinction among desired, intended, and achieved effects. The desired effects of a program represent what is hoped for by various community groups. Desired effects are often implicitly rather than explicitly stated and are often phrased in the language of morals (for example, teenagers should not drink alcoholic beverages). The intended effects of a prevention activity represent the explicit purpose and objectives of the program, such as a reduction in the adolescent mortality rate related to drunken driving. The achieved effects of a prevention program represent both the intended and the unintended changes that are correlated with its implementation; for example, increased understanding of the risks associated with driving under the influence results in increased utilization of designated drivers. Since the desired, intended, and achieved effects of a program or activity can be at variance from one another, it may be unclear from the evaluation research whether the prevention program was successful. As indicated in the foregoing example, the prevention program may accomplish the intended objective in an unintended way without fulfilling community expectations.

The third evaluation issue concerns the distinction between immediate and delayed effects. For several reasons, the immediate effects of a program or activity may be both quantitatively and qualitatively different than the delayed effects (Bell & Battjes, 1985). For example, the effectiveness of an education program intended to reduce fetal and neonatal consequences of substance use and abuse among females but targeted at prepubescents can vary considerably over time. There may be immediate and significant cognitive, affective, and behavioral changes in the intended directions that gradually erode over time, so that statistical differences between the control and experimental groups are insignificant at pubescence. Likewise, the prepubescent changes in knowledge, values, and behaviors may not be transformed into expected behaviors during the childbearing years. Thus, the results of evaluation research may reveal different effects depending on how much time has elapsed between the program and the research.

A fourth issue related to the evaluation of prevention programs and activities concerns the relationship between statistical significance, the strength of an effect, and the size of the sample. Statistical significance is less likely to occur when either the effects of a prevention program are small or the number of units of analysis is small. Since the unit of analysis for many prevention programs is often small (that is, one class, 30 students), the magnitude of the effect must be large in order to achieve statistical significance. However, the same program could very well achieve statistical significance if more individuals, classes, schools, or communities were involved. Thus, in considering the apparent effectiveness of a substance abuse prevention program, we must consider both the strength of the effects and the size of the sample.

The fifth issue to be discussed in the context of evaluation concerns the concept of declining marginal utility. According to this concept, the less the discrepancy between an actual (empirically verified) event and the maximum (or minimum) occurrence of the event, the more difficult it will be to change the event. That is, if the prevalence of substance abuse in a community is much higher than the endemic rate (the minimally attainable rate), then it is relatively easy to reduce the prevalence. As the prevalence decreases, however, it becomes increasingly difficult to further reduce the prevalence rate, and further reductions will require increased resource allocations, more efficient programs, or more effective programs. Figure 7.3 depicts the concept of declining marginal utility as applied to prevention programs.

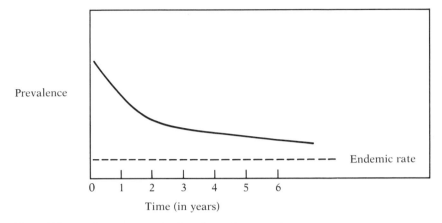

**Figure 7.3**   Declining marginal utility of prevention programs

One year after implementing a prevention program, the prevalence rate may be 70% of what it was before the program. After two years, however, the prevalence is still 50% of its initial value. At the end of the third year the prevalence is 40% of the baseline, and with each succeeding year the prevention program has less impact than it did the previous year.

Clearly, the context of a prevention program is important in determining the apparent effectiveness of the program. A program or activity implemented in a community with a very high prevalence rate can have considerable impact, and the same program in a community with a low prevalence rate may produce little or no discernible change (Bacon, 1978). Likewise, a program that is initially successful in reducing the prevalence of substance abuse in a community can, over time, seemingly become ineffective. Thus, if a program appears to be either effective or ineffective, we must be careful to specify the context in which it was implemented and recognize that it might have very different rules in a different context.

A final caveat regarding the evaluation of substance abuse prevention activities and programs is in order. Prevention professionals have seemingly accepted and endorsed the concept of rigorous evaluation much more readily than their treatment-oriented brethren. Thus, as a rule, the literature on the evaluation of prevention programs more frequently addresses issues of research design than does the literature on treatment. Consider, for example, the basic importance of having both an experimental and a control group in assessing the effectiveness of a program. Whereas control groups are seemingly routinely employed in prevention evaluation research, treatment programs only rarely utilize any form of control group. Hence, although both the effectiveness and scientific rigor of prevention programs have justifiably been questioned, those same criticisms and concerns are applicable to the vast body of "knowledge" regarding treatment.

# Developing Effective Prevention Programs

At the outset of this chapter, we suggested that by reviewing some of the problems and issues encountered in developing substance abuse prevention programs, we might learn to develop more effective prevention programs. Before concluding the chapter, we will identify some of the characteristics of effective prevention programs.

> 1. Prevention activities should be based on a thorough planning process that is empirically validated.

This characteristic has two implications. First, program planners must thoroughly review existing etiological and epidemiological research on substance abuse to determine the antecedents, correlates, and consequences of abuse. In addition, planners should be cognizant of processes of individual and social change. The second implication of an empirically validated planning process is that a needs assessment regarding prevailing local conditions should be conducted (NIDA, 1981). The assessment should minimally focus on two levels, characteristics of the presumed target population and the existing health and human services delivery network.

Too often, prevention programs have been developed with little or no reference to accumulated information from the social, behavioral, educational, or health sciences. For example, Goodstadt's (1978) review of education programs indicated that the implicit model in use during the late 1960s and most of the 1970s was that a change in information would lead to a change in attitudes, which would, in turn, result in a change in drug use behavior. Both theoretically and empirically, however, changes in information do not necessarily result in changes in attitudes, and attitude changes do not necessarily result in behavioral changes. Moreover, the changes in attitudes or behavior that do occur may not be those that were expected or desired (that is, a reduction in drug use behavior).

Similarly, local needs assessments are often forgone on the assumption that national, state, or other data apply to the local community. Such an assumption can result in either an overestimation or an underestimation of the prevalence of substance use and abuse. Overestimation of the initial prevalence can lead to a faulty attribution of success for a prevention program, and underestimation may lead to an equally misleading attribution of failure. Thus, there is no substitute for a local needs assessment as a baseline against which to assess the success or failure of a prevention program.

> 2. Prevention programs must be comprehensive enough to reach their intended targets.

Several issues must be addressed in designing a prevention activity that will match the needs of the intended target population and produce the intended changes. First, several strategies may be necessary—for example, affective, behavioral, and cognitive approaches; creating of alternatives; and changes in social policy. Second, there are several different systems involved—for example, youth, parents or families, schools, community organizations, and the media. Third, there will probably be several levels of needs, such as nonusers, experimental or occasional users, regular users, and the abusers. Fourth, the basic program may require adaptation to meet diverse ethnic and cultural backgrounds as well as age and developmental stages. Finally, promotion of both general health and materials specific to substance abuse should probably be included in the program. It should be noted that although schools provide a convenient arena for prevention programs, parent, peer, and community programs (Manatt, 1979, 1983; NIAAA, 1983) can have considerable impact on drug use behavior. Moreover, the support of these other activities is often essential to the success of the school programs.

> 3. Prevention activities must be intensive enough to promote changes.

This characteristic particularly addresses two weaknesses of many existing prevention programs. First, the program should have enough elements and should devote enough time to each element to permit success. Second, the program must survive its initial "debugging" period and be designed to be sequentially cumulative. Thus, one-shot activities involving a guest speaker, a film, or an all-school assembly are unlikely to have a significant impact on the target population. Likewise, as discussed previously, it may take several years for a program to show the kind of impact it was intended to produce.

> 4. Prevention programs should be both internally and externally consistent.

As used here, internal consistency refers to the correspondence or congruence among the various components of a prevention activity. At a planning and design level, internal consistency means that the purpose, goals, objectives, and activities are congruent with one another. Likewise, the definition of substance use and abuse is consistent with the program components. External consistency, on the other hand, refers to the correspondence between a prevention program and family, school, and community life. That is, to be successful, prevention programs and activities must be cognizant of knowledge, attitudes, and behaviors and must begin with the target population's current status and then move toward whatever changes it hopes to achieve. Many prevention programs have had problems because they either created mixed messages through internal inconsistencies or tried to deliver a message that was at considerable variance from the target population's initial position regarding drug use behaviors, attitudes, and cognitions. For example, law-enforcement personnel often emphasize the illegality of alcohol or drug use as a major risk in such behavior. This emphasis can result in serious discussions related to changes in the law rather than changes in drug use. Likewise, the use of a recovering person as a guest speaker can result in the unintended message that "no matter how bad it gets, you can recover from this affliction."

5. Prevention activities must include thorough training for those who conduct them.

In order for a prevention program to have an impact, the characteristics of the providers are as important as the materials and the audience. Workers should be credible, well prepared, and comfortable with the materials they will be using. In addition, good communication skills, including group facilitation, are important in achieving audience acceptance. Generally, this means that providers must be carefully selected and trained. Otherwise, the prevention program may be rejected by the target population regardless of the effort expended in selecting and developing suitable materials and delivery strategies. Many films, for example, are designed to "trigger," or stimulate, discussions of substance abuse topics. Such films assume the presence of a knowledgeable facilitator to be effective. Likewise, some of the individuals used in mass media messages either have little audience acceptance or are rejected by the intended audience as a credible source of information.

6. Prevention programs should become community owned.

A prevention activity is more likely to be successful and is certainly more likely to survive as a continuing operation if the community assumes its ownership. Community ownership implies that the community (or at least a significant segment) supports the program or activity, participates, accepts responsibility for maintaining the program, and integrates prevention concepts and activities into ongoing social institutions (family, educational, religious, law enforcement, medical, occupational, and human services). Community ownership is facilitated through collaborative efforts with the community rather than by specialists or experts providing prevention programs for or to the community. In addition, community ownership is more likely if the program is designed from the outset to be flexible and adaptable to changing community needs. Planners, managers, and providers would do well to remember that community ownership must be fostered, created, and earned rather than confirmed or awarded on the basis of the program or activity's "obvious" ability to meet community needs.

> 7. Prevention activities must engage in continuous public evaluations.

As the "new kid on the block," prevention programs must engage in thorough and continuous evaluation efforts. Evaluation research is essential to assessing program and component processes, outcomes, impacts, efficiency, and unintended effects. Such assessments provide the information necessary for program improvement and, by making the results public, establish program accountability. Without continuous evaluation it is virtually impossible to determine whether the preceding six characteristics (planning, comprehensiveness, intensity, consistency, training, and community ownership) of substance abuse prevention programs are being achieved. Thus, evaluation is essential to the survival of prevention initiatives.

# ▌ Summary

Social response to substance abuse problems traditionally has focused on treatment or legal approaches. However, the high cost and questionable effectiveness of these approaches have stimulated a growing interest in prevention, which is now viewed as an essential component of the substance abuse services network.

A review of contemporary prevention programs indicates that a number of issues must be addressed if prevention initiatives are to be effective. These issues include the following:

1. disagreement over the definition and measurement of substance abuse problems
2. community and professional resistance to prevention programming

3. controversy over the goals of prevention programs
4. failure to develop adequate causal models of substance abuse
5. failure to utilize sociobehavioral research in designing programs to modify risk factors
6. lack of adequate resources to fully implement programs
7. inadequate time for expected changes to occur
8. insufficient intensity to establish and strengthen behavioral changes
9. failure to define the target population adequately and to match the prevention program to population characteristics
10. use of stringent evaluation models

Several steps can be taken to develop more effective prevention programs. The first step is to utilize empirically validated planning processes that combine information from social, behavioral, educational, and health research. The second and third steps are to ensure that the prevention program is comprehensive and intensive, so it can both reach the intended target population and promote changes in behavior. Fourth, the internal and external consistency of the program must be monitored, in order to avoid mixed messages and to provide a message that can be assimilated by the target population. Fifth, prevention providers must be carefully selected and trained, to achieve audience acceptance of them as credible sources of information. Sixth, in order to survive, prevention programs must be community owned; that is, they must become a part of the community. Finally, continual public evaluations of prevention programs are essential if we are to improve and adapt our programs to changing community needs.

While substance abuse prevention efforts have met with a number of problems, epidemiological studies indicate that most members of our society do not experience acute or chronic substance abuse problems. Informal prevention activities are already in place that can and do work. The challenge is to formalize and systematize these activities to increase their effectiveness. Each prevention effort has helped enhance our knowledge of what is needed and contributed to more successful prevention programming.

# ▌References

Bacon, S. D. (1978). On the prevention of alcohol problems and alcoholism. *Journal of Studies on Alcohol, 39*(7), 1125–1147.

Beauchamp, D. E. (1980). *Beyond alcoholism: Alcohol and public health policy.* Philadelphia: Temple University Press.

Bell, C. S., & Battjes, R. (Eds.). (1985). *Prevention research: Deterring drug abuse among children and adolescents.* Rockville, MD: National Institute on Drug Abuse.

Blane, H. T. (1976). Issues in preventing alcohol problems. *Preventive Medicine, 5,* 176–186.

Blane, H. T., & Chafetz, M. E. (Eds.). (1979). *Youth, alcohol, and social policy.* New York: Plenum Press.

Bourne, P. G. (1974). Approaches to drug abuse prevention and treatment in rural areas. *Journal of Psychedelic Drugs, 6*(2), 285–289.

Brotman, R., & Suffet, F. (1975). The concept of prevention and its limitations. *Annals of the American Academy of Political and Social Sciences, 417*(January), 53–65.

Butynski, W., Record, N., & Yates, J. (1984). *State resources services related to alcohol and drug abuse problems.* Washington, DC: National Association of State Alcohol and Drug Abuse Directors.

Davis, R. E. (1976). The primary prevention of alcohol problems. *Alcohol Health and Research World,* Spring, 10–12.

Drug Abuse Policy Office. (1984). *1984 national strategy for prevention of drug abuse and drug trafficking.* Washington, DC: U.S. Government Printing Office.

DuPont, R. L. (1979). The future of drug abuse prevention. In R. L. DuPont, A. Goldstein, & J. O'Donnell (Eds.), *Handbook on drug abuse.* Rockville, MD: National Institute on Drug Abuse.

French, J. F., Fisher, C. C., & Costa, S. J. (1983). *Working with evaluators— A guide for drug abuse prevention program managers.* Washington, DC: National Institute on Drug Abuse.

French, J. F., & Kaufman, N. J. (1981). *Handbook for prevention evaluation: Prevention evaluation guidelines.* Washington, DC: National Institute on Drug Abuse.

Glynn, T. J., Leukefeld, C. G., & Ludford, J. P. (Eds.). (1983). *Preventing adolescent drug abuse—Intervention strategies.* Rockville, MD: National Institute on Drug Abuse.

Goodstadt, M. D. (1978). Alcohol and drug education: Models and outcomes. *Health Education Monographs, 6,* 263–278.

Grant, M., & Ritson, B. (1983). *Alcohol: The prevention debate.* New York: St. Martin's Press.

Hartford, T. C., Parker, D. A, & Light, L. (1980). *Normative approaches to the prevention of alcohol abuse and alcoholism.* Rockville, MD: National Institute on Alcohol Abuse and Alcoholism.

Jones, C. L., & Battjes, R. J. (Eds.). (1985). *Etiology of drug abuse: Implications for prevention.* Rockville, MD: National Institute on Drug Abuse.

Kandel, D. B. (1978). Convergences in prospective longitudinal surveys of drug use in normal populations. In D. B. Kandel, (Ed.), *Longitudinal research on drug use.* New York: Wiley.

Koch, J. V., & Grupp, S. E. (1971). The economics of drug control policies. *International Journal of the Addictions, 6*(4), 571–584.

Lettieri, D. J., Sayers, M., & Pearson, H. W. (1980). *Theories on drug abuse.* Rockville, MD: National Institute on Drug Abuse.

Low, L. (1979). Prevention. In L. A. Phillips, S. R. Ramsey, L. Blumenthal, P. Cranshaw (Eds.), *Core knowledge in the drug field.* Ottawa, Can.: Non-Medical Use of Drugs Directorate, National Health and Welfare.

Manatt, M. (1979). *Parents, peers and pot*. Rockville, MD: National Institute on Drug Abuse.

Manatt, M. (1983). *Parents, peers and pot II*. Rockville, MD: National Institute on Drug Abuse.

Miller, P. M., & Nirenberg, T. D. (Eds.). (1984). *Prevention of alcohol abuse*. New York: Plenum Press.

Mills, K. C., & McCarty, D. (1979). Preventing alcohol problems: Counting, explaining, and program planning. Paper presented at the annual meeting of the American Public Health Association, New York.

Nathan, P. E. (1983). Failures in prevention: Why we can't prevent the devastating effect of alcoholism and drug abuse. *American Psychologist*, April, 459–467.

National Institute on Alcohol Abuse and Alcoholism. (1982a). *Prevention interventions, and treatment: Concerns and models*. Rockville, MD: Author.

National Institute on Alcohol Abuse and Alcoholism. (1982b). *Special population issues*. Rockville, MD: Author.

National Institute on Alcohol Abuse and Alcoholism. (1983). *Prevention plus: Involving schools, parents, and the community in alcohol and drug education*. Rockville, MD: Author.

National Institute on Drug Abuse. (1981). *Prevention planning workbook, vol. 1*, and *A needs assessment workbook for prevention planning, vol. 2*. Rockville, MD: Author.

Pekkanen, J. R. (1980). Drug law enforcement efforts. In *The facts about "drug abuse."* The Drug Abuse Council. New York: Free Press.

Robinson, D. (1982). Alcoholism: Perspectives on prevention strategies. In E. M. Pattison & E. Kaufman (Eds.), *Encyclopedic handbook of alcoholism*. New York: Gardner Press.

Rossi, P. H., & Freeman, H. E. (1985). *Evaluation—A systematic approach* (3rd ed.). Beverly Hills, CA: Russell Sage Foundation.

Sanford, N. (1972). Is the concept of prevention necessary or useful? In S. E. Golan & C. Eisdorfer (Eds.), *Handbook of community mental health*. New York: Appleton, Century, Crofts.

Schaps, E., DiBartolo, R., Palley, C. S., & Churgin, S. (1978). *Primary prevention evaluation research: A review of 127 program evaluations*. Prepared for the National Institute on Drug Abuse.

Segal, M., Palsgrove, G., Sevy, T. D., & Collins, T. E. (1983). The 1990 prevention objectives for alcohol and drug misuse: Progress report. *Public Health Reports*, 98(5), 426–435.

Swisher, J. D. (1979). Prevention issues. In R. L. DuPont, A. Goldstein, & J. O'Donnell (Eds.), *Handbook on drug abuse*. Rockville, MD: National Institute on Drug Abuse.

# Program Planning and Evaluation

Whether substance abuse programs are oriented toward treatment or prevention, their success depends as much on excellence in planning and management as it does on the quality of their service. Programs flourish when they can demonstrate their attainment of clear and carefully developed goals. They fail when their objectives are diffuse, their activities poorly organized, or their accomplishments unmeasured.

> While serving as a consultant . . . I observed that programs seldom fail because of clinical issues. Invariably, it seemed that failure resulted from insufficient administration, lack of political know-how, or a short supply of appreciation due to the absence of good evaluation. Whatever the causes, programs seemed most vulnerable in the non-clinical areas. And, again in my own experience, these problems usually relate to an inadequate design and implementation process [Wrich, 1984, p. 4].

Although Wrich's statement refers primarily to employee assistance programs, his generalization is equally applicable to substance abuse programs of other kinds. Counselors must involve themselves in program planning and evaluation if for no other reason than to safeguard the existence and growth of their clinically excellent programs. Effectiveness at all levels depends on careful attention to the planning process.

# Program Planning

> Good management is concerned with achieving results, not with doing tasks. It is therefore necessary to know what results are required before doing anything. The more precisely the results can be defined, the easier it is to plan, organize and control work and motivate people [Nickson, 1978, p. 177].

Nickson's notion that desired results should be seen in terms of outputs rather than inputs seems at first glance to be obvious. In fact, however, many counselors tend to focus more on the means they use than on the ends they reach, measuring their achievements by the number and type of activities performed instead of examining the ultimate effects of these activities. "A human service professional must ask not how many clients will be seen for how many hours (input), but what kind of impact he or she hopes to have on these clients' lives (output)" (Lewis & Lewis, 1983, p. 6). Substance abuse counselors, like other helping professionals, need to assess their work according to their success in meeting real client and community needs and in attaining objectives that can be measured in terms of client and community change. Effective programming depends on a step-by-step planning process that includes the following basic components:

1. assessing needs
2. identifying desired outcomes
3. devising alternative methods for reaching goals and judging among them
4. developing implementation and evaluation plans
5. budgeting

These steps formulate a generic process that is appropriate for activities of such varied scope as developing an agencywide strategy, planning for changes in an existing program, or devising a treatment plan for an individual client.

## Assessing Needs

The program planning process should always begin with a needs assessment, which for our purpose can be defined as a research and planning activity that seeks to identify the extent and types of existing and potential drug and alcohol abuse problems in a community, the current services available in the community, and the extent of unmet needs or underutilized resources in order to plan appropriate prevention (or treatment) services [National Institute for Drug Abuse (NIDA), 1981a].

Planners need to gather data about existing problems and resources before they can even begin to formulate agency or program goals, let alone plan for the provision of specific services.

**Problem identification**    Needs assessment starts with an attempt to define the problems that services will be designed to solve. Somehow, planners must gather data that will help identify whatever gap exists between the current state of affairs and a more desirable situation. In the substance abuse field, four types of information about problems seem especially important: drug use indicators, problem behavior indicators, psychological or developmental characteristics, and social or economic conditions (NIDA, 1981b). These types of data are described, along with examples of their use, in Exhibit 8.1.

Information about current drug use is obviously important in the process of identifying problems, but practitioners often overlook the complexity of this aspect of the needs assessment. Knowing the number of drug arrests, persons in treatment, or drug emergencies in a community may help provide a convincing case that something should be done, but it does not necessarily provide enlightenment about *what* should be done. Counselors and prevention specialists frequently work under the assumption that a given problem can be solved by a given intervention (for example, providing accurate information will prevent drug use by adolescents). In fact, however, drug use data do not provide guidance for program planners unless they are accompanied by documentation of the correlations between variables (for example, between knowledge and initial drug use) and the results of previous studies. For instance, providing accurate information about drugs has *not* been proved to prevent substance abuse among adolescents; yet many practitioners persist in assuming that data showing the existence of a drug problem automatically point the way toward a particular educational approach.

Drug use data are further complicated by the distinction between prevalence and incidence rates. As we have seen, prevalence refers to the number of cases within a population, and incidence refers to the number of *new* cases occurring among members of the population within a certain period.

> *Substance abuse treatment needs assessments are usually studies of prevalence:* Treatment services are most needed in areas where

# ▌ Exhibit 8.1

## Four Types of Problem-Oriented Data

| Data Type | Description | Example |
|---|---|---|
| 1. Drug use indicators | Statements on the incidence and prevalence of drug use. Usually broken down by drug type and demographic characteristics of the users. Also encompasses figures on drug arrests, numbers of persons in treatment, drug emergencies, and the like. | "Sixty-three percent of the 14- to 18-year-olds in four county high schools report five or more uses of illegal psychoactive substances." |
| 2. Problem behavior indicators | These are secondary indicators that are believed to be correlated with drug usage. They include crime rates, vandalism, truancy, school dropout rates, and the like. | "Over the past four years, juvenile arrests have risen by 285%." |
| 3. Psychological or developmental characteristics | Certain developmental characteristics, usually of a psychological nature, are believed to be correlated with potential for future drug use. These include aspects of family interaction, development of self-esteem or values, and interaction skills. | "Sixty percent of the third-graders at Herbert Hoover Elementary School scored 'negative' or 'very negative' on the 'As I See Myself' self-concept questionnaire." |
| 4. Social or economic conditions | These data are concerned with the environmental conditions that correlate highly with drug use. Some of these are thought to be poor housing conditions, persistent unemployment, discrimination, and the like. | "In the eight-block area bounded by Broadway, Main, Elm, and Walnut streets, the unemployment rate is 32%." |

*Note:* From *Prevention Planning Workbook* (p. 6) by the National Institute for Drug-Abuse, 1981 (DHHS Publication No. 81-1061). Washington, DC: U.S. Government Printing Office.

prevalence . . . is high; but incidence studies may also be utilized in future-oriented planning for treatment. On the other hand, *prevention needs assessment will primarily utilize incidence studies:* Substance abuse prevention services are most needed in areas where the incidence . . . is high.

Remember that, in general, the highest priority for substance abuse prevention services should be where individuals without such services would have the highest probability of beginning to abuse drugs and alcohol. If other data are not available, prevalence data may be utilized as an indication of incidence for a prevention needs assessment study. In most cases, if the prevalence is high, the incidence rate will also be high. There are exceptions to this, however, as, for example, drug use in various age groups. Among young teenagers, few individuals have had the opportunity to use drugs for very long, and the ratio of incidence to prevalence may be very high. In the 30 to 35 age group, the opportunity may have been available for some time, so there will be fewer new cases in relation to the number of existing cases [NIDA, 1981a, pp. 12–13].

Thus, what might appear at first glance to be the simplest aspect of a needs assessment — measuring the amount of drug use in the community — may in fact be complex, requiring careful thought on the part of the program planner before connections between drug use and potential interventions can be made.

Even greater care is required when information concerning problem behaviors, psychological characteristics, or socioeconomic conditions is gathered.

It is important to note that once certain problem behavior indicators have been chosen for assessment, they will have a great impact on what the programs eventually look like. This is because the programs, if responsive to the needs assessment, will set out to correct problems that surface during the assessment. This means that the problems you set out to find are likely to be the ones that you indeed find and design programs around. Hence, the needs assessment must be planned carefully because of its impact on program design [NIDA, 1981b, p. 7].

Planners tend to select certain behaviors or characteristics to measure because they assume that the targeted variables are, in fact, correlated with substance abuse. Programs may then be designed to bring about change in these areas without clear indications that such correlations actually exist. Again, such shortcomings will be lessened if planners present substantiation for their assumptions, use their own program evaluations as a basis for further examination of the connections between drug use and other characteristics or behaviors, and insist on clarity in all program objectives.

**Assessment methods**   A number of methods and tools are available for assessing needs. The approach chosen for a specific study depends on both data needs and adequate resources. Among the most common approaches are community surveys, studies of social indicators, canvassing of local agencies, open forums, and interviews of key informants.

*Surveys* provide the best opportunity to gather direct information about problems and community attitudes.

> Surveys that are carefully designed and conducted provide the most direct, scientifically valid, and reliable information about the needs and utilization patterns of individuals and families. Of all the approaches to need assessment, the citizen survey approach alone is capable of eliciting from individuals specific information about their own needs and utilization of services [Bell, Nguyen, Warheit, & Buhl, 1978, p. 287].

Surveys can be administered either to a sample of community members or to all members of a target group (for example, a high school freshman class) and can involve written questionnaires, telephone interviews, or personal questioning. The design of the instrument determines the kind of information it will elicit, making it important to put as much effort into planning the survey as into carrying it out. Effective use of surveys requires a major commitment in time and money, as well as a high degree of expertise. For this reason alone, the use of the survey approach is somewhat limited. Most agencies would find it difficult to assess needs by using a survey for every new program they were considering. Even small agencies, however, should attempt to use some form of survey at fairly regular intervals in order to keep their data on needs as current as possible.

*Social indicators* are quantitative measures of community characteristics that might correlate with service needs. This approach is frequently used in combination with other methods to form a comprehensive needs assessment, since planners can use secondary data, rather than personally gathering all of the necessary information on the spot. Once planners have decided what information might be useful, they can use a combination of local data with more general information gleaned through sources such as census reports, governmental publications, statistics gathered by national or local organizations, and needs assessments carried out by planning or health departments. Data concerning demographic characteristics, socioeconomic variables, health, education, housing, employment patterns, family patterns, safety, and law enforcement all play a part in determining what services are likely to be needed in a particular area or among members of a target population. These data, unlike information obtained directly from clients, act as indirect indicators of community needs.

> Data on juvenile delinquency, driving while intoxicated arrests, school problems and truancy, drug seizures, family problems, family violence, and high unemployment reflect personality characteristics, social and interpersonal variables, and behaviors that may be used as indirect indicators of existing or potential substance abuse problems in the community. . . . The use of an indirect indicator always involves the assumption that the indicator is somehow correlated with substance use or potential substance use. Such an assumption need not imply any causal relationship. . . . And it is neither necessary nor reasonable to assume that each occurrence of the indicator will be accompanied by a substance abuse problem. The assumption is merely that the conditions under which the indicator occurs are also conditions under which substance abuse problems are frequently found. . . . Whenever possible, the assumption should be substantiated with data or with findings from the literature [NIDA, 1981a, p. 49].

Thus, appropriate use of social indicators requires careful analysis of existing data to ensure that the variables studied do have a good chance of being related in some way to substance use or abuse.

*Soliciting information from local agencies* also helps in the development of realistic plans. Interviews or questionnaires can be used to elicit information answering two types of questions. First, what sources of help and money are available in the community? Second, what gaps in community services have been recognized by service providers? Having accurate information about the programs already available can eliminate needless duplication. At the same time, it can point the way toward services that are needed by community members but not provided by existing agencies. Program managers are often willing to identify special problems or client groups that their agencies are unable to address. Of course, this type of information is largely subjective and must be used in connection with other types of assessment data.

*Open forums and meetings* give community members a chance to speak out about their needs and priorities. Barton (1978, p. 38) points out that "for conditions to become recognized as problems, there must be a process of perceived, collective definition in which a given condition is selected and identified as a social problem." The fact that substance abuse professionals perceive a situation as problematic does not necessarily mean that the community sees that situation in the same light. Only the community as a whole can decide what degree of drug or alcohol use is acceptable and how many drug-related problems it is willing to bear. If community support and resources are needed for a given program, practitioners must learn how people outside of the service-providing network feel about the issue.

> Human service professionals often believe that they can identify the negative or positive conditions that exist in a community. Yet the identification of problem situations is affected by a variety of perceptions, values, experiences, and sociocultural factors. Only members of a given community can decide whether a condition is tolerable or unacceptable, central to the quality of life or tangential. Needs assessment must also take into account potential consumers' perceptions of their own needs [Lewis & Lewis, 1983, pp. 23–24].

One way to address this issue effectively is through community meetings. Whether these are informal get-togethers or formal hearings, many elements of the community can be encouraged to present views that might not otherwise have been considered. New ideas can be developed, and the community's commitment to the new program can be enhanced through a sense of participation in the decision-making process.

*Key informants* can also play an important role in the assessment of community needs. In any area it is possible to find neighborhood leaders, political figures, or others whose positions make them sensitive to community needs. Planners can use meetings, individual interviews, or even questionnaires to tap into this valuable information resource, asking respondents to share their admittedly subjective perceptions about current problems and community members' ideas about them. In the substance abuse field attention can be focused on key people who have contact with target populations. Among the categories of people who might be considered are (NIDA 1981a, p. 30):

- teachers, counselors, and other school officials
- police, parole and probation officers, judges, public defenders, and other law enforcement personnel
- public officials
- local clergy, private therapists, community mental health center personnel, and Alcoholics Anonymous personnel
- doctors, nurses, and other health professionals
- drug and alcohol abuse prevention and treatment program staff and clients
- students
- social workers and personnel from the welfare agency
- prevention clients (for example, youth, women, minorities, elderly)

Subjective opinions can never replace objective data, but the sensitive analyses of key informants can help narrow the focus of the assessment by pointing in the direction of needed sources and assisting in their analyses.

The use of data-gathering instruments, no matter how expert, cannot complete the needs assessment process.

> The process of need identification and assessment involves two distinct steps: (a) the application of a measuring tool or an assortment of tools to a defined social area; and, following this attempt at measurement, (b) the application of judgment to assess the significance of the information gathered in order to determine priorities for program planning and service development [Siegel, Attkisson, & Carson, 1978, p. 216].

Possession of accurate data makes it possible for planners to analyze the current situation and set priorities based on reality. Needs assessment makes goal setting possible.

## Identifying Desired Outcomes

Goal setting is the heart of the planning process. If needs assessment allows planners to identify community problems, goal selection lets them begin finding solutions.

All too often, substance abuse professionals focus on means, rather than on ends, insisting that certain services, and only those services, will bring about desired client outcomes. In fact, however,

> We cannot say unequivocally that a specific service will consistently bring about a specific client outcome. We can say that, given a set of objectives concerning desirable client outcomes, we can select from among a number of alternate interventions and build a program with a reasonable chance for success [Lewis & Lewis, 1983, p. 28].

The key to effective planning, then, is to focus on desired outcomes before even beginning to consider the activities that might lead to these ends.

In general, *goals* are defined as broad statements of the outcomes sought by an agency or program. *Objectives* are more specific, limited, and measurable. Ideally, attainment of all of a program's objectives will mean that its general goals have been reached. It is less important to distinguish between goals and objectives, however, than to ensure that some statement of outcome is used to determine the selection of program activities. Outcomes should be stated so that they are:

- *behavioral:* clear, concrete, specific, operational
- *measurable:* or in some way at least verifiable—it is clear when they have been accomplished
- *realistic:* not set too high, capable of being accomplished with available resources
- *worthwhile:* not set too low, not petty or meaningless
- *adequate:* that is, goals that are substantial translations of the mission of the system and that de facto satisfy real needs and wants (Egan & Cowan, 1979)

Once planners have prepared concrete and realistic outcome statements, they can begin to identify an array of activities that might lead to the desired accomplishments. When clear objectives form the basis of program planning, resulting activites tend to be more innovative than they are in situations where planners assume that certain kinds of services are mandatory. Moreover, appropriate outcome statements simplify evaluation by providing measurable standards and milestones.

## Devising and Selecting Alternatives

When their objectives are clear, planners can identify alternative methods for accomplishing them, ideally considering a wide range of options before narrowing the program's focus. Brainstorming, for instance, can generate a large number of alternatives. Many of the activities listed might at first glance appear impractical, but untried approaches should receive as much consideration at this point as more customary methods. As Elkin (1977, p. 74) points out, "The established way of doing something . . . must be assessed as one alternative rather than as a sacred cow." Good decision making requires that the planner devise as many alternatives as possible, consider the potential consequences of each, and search for any data that might possibly be relevant, always maintaining an openness to new information. The effective decision maker (Janis & Mann, 1977, p. 11):

1. thoroughly canvasses a wide range of alternative courses of action
2. surveys the full range of objectives to be fulfilled and the values implicated by the choice
3. carefully weighs whatever he knows about the costs and risks of negative consequences, as well as the positive consequences, that could flow from each alternative
4. intensively searches for new information relevant to further evaluation of the alternatives
5. correctly assimilates and takes account of any new information or expert judgment to which he is exposed, even when the information or judgment does not support the course of action he initially prefers
6. reexamines the positive and negative consequences of all known alternatives . . . before making a final choice
7. makes detailed provisions for implementing or executing the chosen course of action

In the substance abuse field there is a pressing need for more effective treatment alternatives. People involved in program planning need to consider what Simon (1976) calls an optimizing approach to decision making, rather than a satisficing approach. Satisficing involves setting minimal criteria, considering alternatives in terms of whether they meet these criteria, and halting the process when a reasonable alternative has been encountered. An optimizing strategy, in contrast, examines as many alternatives as possible, weighing each, and stops the search only when the best possible options have been found. Planning for substance abuse treatment programs has tended to be based on a few minimally acceptable methods. An optimizing approach, which would open the field to innovation, is needed.

## Developing Implementation and Evaluation Plans

Once planners have completed the steps of assessing needs, setting goals, generating alternative methods, and deciding on preferred activities, they can develop the mechanisms for putting their plans into action. At this point program developers should have in hand general statements of goals, lists of concrete objectives, and a set of specified methods or services selected to meet each objective. Every service listed should be clearly designed to meet a specified outcome objective; any activity that fails to connect with one of the objectives should be eliminated.

Each service that has withstood this final test should now be given an implementation plan. The questions to be asked at this point are (Young, 1978, p. 16):

1. What are the major activities necessary to implement the methods selected?
2. Who will be responsible for performing each activity?
3. What are the starting and completion dates for major activities?
4. What are the basic resources needed to perform each activity?

The answers to these questions form the framework for an implementation plan specifying who is to perform what activities, when, and with what resources.

The development of a plan for evaluation takes place concurrently with the initial program development process. While programming decisions are being made, planners are also considering how to evaluate the success of the services to be delivered. The objectives that have been clearly specified in the interest of program efficiency also point the way toward effective evaluation. If evaluation criteria are identified at this point, planners can also create evaluation implementation plans simply by deciding on methods for continually gathering data.

## Budgeting

Wildavsky (1974, p. 2) calls a budget "a series of goals with price tags attached," making it plain that planning and budgeting are inextricably linked.

> The budget itself is simply a projection of operational plans, usually for a one-year time span, with the plans being stated in terms of the allocation of dollars for varying functions or activities. Whether the budget helps or hinders the agency's efforts to set and meet its goals depends on the degree to which it is placed in perspective as a tool at the service of program planers. . . . The budget, then, should be the servant, rather than the master, of planning [Lewis & Lewis, 1983, p. 51].

Creating the annual budget depends on forecasting expected revenues and needs. Analysis of budgetary needs involves scrutinizing implementation plans and making accurate estimates of the costs of the chosen activities. If this analysis forms the basis of the budgeting, the budget becomes what it should be: a decision-making tool transforming goals into realities.

# ▎Evaluation

The purposes of evaluation are (1) to let us know whether services have taken place as expected and (2) to determine whether these services have succeeded in bringing about the desired client and community outcomes. Accomplishment of these distinct purposes requires two types of evaluation. *Process evaluation* assesses the agency's activities to determine whether a program is actually operating in accordance with plans and expectations. *Outcome evaluation* attempts to verify the impact of services by measuring the degree to which clients have changed as a result of the program's interventions. A useful evaluation plan must contain elements of each.

## Process Evaluation

Process evaluation involves collecting and analyzing information that can verify whether planned services have been delivered consistently to the appropriate number and types of clients.

> A large proportion of programs that fail to show impacts are really failures to deliver the interventions in ways specified. Actually, there are three potential failures: first, no treatment is delivered at all (or not enough); second, the wrong treatment is delivered; and third, the treatment is unstandardized, uncontrolled, or varies across target populations. In each instance, the need to monitor the

actual delivery of services and identify faults and deficiencies is essential [Rossi, Freeman, & Wright, 1979, p. 132].

Process evaluation lets program planners know whether clients have been reached in the numbers projected and whether the degree and quality of services meet expectations. This information makes outcome evaluations more meaningful by specifying what number, type, and range of services have brought about the outcomes being assessed.

> This type of evaluation normally takes the form of a comparison with identified standards for program implementation. This process depends on the existence of clearly defined, measurable program objectives. It also depends on the presence of an information system that can provide answers to the basic process evaluation question: Exactly what services were provided, by whom, for whom, and how many, in what time period, at what cost? When this information is used to compare accomplishments with objectives, guidelines for needed program improvements become clear, comparison of alternate methodologies becomes feasible, and accountability becomes a reality [Lewis & Lewis, 1983, p. 150].

**Goals and objectives**  Because process evaluation depends on the evaluator's ability to identify gaps between planned activities and actual accomplishments, it can be performed only when the program's objectives are clear and measurable. Each goal should specify some condition that the program will bring about, and each goal must be divisible into quantifiable objectives. Caines, Lewis, and Bates (1978) provide a hypothetical example involving a community information and referral agency. This agency has conducted a needs assessment leading to the estimate that approximately 2000 alcohol-dependent individuals with incomes at or below the poverty level live in the target community and are receiving no services. The program goal is that, within three years, 2000 alcoholics at or below the poverty level will be referred to appropriate financial, rehabilitative, and family services.

Once all the terms contained in such a program goal have been defined (What is meant by *alcoholic?* What are the boundaries of the *community?* How is the *poverty level* defined?), planners can decide what activities must take place within what time span if the goal is to be reached. In this example the objectives for the first four months of the program might include the following:

1. identification of all appropriate services in the community within three months
2. establishment of facilities and equipment to provide referral services within two months

3. employment and training of referral and administrative staff within two months
4. completion of an operational program within three months
5. establishment of liaison with all referral agencies within four months

Such objectives can be considered measurable only if they contain clear criteria and standards. The criterion is what is to be measured; the standard is the quantity or quality desired. For example, the first objective above is *identification of all appropriate services in the community within three months.* One criterion, *services,* involves several standards: *all, appropriate,* and *in the community.* The other criterion is *time* and also involves a specified standard: *three months.* If all criteria and standards are clearly defined before the fact, the evaluator can readily determine whether the objective has been met by considering it in terms of the predetermined standards after three months has elapsed.

These time-oriented objectives make it possible for the agency to conduct an ongoing evaluation rather than awaiting an annual report. If, at the end of four months, liaisons with all referral agencies have not been completed, managers can analyze the difficulty and take action either to improve these links or to adjust the plans for subsequent activities. In agencies without clear, time-oriented objectives, such problems go unrecognized, and the failure to attain overall goals is frequently unexplained.

**Management information systems.** The criteria and standards that form each objective also lead the way toward the kind of information that will be needed in order to measure program accomplishments. For example, the hypothetical information and referral agency discussed above had as one of its goals the referral of alcoholics *at or below the poverty level.* Information about income must therefore be obtained routinely from each client in order to determine whether the specified target population is being reached. Service delivery information is also needed, in order to determine whether treatment is being provided in accordance with plans.

Thus, the data needed for evaluation can be identified by examining each specified objective and clarifying the criteria and standards to be met. Once information requirements have been specified, planners can easily decide on the most appropriate source for the data. What is most important is that the collection of information needed for evaluation be built into the agency's routine operating procedures. As a part of program development, planners should decide who within an agency will record the necessary information, what methods or forms should be used, how the information should be reported and maintained, and who should be responsible for its analysis. Process evaluation becomes simplified through the creation of an integrated management information system that includes (Lewis & Lewis, 1983, p. 155):

- information related to the community, such as demographic information, data on social and economic characteristics, identification of underserved populations, and listings of external services and resources
- information concerning individual clients, groups of clients, and the client population as a whole, including such data as presenting problem, history, type of service received, length of service, socioeconomic and family characteristics, employment, and even measurements of satisfaction and service outcome
- service information, including types of service provided by units within the agency, number of clients served, number of admissions and discharges in a given time period, and specification of service-related activities
- staff information, including time spent in varying activities, number of clients served, volume of services, and differences among separate programs within the agency
- resource allocation information, including total costs, costs for specific types of services, and data needed for financial reporting

These data do not require complex or expensive computer systems and can be obtained through normal agency routines. Planners and evaluators need to be concerned less about the amount of information available than about its appropriateness.

> The key to system effectiveness is the degree to which it meets the agency's unique planning, management, and evaluation needs. Agency personnel need to identify as specifically as possible the kinds of data needed, the source of these data, and the frequency with which they should be distributed. Beyond this, planning for effective gathering and disseminating of information involves working out the type of system that is most appropriate for the agency's functions, size, and degree of complexity. The same kinds of planning processes are needed for a small agency using one client data form as for the large institution with a full-fledged information department [Lewis & Lewis, 1983, p. 156].

Of course, all of this information about the agency's activities is important only to the degree that it helps to explain the client changes that have been achieved. Evaluation, if it is to be useful, must focus on outcome as well as process.

## Outcome Evaluation

Outcome evaluation in the drug and alcohol field has been plagued by a number of problems, including overly narrow and insensitive outcome measurements, difficulties in locating subjects for follow-up, and doubts about the accuracy of client self-reports. These problems, however insoluble they may seem to be on the surface, must be overcome in the interest of treatment effectiveness. Valid outcome research is needed both to enhance program planning and management and to improve the decisions made by each counselor concerning every client.

> Treatment is a dynamic process that gains its direction principally from the ongoing evaluation that a therapist makes. Within the framework of this assumption, sophisticated treatment is, in fact, a process of continuous patient evaluation. This evaluation process provides the data base for the selection and implementation of the specific treatment techniques which are to be applied to each individual patient [Caddy, 1980, p. 168].

Information about the effectiveness of treatment interventions is needed for decision making, whether the decisions at hand concern the development of a program or the design of an individual treatment plan. This information can be trusted only if it is based on both appropriate outcome measurements and effective follow-up procedures.

**Outcome measures**   Traditionally, outcome evaluation research in the substance abuse field has been based on simplistic measures. Caddy (1980, p. 156) writes that a "dichotomous representation of the options available to the 'alcoholic' has been employed as the principal, and often the only, index of outcome in many alcoholism treatment evaluation studies", pointing out that this research focus can be attributed to a traditional view of alcoholism. Since the disease concept sees alcoholics as unable to control their drinking, the only possible options seen by many evaluators are (1) that alcoholics are drinking abusively or (2) that they are completely abstinent (that is, their alcoholism has been arrested). Research on drug treatments has been similarly limited. As Maisto and Cooper (1980, p. 2) point out, "Drug research is also characterized by poorly defined and limited measures of outcome. In this regard, studies often only report nominal measures of drug use, e.g., addicted and drug-free."

A multivariate concept of drug and alcohol problems brings a change in the focus of outcome evaluation. First, drinking and drug-taking behaviors are considered as continuous rather than nominal variables. Second, a number of additional outcome criteria are utilized in addition to measures of posttreatment substance use.

Considering drug or alcohol use as a continuous variable takes into account the complexity of this behavior and allows the evaluator to recognize the existence of varying degrees of involvement.

> From the disease-model perspective, treatment outcome is a dichotomous variable: either the patient is abstinent or has relapsed. Since alcoholism is defined as a progressive disorder characterized by loss of control, the amount of drinking is immaterial—it is assumed that the level will ultimately increase in severity as an inevitable consequence of relapse. Given this orientation, treatment outcome is a simple question of ascertaining whether the patient is drinking or abstinent at any fixed point in time. Treatment assessment of this type resembles a "dipstick method" in which the dipstick either comes up "dry" (abstinent) or "wet" (drinking). . . . We cannot tell whether a dipstick reading at point X in time indicates that the level of drinking is increasing, decreasing, or remaining stable [Marlatt, 1983, p. 1102].

Instead of using a "dipstick," the evaluator should use a more accurate gauge that follows individual clients over time and allows for some recognition of the direction of change. A practitioner following a multivariate approach might be as interested in how an individual client changes and adjusts in response to life events as in how a group's "success" can be measured at a certain point. Many psychosocial criteria in addition to drinking or drug-taking behaviors can also be considered more appropriately as continuous rather than nominal variables. For instance, it might be more useful to know the number of days a client works during a given period instead of asking the dichotomous question of whether he or she is employed at any given moment.

As researchers move away from a dichotomous view of treatment outcome, they move toward a recognition that multiple outcome variables should be assessed.

> Compared to more simplistic models, the variables one assesses at outcome are considerably more inclusive when following a multivariate approach. In the alcohol field, outcome research . . . has demonstrated the need for assessing the client's emotional, vocational, interpersonal, and physical health in addition to drinking behavior. Similarly, drug researchers are moving from single measures focusing on drug use toward using a number of diverse measures of life functioning [Maisto & Cooper, 1980, p. 9].

Although drinking and drug-taking behaviors will always remain as major—even primary—criteria of treatment success, they are not the only variables that indicate the degree of a client's rehabilitation. In the interests of consistency across studies with varying populations, Emrick and Hansen (1983) suggest that the following criteria could serve as core indexes to be used in all treatment evaluation studies, at least in the alcoholism field:

*treatment completion:* defined by the care-giver's perception that the client has completed the treatment offered; measured by discharge status

*recidivism:* defined by the number of subsequent, equally restrictive entries into substance abuse treatment; measured by self-reports, collateral information, and agency records

*mortality:* measured by the time from treatment admission to day of death, with death classified in terms of its relationship to alcohol abuse

*treatment use:* defined as use of any medical treatment; measured by both self-reports and records

*physical health:* defined as the number of days the client experiences medical problems, takes prescribed medication, or receives hospital treatment, as well as by physical disability pensions and self-perceptions concerning health

*drinking behavior:* defined as the number of days the client is abstinent with or without environmental or pharmacological constraints, drinks moderately, or drinks heavily; measured through multiple avenues, including interviews with clients, information from collaterals, and chemical test results

*other substance use:* defined as the number of days abstinent or using psychoactive drugs other than alcohol; measured by interviews, collateral information, chemical tests, and other measures

*legal problems:* defined in terms of alcohol-related or non-alcohol-related arrests or charges and in terms of the number of days engaged in illegal activities; measured through self-reports, collateral information, and official records

*vocational functioning:* defined by employment status, number of days worked, sources of income, perception of problems, and need for employment counseling; measured by client and collateral information

*family/social functioning:* defined in terms of the client's satisfaction with interpersonal relationships and recreation

*emotional functioning:* defined by the client's report of psychiatric symptoms or treatment need; measured through the use of psychological instruments

The list of potential criteria presented by Emrick and Hansen represents an effort both to broaden outcome evaluation and to seek consistent and objective methods of measurement. Ideally, the use of these methods should not be reserved for researchers but should form part of the routine evaluations performed every day by treatment practitioners. This ongoing process can be expedited through the use of existing instruments, many of which have been designed for the purpose of measuring treatment outcomes.

**Assessment instruments**   Substance abuse practioners often find it difficult to design valid instruments to evaluate outcomes. Rather than focusing too narrowly on dichotomous questions concerning drug or alcohol use, they can use instruments designed by other evaluators. Such standardized instruments, in addition to making evaluation more practical for small agencies, facilitate comparisons among programs. Many instruments are available, among them the following, all of which have been reproduced in full or in part in a handbook developed by the National Institute on Alcohol Abuse and Alcoholism (NIAAA) (Lettieri, Nelson, & Sayers, 1985):

1. *Behavior Rating Scale—Social, Employment, Economic, Legal, Drinking* (Brandsma, Maultsby, & Welsh, 1980). This instrument forms the basis for interviews performed both before treatment and afterward. Separate scales assess social functioning, employment, economic status, legal issues, and drinking behaviors and attitudes. The authors used the 64-item scale to follow up on problem drinkers who had completed outpatient treatment.

2. *Alcohol Dependence Scale* (Horn, Skinner, Wanberg, & Foster, 1984). The ADS is a brief, self-administered instrument made up of 25 multiple-choice items. It was designed for use at intake and as a follow-up instrument to assess one aspect of treatment outcome. The scale measures such aspects of alcohol dependence as withdrawal symptoms, obsessive/compulsive drinking style, tolerance, and drink-seeking behavior.

3. *Client Follow-Up Interview* (Kelso & Fillmore, 1984). This assessment tool is a structured interview that can be given at intake, discharge, and follow-up. The interview assesses client functioning in a number of areas, collecting information relating to psychological functioning, alcohol consumption, drug use, physical health, personality, treatment factors, social relationships, employment, legal problems, life events, attitudes, and coping responses.

4. *Addiction Severity Index* (McLellan, Luborsky, Woody, & O'Brien, 1980). This index is a well-tested instrument that assesses seven areas: medical status, employment status, drug use, alcohol use, legal status, family/social relationships, and psychological status. Completion of the structured interview leads to severity ratings for each area, from 0 (no treatment necessary) to 9 (treatment needed to intervene in life-threatening situation). The index has been found suitable for repeated administration in follow-up.

5. *Health and Daily Living Form* (Moos, Cronkite, Billings, & Finney, 1984). The HDL Form was developed for use in a longitudinal follow-up study of treatment outcome. The 200-item instrument can be administered either by the client or by an interviewer. It assesses health-related functioning, social func-

tioning and resources, family functioning and home environment, children's health and functioning, life-change events, coping responses, and family-level composite. This is one of the very few instruments that take into account life circumstances and events outside of the treatment milieu. Moos and his colleagues have also developed more specialized scales dealing with family and work environments.

6. *DUI Probation Follow-Up Project Life Activities Questionnaire* (National Highway Traffic Safety Administration, 1981). This questionnaire was designed to follow up on clients who had been seen after DUI violations. The information gathered through use of the interviewer-administered instrument can supplement such outcome criteria as recidivism and accident involvement. Questions relate to living situations, employment, health, alcohol use, social factors, marriage, and life-style.

7. *National Alcohol Program Information System (NAPIS), ATC Client Progress and Follow-Up Form* (NIAAA, 1979). The institute developed this instrument for use as a six-month follow-up tool for clients who had been treated in NIAAA-funded alcoholism treatment centers (ATCs). It provides a good example of a general follow-up instrument, including questions related to marital status, employment, financial support, household drinking, motor vehicle records, institutionalization, drinking behaviors, and client self-perceptions.

8. *ATC Follow-Up Study Questionnaire* (Ruggles, Armor, Polich, Mothershead, & Stephen, 1975). This questionnaire was developed for 18-month follow-up interviews of clients treated in NIAAA-funded alcohol treatment centers. The assessment covers a variety of areas, including family situation, employment, alcohol consumption and problems, treatment history, legal issues, and perceptions of drinking problems.

9. *Time-Line Follow-Back Assessment Method* (M. B. Sobell et al., 1980). This assessment method provides a model that may be ideal for gathering information about drinking behavior as a continuous variable. An interview is used to solicit reports of daily drinking as clients remember its having occurred over a specific period. A blank calendar is filled in, with codes identifying each day as follows:

A: abstinent
L: <6 standard drinks
D: >6 standard drinks
JA: jail, alcohol related
JN: jail, not alcohol related
HA: hospital, alcohol related
HN: hospital, not alcohol related
R: residential treatment

Clients are generally able to recall daily drinking behaviors by identifying anchor points or extended periods of invariant drinking behavior. Similar time-line mechanisms can be used to gather information about other drug use.

Substance abuse treatment providers can evaluate outcomes either by developing their own mechanisms or by using instruments such as those listed above.

**Follow-up procedures**    Effective outcome evaluation depends both on the selection and measurement of appropriate criteria and on the use of well-planned procedures. Even when evaluators utilize valid and reliable outcome measurements, they need to take further steps to ensure the accuracy of their data. Traditionally, research and evaluation in the substance abuse field have been troubled as much by procedural deficits as by poor criterion selection. If evaluation is to be useful at all, it must be based on methods that encourage accuracy in the data collected from clients and collateral resources, and that minimize loss of clients to follow-up (when clients can't be located). Fortunately, a number of studies have indicated that self-reports of drinking behaviors can be reasonably valid, especially if they are backed up by indicators from other sources (Maisto & Cooper, 1980; L. C. Sobell, Maisto, Sobell, & Cooper, 1979; L. C. Sobell & Sobell, 1975, 1978). Similarly, problems of attrition do appear to be surmountable if careful follow-up procedures are planned and given priority (Caddy, 1980). Completeness and accuracy in follow-up are possible if outcome evaluation, like process evaluation, becomes an integral part of the treatment program.

As far as individual clients are concerned, the focus on outcome follow-up should begin at the first intake interview.

> At the time of intake, patients are briefed about the need for follow-up interviews; during this briefing, the evaluator should stress the importance of the continuity of care function that such interviews provide and suggest that the patient should consider agreeing to be followed up for a specified posttreatment interval. Then, prior to each patient's termination of or discharge from therapy, the evaluator should again discuss the value of follow-up with the patient and request or confirm his/her involvement in the follow-up process [Caddy, 1980, p. 170].

This consistent attention to evaluation from intake through treatment and follow-up helps to establish the clients' understanding of its importance and to encourage their commitment to participate. This approach also improves the planning done by evaluators, since comparable measurements need to be taken both before and after treatment.

Clients leaving treatment with an understanding that follow-up contacts will ensue are likely to maintain their intent to cooperate if regular and positive contacts are made.

> Follow-up should be based on a model of frequent and continued contact, rather than a shotgun approach involving contact only after a specified posttreatment interval. . . . Follow-up based on frequent and continued contacts, with both patients and their respective CISs [collateral information sources], offers several advantages over the traditional one-shot approaches. First, it greatly facilitates the tracking of those patients whose geographical mobility is high. Second, it probably enhances the validity of reports by patients and their collaterals, for it maximizes the opportunity for the establishment of rapport between the interviewer and the interviewee. Finally, it offers an extremely low cost continuity of care after formal treatment has ended. Such care may influence the course of recidivism and/or help consolidate the gains made during the course of treatment [Caddy, 1980, p. 161].

Thus, frequent contacts aid the evaluation process in several ways. The ongoing relationship between treatment providers and former clients enhances cooperation and commitment; the regularity of contact makes it far less likely than usual that clients will be "lost" during follow-up; and the relationship may also prevent some problems from occurring at all and allow for immediate intervention in others.

Routine and frequent contacts are likely to increase the accuracy of client self-reports, but other sources of information must also be used before evaluators can have complete confidence in the information they have acquired. Multiple sources and measures should be used, not because clients are disbelieved but because no one measure can possibly be adequate to assess such complex behaviors as drinking, drug use, and life functioning.

> Questions about the reliability and validity of outcome data can best be answered by basing outcome conclusions upon a convergence of multiple indicators of outcome. Thus, treatment outcome information should be derived from as many sources as possible, including (a) subjects' self-reports; (b) multiple collateral informants (e.g., friends, relatives, employers, probation officers, neighbors); (c) infield probe breath samples of subjects' BAC (blood alcohol content); (d) urine testing for drugs; (e) Nalline testing for narcotics; (f) official records to verify subjects' self-reports of incarceration, employment, driving infractions, disabilities, marriages, deaths, and so on; (g) periodic liver function tests to assess recent episodes of heavy drinking; and (h) any other measures which can be developed. When a variety of relatively independent measures of outcome are employed and are mutually corroborative, evaluators can have confidence in the validity of their outcome conclusions [L. C. Sobell & Sobell, 1980, pp. 181–182].

Treatment providers may be overwhelmed by the prospect of maintaining frequent contacts with former clients and, at the same time, using multiple sources of information to measure treatment outcome. They might well consider the notion of performing outcome evaluation studies following up a limited number of randomly selected subjects. A complete evaluation of all members of a random sample is more useful than a partial and biased study of a larger number of clients.

The effectiveness of this approach to outcome evaluation depends on the quality of the relationship between interviewer and interviewee, evaluator and client. Caddy (1980, p. 160) points out that

> a sophisticated and skilled interviewer who is able to establish a high level of rapport with a patient during the follow-up interview (and who can offer some continuity of care) will be far more successful in maintaining the sort of contact with a patient which facilitates the gathering of valid data than would be a less clinically skilled "door step" interviewer.

Each agency or program needs to develop mechanisms that are appropriate to its goals and staffing, sometimes having to balance a desire for interviewer objectivity, which would argue in favor of using outside evaluators, with an equally valid desire for making follow-up a more integral part of treatment. Whoever the follow-up interviewers are, they must be trained to work with clients in an accepting and nonjudgmental manner, setting an atmosphere that encourages honest reporting. Caddy (p. 158) suggests "structuring the therapeutic and follow-up relationships to include the philosophy that (a) the patient will not be punished or negatively judged for reporting drinking behavior which occurs during or after treatment, and (b) positive consequences will always follow the factual reporting of all data."

Evaluation, whether of process or of outcome, must be based on an openness to new information, whatever that information may be. Its purpose is not merely to justify support for current practices, but, rather, to help practitioners make desirable changes. Objective evaluation takes planning to its logical conclusion by comparing the program's accomplishments with its goals. Without this important step the quality of substance abuse counseling could never be assured.

## ▌ Summary

Excellence in planning and evaluation can be as important to the success of a substance abuse program as the quality of its clinical treatment. In fact, good program management seems to go hand in hand with good client services. Substance abuse counselors, like other human service and health professionals, need to focus on meeting objectives that can be evaluated in terms of measurable client and community outcomes.

Effectiveness in programming depends on the careful implementation of a planning process that includes the following steps: (1) assessing needs, (2) identifying desired outcomes, (3) devising alternative methods for reaching goals and judging and selecting among them, (4) developing implementation and evaluation plans, and (5) budgeting. Variations of the same steps are appropriate for such divergent activities as developing long-term agency strategies, making changes in specific programs, or even devising individual client treatment plans.

Program planning leads directly toward evaluation, which lets us know whether services have taken place as expected and whether desired client outcomes have been reached. Two types of evaluation are needed to provide this information. Process evaluation involves collecting and analyzing data to verify whether programs are operating in accordance with plans. Outcome evaluation attempts to measure the degree to which clients have changed as a result of the services provided.

In the substance abuse field, outcome evaluation has been plagued by problems such as insensitive outcome measurements and poorly planned follow-up procedures. Evaluation can be improved if treatment facilities consider drinking and drug-taking behaviors as continuous, rather than dichotomous, variables; if they measure a number of outcome criteria; and if they carefully plan follow-up procedures. Attention to the results of truly objective evaluations can bring about what all substance abuse professionals desire: more effective programs that increase our ability to meet the unique needs of each client we serve.

# ▌References

Barton, A. K. (1978). A problem, policy, program model for planning community mental health services. *Journal of Community Psychology, 6*, 37–41.

Bell, R. A., Nguyen, T. D., Warheit, G. J., & Buhl, J. M. (1978). Service utilization, social indicator, and citizen survey approaches to human service needs assessment. In C. C. Attkisson, W. A. Hargreaves, M. J. Horowitz, & J. E. Sorensen (Eds.), *Evaluation of human service programs* (pp. 253–300). New York: Academic Press.

Brandsma, J. M., Maultsby, M. C., & Welsh, R. J. (1980). *Outpatient treatment of alcoholism: A review and comparative study.* Baltimore: University Park Press.

Caddy, G. R. (1980). A review of problems in conducting alcohol treatment outcome studies. In L. C. Sobell, M. B. Sobell, & E. Ward (Eds.), *Evaluating alcohol and drug abuse treatment effectiveness: Recent advances* (pp. 151–176). New York: Pergamon Press.

Caines, K., Lewis, J. A., & Bates, L. E. (1978). *A manual for self-evaluation of human service agencies.* San Francisco: University of San Francisco.

Egan, G., & Cowan, M. A. (1979). *People in systems: A model for development in the human service professions and education.* Pacific Grove, CA: Brooks/Cole.

Elkin, R. (1977). A systems approach to planning and managing programs for the handicapped. In D. Borst & P. J. Montana (Eds.), *Managing nonprofit organizations.* New York: AMACOM.

Emrick, C. D., & Hansen, J. (1983). Assertions regarding effectiveness of treatment for alcoholism: Fact or fantasy? *American Psychologist, 38,* 1078–1088.

Horn, J. L., Skinner, H. A., Wanberg, K., & Foster, F. M. (1984). *Alcohol Dependence Scale (ADS).* Toronto: Addiction Research Foundation of Ontario.

Janis, I., & Mann, L. (1977). *Decision making: A psychological analysis of conflict, choice, and commitment.* New York: Free Press.

Kelso, D., & Fillmore, K. M. (1984). *Overview: Alcoholism treatment and client functioning in Alaska.* Anchorage: Center for Alcohol and Addiction Studies, University of Alaska.

Lettieri, D. J., Nelson, J. E., & Sayers, M. A. (1985). *NIAAA treatment handbook series 2: Alcoholism treatment assessment research instruments.* DHHS Publication No. ADM 85-1380. Washington, DC: U. S. Government Printing Office.

Lewis, J. A., & Lewis, M. D. (1983). *Management of human service programs.* Pacific Grove, CA: Brooks/Cole.

Maisto, S. A., & Cooper, A. M. (1980). A historical perspective on alcohol and drug treatment outcome research. In L. C. Sobell, M. B. Sobell, & E. Ward (Eds.), *Evaluating alcohol and drug abuse treatment effectiveness: Recent advances* (pp. 1–14). New York: Pergamon Press.

Marlatt, G. A. (1983). The controlled drinking controversy: A commentary. *American Psychologist, 38,* 1097–1109.

McLellan, A. T., Luborsky, L., Woody, G. E., & O'Brien, C. P. (1980). An improved diagnostic instrument for substance abuse patients: The Addiction Severity Index. *Journal of Nervous and Mental Disorders, 168,* 26–33.

Moos, R. H., Cronkite, R. C., Billings, A. G., & Finney, J. W. (1984). *Health and Daily Living Form Manual.* Palo Alto, CA: Social Ecology Laboratory, Veterans Administration and Stanford University Medical Centers.

National Highway Traffic Safety Administration. (1981). *A description of Life Activities Inventory and scoring procedures, 1980 annual report. Volume 6. Final report—CDUI Project, Alcoholism Division, County of Sacramento Health Department.* DOT Publication No. HS-6-01414. Washington, DC: Author.

National Institute on Alcohol Abuse and Alcoholism. (1979). *National Alcoholism Program Information System (NAPIS).* Washington, DC: U. S. Government Printing Office.

National Institute on Drug Abuse. (1981a). *A needs assessment workbook for prevention planning.* DHHS Publication No. ADM 81-1061. Washington, DC: U.S. Government Printing Office.

National Institute on Drug Abuse. (1981b). *Prevention planning workbook.* DHHS Publication No. ADM 81-1062. Washington, DC: U.S. Government Printing Office.

Nickson, R. W. (1978). *How to be a successful manager.* London: Thorsons Publishing.

Rossi, P.H., Freeman, H.E., & Wright, S.R. (1979). *Evaluation: A systematic approach.* Beverly Hills, CA: Sage.

Ruggles, W. L., Armor, D., Polich, J. M., Mothershead, A., & Stephen, M. (1975). *A follow-up study of clients at selected alcoholism treatment centers funded by NIAAA.* Palo Alto, CA: Stanford Research Institute.

Siegel, L. M., Attkisson, C. C., & Carson, L. G. (1978). Need identification and program planning in the community context. In C. C. Attkisson, W. A. Hargreaves, M. J. Horowitz, and J. E. Sorensen (Eds.), *Evaluation of human service programs* (pp. 215–252). New York: Academic Press.

Simon, H. A. (1976). *Administrative behavior: A study of decision-making processes in administrative organizations.* New York: Free Press.

Sobell, L. C., Maisto, S. A., Sobell, M. B., & Cooper, A. M. (1979). Reliability of alcohol abusers' self-reports of drinking behavior. *Behavior Research and Therapy, 17,* 157–160.

Sobell, L. C., & Sobell, M. B. (1975). Outpatient alcoholics give valid self-reports. *Journal of Nervous and Mental Disease, 161,* 32–42.

Sobell, L. C., & Sobell, M. B. (1978). Validity of self-reports in three populations of alcoholics. *Journal of Consulting and Clinical Psychology, 46,* 901–907.

Sobell, L. C., & Sobell, M. B. (1980). Convergent validity: An approach to increasing confidence in treatment outcome conclusions with alcohol and drug abusers. In L. C. Sobell, M. B. Sobell, & E. Ward (Eds.), *Evaluating alcohol and drug abuse treatment effectiveness: Recent advances* (pp. 177–183). New York: Pergamon Press.

Sobell, M. B., Maisto, S. A., Sobell, L. C., Cooper, A. M., Cooper, T., & Sanders, B. (1980). Developing a prototype for evaluating alcohol treatment effectiveness. In L. C. Sobell, M. B. Sobell, & E. Ward (Eds.), *Evaluating alcohol and drug abuse treatment effectiveness: Recent advances* (pp. 129–150). New York: Pergamon Press.

Wildavsky, A. (1974). *The politics of the budgetary process* (2nd ed.). Boston: Little, Brown.

Wrich, J. T. (1984). President's message. In the newsletter of the Employee Assistance Society of North America, Oak Park, IL.

Young, K. M. (1978). *The basic steps of planning.* Charlottesville, NC: Community Collaborators.

# AUTHOR INDEX

# SUBJECT INDEX